Suicide in Schools

Suicide in Schools provides school-based professionals with practical, easy-to-use guidance on developing and implementing effective suicide prevention, assessment, intervention and postvention strategies. Utilizing a multi-level systems approach, this book includes step-by-step guidelines for developing crisis teams and prevention programs, assessing and intervening with suicidal youth, and working with families and community organizations during and after a suicidal crisis. The authors include detailed case examples, innovative approaches for professional practice, usable handouts, and internet resources on the best practice approaches to effectively work with youth who are experiencing a suicidal crisis as well as those students, families, school staff, and community members who have suffered the loss of a loved one to suicide. Readers will come away from this book with clear, step-by-step guidelines on how to work proactively with school personnel and community professionals, how to think about suicide prevention from a three-tiered systems approach, how to identify those who might be at risk, and how to support survivors after a traumatic event—all in a practical, user-friendly format geared especially for the needs of school-based professionals.

Terri A. Erbacher, PhD, is a school psychologist for the Delaware County Intermediate Unit and a clinical assistant professor at Philadelphia College of Osteopathic Medicine. She has served on the executive boards of Philadelphia's chapter of the American Foundation for Suicide Prevention, Survivors of Suicide, and Pennsylvania's Youth Suicide Prevention Initiative. She was named Pennsylvania's school psychologist of the year in 2011 and has won multiple awards in recognition of her clinical practice and expertise in crisis response, suicide risk assessment and prevention, and traumatic loss.

Jonathan B. Singer, PhD, LCSW, is an assistant professor at Temple University's School of Social Work, where his clinical and research interests focus on family-based interventions for suicidal and cyberbullied youth and the role of technology in prevention and intervention. He served as an advisor for the City of Philadelphia's Youth Suicide Prevention Task Force, Non-homicide Child Death Review, and Pennsylvania Youth Suicide Prevention Initiative. He is the founder and host of the award-winning Social Work Podcast.

Scott Poland, EdD, is a professor and co-director of the Suicide and Violence Prevention Office at Nova Southeastern University in Florida. As a pioneer in school suicide prevention, he published his first book on the subject in 1989 and authored or coauthored every chapter on suicide for the National Association of School Psychologists's *Best Practices in School Psychology* volumes. He previously served as the prevention division director of the American Association of Suicidology and has testified about the mental health needs of children before the US Congress.

Routledge
Taylor & Francis Group

School-Based Practice in Action Series
Series Editors
Rosemary B. Mennuti, EdD, NCSP
and
Ray W. Christner, PsyD, NCSP
Cognitive Health Solutions, LLC

This series provides school-based practitioners with concise practical guidebooks that are designed to facilitate the implementation of evidence-based programs into school settings, putting the best practices *in action.*

Assessment and Intervention for Executive Function Difficulties
George McCloskey, Lisa A. Perkins, and Bob Van Divner

Resilient Playgrounds
Beth Doll

Comprehensive Planning for Safe Learning Environments
A School Counselor's Guide to Integrating Physical and Psychological Safety—Prevention through Recovery
Melissa A. Reeves, Linda M. Kanan, Amy E. Plog

Behavioral Interventions in Schools
A Response-to-Intervention Guidebook
David M. Hulac, Joy Terrell, Odell Vining, and Joshua Bernstein

The Power of Family-School Partnering (FSP)
A Practical Guide for School Mental Health Professionals and Educators
Cathy Lines, Gloria Miller, and Amanda Arthur-Stanley

Implementing Response-to-Intervention in Elementary and Secondary Schools
Procedures to Assure Scientific-Based Practices, Second Edition
Matthew K. Burns and Kimberly Gibbons

A Guide to Psychiatric Services in Schools
Understanding Roles, Treatment, and Collaboration
Shawna S. Brent

Comprehensive Children's Mental Health Services in Schools and Communities
Robyn S. Hess, Rick Jay Short, and Cynthia Hazel

Responsive School Practices to Support Lesbian, Gay, Bisexual, Transgender, and Questioning Students and Families
Emily Fisher and Kelly Kennedy

Pediatric School Psychology
Conceptualization, Applications, and Leadership Development
Thomas J. Power and Kathy L. Bradley-Klug

Serving the Gifted
Evidence-Based Clinical and Psychoeducational Practice
Steven I. Pfeiffer

Early Childhood Education
A Practical Guide to Evidence-Based, Multi-Tiered Service Delivery
Gina Coffee, Corey E. Ray-Subramanian, G. Thomas Schanding, Jr., and Kelly A. Feeney-Kettler

Implementing Response-to-Intervention to Address the Needs of English-Language Learners
Instructional Strategies and Assessment Tools for School Psychologists
Holly Hudspath-Niemi and Mary Lou Conroy

Conducting Student-Driven Interviews
Practical Strategies for Increasing Student Involvement and Addressing Behavior Problems
John Murphy

Single Case Research in Schools
Practical Guidelines for School-Based Professionals
Kimberly J. Vannest, John L. Davis, and Richard I. Parker

Working with Traumatic Brain Injury in Schools
Transition, Assessment, and Intervention
Paul B. Jantz, Susan C. Davies, and Erin D. Bigler

Ecobehavioral Consultation in Schools
Theory and Practice for School Psychologists, Special Educators, and School Counselors
Steven W. Lee and Christopher R. Niileksela

Suicide in Schools
A Practitioner's Guide to Multi-level Prevention, Assessment, Intervention, and Postvention
Terri A. Erbacher, Jonathan B. Singer, and Scott Poland

Suicide in Schools

A Practitioner's Guide to
Multi-level Prevention, Assessment,
Intervention, and Postvention

**Terri A. Erbacher,
Jonathan B. Singer, and Scott Poland**

NEW YORK AND LONDON

First published 2015
by Routledge
711 Third Avenue, New York, NY 10017

and by Routledge
27 Church Road, Hove, East Sussex BN3 2FA

Routledge is an imprint of the Taylor & Francis Group, an informa business

© 2015 Terri A. Erbacher, Jonathan B. Singer, and Scott Poland

The right of Terri A. Erbacher, Jonathan B. Singer, and Scott Poland
to be identified as authors of this work has been asserted by them in
accordance with sections 77 and 78 of the Copyright, Designs and
Patents Act 1988.

Library of Congress Cataloging-in-Publication Data

Erbacher, Terri A.
    Suicide in schools : a practitioner's guide to multi-level prevention,
assessment, intervention, and postvention / by Terri A. Erbacher,
Jonathan B. Singer, and Scott Poland.
        pages cm.—(School-based practice in action series)
    Includes bibliographical references and index.
    1. Youth—Suicidal behavior—United States.   2. Students—Suicidal
behavior—United States.   3. Suicide—United States—Prevention.
4. Educational counseling—United States.   5. Youth—Suicidal
behavior—United States—Case studies.   6. Students—Suicidal
behavior—United States—Case studies.   7. Suicide—United
States.—Prevention—Case studies.   I. Singer, Jonathan B.   II. Poland,
Scott.   III. Title.
HV6545.8.E737   2015
371.7'13—dc23
2014026248

ISBN: 978-0-415-85702-4 (hbk)
ISBN: 978-0-415-85703-1 (pbk)
ISBN: 978-0-203-70297-0 (ebk)

Typeset in Baskerville
by Apex CoVantage, LLC

In memory of:
Joseph M. Erbacher
Don Poland

Contents

1 Overview and Introduction   1

2 Training Gatekeepers   19

List of Figures

List of Tables

Foreword

We are delighted to see the growth of the *School-Based Practice in Action Series* over the years. This project grew out of a discussion between us several years ago while attending a professional conference. At that time, we were each at different points in our careers, yet we both realized and faced the same challenges for education and serving children and families. Acknowledging the transformations facing the educational system, we shared a passion and vision in ensuring quality services to schools, students, and families. This idea involved increasing the strong knowledge base of practitioners together with an impact on service delivery. This would require the need to understand theory and research, albeit we viewed the most critical element as having the needed resources bridging empirical knowledge to the process of practice. Thus, our goal for the *School-Based Practice in Action* series has been to offer resources for readers based on sound research and principles that can be set directly "into action." This series resulted in a total of 19 books on topics that we deemed extremely important for you to have at your fingertips. After a number of wonder years working with amazing authors, our mission is complete with this, our final book, dealing with suicide in schools. May this breathe life into each and every one of you as you work daily against the loss of life and face the challenges of assessment and interventions for suicide in schools.

This book, as with the others in the series, offers information in a practice-friendly manner, and provides a web-link to obtain reproducible and usable materials that are a supplement to the content of the book. Within the text, readers will find the icon presented here that will cue them to documents available on the website. These resources are designed to have a direct impact on transitioning research and knowledge into the day-to-day functions of school-based practitioners. We recognize that the implementation of programs and the changing of roles come with challenges and barriers, and as such, these may take on various forms depending on the context of the situation and the voice of the practitioner. To that end, the books of the *School-Based Practice in Action* series may be used in their entirety and present form for a number of practitioners;

however, for others, these books will help them find new ways to move toward effective action and new possibilities. No matter which style fits your practice, we hope all of our books will influence your work and professional growth.

Working with Dr. Terri A. Erbacher, Dr. Jonathan B. Singer, and Dr. Scott Poland has been an honor. We are grateful to have brought the leaders in the field on this topic to be the final book in the series. Their book, *Suicide in Schools: A Practitioner's Guide to Multi-level Prevention, Assessment, Intervention, and Postvention,* is a gem. Given that suicide is the third leading cause of death for those aged 15–24 years, this topic is vital. However, working with suicidal youth often presents as both a professional challenge and a personal fear for clinicians. The authors base this book on the most recent research regarding youth suicide. From empirical research and their own clinical practice, they offer guidelines and strategies on how to identify often hidden warning signs and risk factors, to work within a systems perspective, and to build a therapeutic alliance. Through the utilization of assessment tools they provide, the authors provide a clear and comprehensive process to conduct suicide risk assessment interviews effectively, to determine level of suicide risk, and to offer follow-up interventions. Because of their practical experience, the authors go further and provide ways to monitor suicidal behavior over time, as well as to aid in the development of effective treatments for suicidal youth. The authors also address the issues involved in postvention in the aftermath of suicide, providing specific suggestions to accomplish throughout the first 24 hours and beyond. There is specific guidance offered for "caring for the caregiver." This is one of the most practical and user-friendly books we have read on this topic, and we are so pleased to have it as part of our series.

Finally, we want to extend our thank you to Ms. Anna Moore and Routledge Publishing for their ongoing support of a book series focused on enriching the practice and service delivery within school settings. Their openness to meet the needs of school-based practitioners made the *School-Based Practice in Action* series possible. In addition, we must thank Mr. Dana Bliss, whose foresight and collaboration made our idea for a book series a reality. We hope that you have enjoyed reading and implementing the materials in this book and all of the books in the series as much as we have enjoyed working with the authors on developing these resources. Best wishes in your work with schools, children, and families. Thank you for allowing us to dream.

Rosemary B. Mennuti, EdD, NCSP
Ray W. Christner, PsyD, NCSP
Series Editors, School-Based Practice in Action Series

Acknowledgments

We are grateful to our series editors, Roe Menutti and Ray Christner, for encouraging us to undertake this project and providing support and guidance throughout. We would also like to thank Anna Moore, our Routledge editor, and Lori Young, David Estrin, and Jennifer Marine, our copy editors, for shining a light on our blind spots and making the text a better version of itself. We thank Melody Regino, Jan Ulrich, and Patti Clark for adding depth to the text by sharing their unique experiences. Last, but certainly not least, we are grateful to the many graduate students who provided editorial feedback and research assistance: Sarah Biemuller, Mollie Cherson, Jacqueline Farace, Rachel Flood, Caitlin Gilmartin, Hannah Kahn, Chip Schofield, Aleida Silva-Garcia, and Claire Talarico.

This book would not be all that it is without my co-authors and to them I am grateful for their insights and expertise. I am also thankful for the many mentors and supporters that have guided me along the way, including those at the Delaware County Intermediate Unit, the Delaware County Suicide Prevention Task Force, Survivors of Suicide, and AFSP—Greater Philadelphia. And to my biggest cheerleader, my mother, who has taught me the gift of unconditional acceptance. Finally, I am ever thankful to my husband, Scott, for accepting me as I am and for picking up the pieces while I wrote this book.

—Terri A. Erbacher

Everything I put in this book has its origins in the experiences I have had with suicidal youth and their families. I hope that I have done justice to your experience. I'm grateful to the school personnel who do their job ethically, professionally, and in the service of youth and families. I'm grateful to my own family. My wife Randi somehow made the time and space for me to write this book while she was a doctoral student, a professor, and mother to our three kids (and best huggers ever): Emerson, Max, and Luca.

—Jonathan B. Singer

My father died by suicide, but prevention did not become my highest priority until I became the Director of Psychological Services for a massive Texas school system and was faced with three student suicides, and I discovered that youth suicide is a difficult issue to address in schools. I have been on a quest ever since to share what I believe schools need to know and do. I am grateful to the many professionals who have been so receptive in the more than 1000 presentations that I have made about suicide prevention. I am especially thankful for the support of my family and Nova Southeastern University.

—Scott Poland

1 Overview and Introduction

Are You Prepared?

Situation 1

Imagine it's a cold day in December. You are in your office, space heater chugging along; the view outside is bleak and grey. You get a text from your vice principal, "Did you hear?" Just then the phone rings. Mrs. Beckman, the mother of one of your students, Ariel, is calling from the hospital. "She tried to kill herself [sobbing]." "Mrs. Beckman? Who tried to kill herself?" She can't be talking about Ariel. Ariel is not on your radar as a student at risk for suicide. As a high school junior (16 years old), she is involved in the stage crew for the school plays, seems to have friends, and has okay grades. "Ariel tried to kill herself. I found her when I went in to wake her up this morning. She was lying on her bed, sweating, looking really yellow, and was covered in vomit. I thought she was sick with the flu. And then I saw the bottle of Tylenol next to the bed. I freaked out. I shook her. Her eyes opened. I yelled at her 'What did you do???' She started crying and whispered the words, 'Mom, I took a lot of Tylenol last night. I'm so sorry.'" Mrs. Beckman stopps talking. She is breathing quickly. You realize that you are too. You know what had happened next: 911, ambulance, emergency department, activated charcoal, more vomiting, and a checkbox on the electronic medical record next to suicide attempt. "The doctors told me . . . [sobbing] she might die. They said something about her organs failing." A wave of sadness rushes over you, "Mrs. Beckman, I'm so sorry." You know that an overdose of acetaminophen (Tylenol) left untreated for 8–12 hours is almost always fatal. You get off the phone with Mrs. Beckman. You take a deep breath. The sky is still grey, but you don't feel cold anymore. You respond to your vice principal's text, "Just heard. Your office or mine?"

Is your school prepared to handle this situation? If Ariel recovers, does your school have a policy to deal with her return to school? Are you prepared to deal with the many questions anticipated by Ariel's peers? Does your school's crisis plan include the steps to take if Ariel dies? Is your school liable in any way if Ariel dies? Are you ready to handle Ariel's grieving peers? What about her closest friends? What about Ariel's teachers? Are you prepared to deal with questions from the media? Does your school have a way to identify students like Ariel who might not be on anyone's radar? Do you have a way to train and educate students and staff to identify and report suicide risk? How would you ensure your own self-care after running crisis intervention for days on end? **After reading all of these questions, do you feel your school is prepared?**

Situation 2

Imagine Jeremiah, who is an eighth-grade middle school student. His mother passed away when he was in second grade, and he has always appeared somewhat sad and distant from peers. Jeremiah's language arts teacher has become concerned with Jeremiah's most recent creative writing essay as it is dark, depressing, and horrifying. Jeremiah's teacher is unsure if Jeremiah is simply writing imaginatively or if his writing is an expression of his own feelings of despair. His teacher decided to err on the side of caution and ask the school psychologist to stop by her room as soon as possible. The school psychologist responded immediately.

Would the teachers in your school have immediately referred Jeremiah to the school psychologist or another staff member? Are the teachers in your school aware of what steps to take if they become concerned about a student such as Jeremiah? More importantly, do they grasp the importance of acting upon these concerns immediately? Have they been trained on the warning signs of suicide? Are your school counselors, social workers, and/or school psychologists prepared to handle Jeremiah from here? Do they know what steps to take, with whom to collaborate, and whom to call? Are they familiar with conducting a suicide risk assessment or screening? Do they know how and when to refer for additional supports? Are there protocols to follow in your crisis plan for responding to potentially suicidal students? **Do you think your school is prepared?**

If you were able to successfully answer all of these questions, we applaud you on your high level of preparation and thank you for reading this far. We appreciate your sharing this book with colleagues who do not have your level of expertise in suicide prevention, intervention, and postvention. If you did not have the answers, however, we are so glad you are reading this book. You will learn essential concepts and skills for responding to suicidal thoughts and behaviors (STB) in schools.

Purpose of This Book

Suicide is frightening. Many of us working in schools are terrified of not doing all the right things if suicidal students present themselves in our office or classroom. It is anxiety provoking to wonder if we are prepared to respond to the tragedy of suicide loss quickly and effectively. Most of us in schools, even school mental health professionals (SMHPs), are not fully trained or prepared to deal with suicide *prevention, intervention,* and *postvention.*

One study of school psychologists found that only 61% of respondents had coursework in any type of crisis intervention during their training

(Bolnik & Brock, 2005). Comparing this to training in suicide specifically, a recent doctoral dissertation found that only 12% of school psychologists reported completing coursework in suicide *prevention* strategies and 13% had coursework in *intervention* or *postvention* strategies, and only 35% of school psychologists who participated in the study felt competent to do a suicide risk assessment (Stein-Erichsen, 2011). Overall, school psychologists report having very little training in skills related to suicide despite the fact that 50% of respondents in this study had dealt with at least one completed suicide in their school (9% had four or more suicides). They are the ones often turned to in such an event—ready or not. The message is clear. If our school psychologists are not feeling confident in their skills and are not receiving coursework through their university-based training, the likelihood that other school staff members have the skills needed to prevent and respond to suicide is slim.

This book is a hands-on guide that includes practical action steps to effectively implement suicide prevention strategies, intervene with a potentially suicidal student, and respond with best practice strategies to a suicide loss in your school community. We cover the role of SMHPs—counselors, nurses, school psychologists, and social workers—and the roles of administrators, teachers, and ancillary school staff. This text is not designed to take the place of your district's crisis response manual but is a broader and more current review of best practice guidelines for suicide prevention, intervention, and postvention in schools. In addition to being a practical guide for staff on the ground level, this text can be used by administrators and crisis teams to review and update their school district's policies around suicide risk. Every school and school district is unique and presents with distinct characteristics requiring an individualized approach, but each school district should have policies in place. We hope this text helps.

Expert tip: Any member of the school community, student or adult, can prevent a student from dying by suicide, and any member of the larger community can be affected by an attempted suicide or suicide death of a student or school staff member.

We have written this text for all school personnel and community members who may come across suicidal or grieving children and teens. We distinguish between insights and recommendations based on empirical support, expert consensus guidelines, professional standards, and our own experiences as suicidologists. This text is a not a substitute for actual training in building the necessary skills to prevent, respond to, and intervene in youth suicide but serves as a resource for professionals dealing with a suicidal crisis. In addition, this text provides graduate students with a comprehensive overview of suicide-related issues in the school.

Responding effectively to a suicide crisis is a difficult but not impossible task. The difference between a thoughtful response and a knee-jerk reaction can be the difference between effective crisis response (Chapter 3) and a wrongful death lawsuit (Chapter 4); this is especially true as we better understand the risk of suicide contagion and the risk of suicide loss in exacerbating mental or physical conditions already present in survivors (Knieper, 1999).

Overview: Key Goals of This Text

This book is intended for use by all school personnel, including administrators, SMHPs, crisis team members, teachers, and other school staff as well as professionals outside of school working with youth. Whenever we refer to *you* in this book, we are referring to all professionals mentioned above. We do this to relate information directly to *you*, our reader, as our goal is to present this difficult information in a user-friendly way. You will gain new knowledge about suicide and learn how to apply the principles and skills to your daily work. Many of you will read this text in its entirety, but chapters also stand alone to be read as needed.

In Chapter 1, you will soon learn about risk factors, warning signs, and protective factors for youth suicide. In this chapter, we share unique historical and personal perspectives from our experiences in the field, define key terms, identify the scope of this public health problem, and present global recommendations for schools.

Chapters 2 through 5 address school *suicide prevention* strategies. Chapter 2 is great for all school staff to read as it provides an overview and discussion of gatekeepers; those who can identify a youth at risk for suicide with the knowledge to refer that student to appropriate level of services. Chapter 3 focuses on crisis teams, including the importance of working with a comprehensive team and the integration of suicide procedures and protocols into your school crisis plans with efficacy. Chapter 4 reviews current case law and liability if a student dies by suicide as well as your school's legal and ethical responsibilities. Chapter 5 takes you through the effective implementation of evidence-based suicide prevention programs, differentiating between the three tiers of universal, selective, and indicated prevention. Should your school and community want to take a proactive approach, this chapter presents many options.

Chapters 6 and 7 discuss *suicide intervention* strategies with potentially suicidal youth. Intervening with a student who presents with STB is perhaps one of the most common tasks of school personnel with regard to suicide. These two chapters take you through all of the applied steps to conduct ethical suicide risk screenings and comprehensive assessments. We address the challenges of notifying parents or guardians, making referrals, integrating youth back to school after a suicide attempt, and using a systems approach to consult with other school staff, families, and community agencies. Finally, we address monitoring suicide risk over time, planning treatment, and keeping students safe. These chapters provide the most benefit for SMHPs and mental health practitioners working with youth outside of school. However, they will help crisis team members, administrators, and other school staff better understand the procedures followed by the SMHPs and how these impact students in the school or classroom.

Chapters 8 and 9 focus on *suicide postvention*—how to effectively respond in the aftermath of a suicide loss. Chapter 8 focuses on immediate interventions and provides practical, hands-on suggestions for tasks to be completed during the first 24 hours upon hearing of a suicide death. We discuss how to triage students who need the most support and apply the framework of the three tiers of universal, selective, and indicated strategies to postvention. Chapter 9 addresses longer-term response for a school and community that are grieving, including practical issues such as attending a funeral, dealing with the empty desk, creating a memorial, and the complex differences between grief and trauma. As these chapters focus on a comprehensive response in the aftermath of a school crisis, they are beneficial for all school personnel to read. These chapters evolved primarily out of one of our author's (Erbacher) years of experience providing postvention response to various school districts in the aftermath of suicide loss.

Chapter 10 focuses on *self-care*, and the personal, professional, and organizational factors that can contribute to *burnout, compassion fatigue,* and *vicarious traumatization* for school personnel who respond to suicide risk. Please do not skip this chapter. Learn what you and your school can do to maintain your health and personal wellness *before* burnout and fatigue overwhelm you.

While each chapter includes a case study, Chapter 11 presents a *final illustrative case example* demonstrating the complexity of managing suicide risk in the school setting in order to apply skills and provide a pragmatic understanding of principles learned. Chapter 12 provides a multitude of *resources*, including organizations focusing on suicide prevention and intervention, books for professionals and survivors of suicide, and websites to visit for further information.

Added bonus: Don't forget the online eResources. We have provided over 40 handouts, checklists, forms, and sample letters that you can adapt and use. Need a PowerPoint presentation for an in-service on suicide risk in schools? Need a visual rating scale for elementary school students? Need a Safety Plan form? They are all in the eResources (you will find this eResource icon throughout the text when indicated). Please take a minute, go to the site, and figure out what eResources will make your job easier and what is available should you need these resources later.

The Role of the School in Suicide Prevention

In 1999, the U.S. Surgeon General issued a *Call to Action to Prevent Suicide* in which he framed suicide as a preventable public health problem (National Research Council, 2002). The assumption was, and is, that if everyone takes responsibility for recognizing and responding to suicide risk, then the majority of suicide deaths can be prevented. Prevention of youth suicide should be addressed where our youth spend the majority of their day—at school. As schools should maintain a safe environment that works to prevent suicide and where students feel comfortable sharing concerns, it is crucial for all school staff to be familiar with and watchful for risk factors and warning signs of suicidal behavior. Crisis team personnel, including SMHPs and administrators, should be trained to intervene when a student is identified at risk for suicide. They are the ones who conduct suicide risk assessments, warn/inform parents, provide recommendations and referrals to community services, and often provide follow-up counseling and support at school.

Suicide loss impacts the entire school community, with the potential for students to show declines in mental wellness, behavior, attendance, and grades. If that is not enough to convince your school boards or stakeholders about the importance of addressing this issue, remind them that schools have even been sued following a student suicide.

Key Terms

When discussing suicide deaths, we refrain from using older terminology that we encourage you to refrain from as well. The term *committed* suicide is a holdover from the time when suicide was a crime; one could also *commit* murder. Instead, we say an individual *died by suicide* or *took his or her own life*, as these statements do not pass judgment on the act. We also refrain from referring to a *failed* suicide attempt or a *successful* one. The implication is that the person who survived a suicide attempt failed at it—certainly the wrong message to send. Instead we describe suicide attempts as *aborted* (i.e., the person stops him or herself) or *interrupted* (i.e., an outside circumstance stops the individual). Throughout this text, we use the abbreviation STB to refer to suicidal thoughts and behaviors. These can include ideation, planning, attempts, or death. Table 1.1 identifies other important terms and definitions adapted from research consensus in the identification and treatment of suicidal behavior (Bryan & Rudd, 2011; U.S. Department of Health and Human Services, 2012; Whitlock, Wyman, & Barreira, 2013).

Historical Perspectives of Suicide in Schools

More than 25 years ago, one of the co-authors of this text, Scott Poland, wrote *Suicide Intervention in the Schools* (Poland, 1989), one of the first books addressing youth suicide risk and schools. At the time, very little was known

Table 1.1 Definitions of Key Terms

Term	Definition
Suicide ideation	Thoughts of ending one's own life, regardless of how intense these suicidal thoughts are.
Suicidal behavior	Any behavior resulting in an attempt or preparation for an attempt; this may include practicing or rehearsing for the attempt.
Suicide attempt	A non-fatal self-directed potentially injurious behavior with any intent to die as a result of the behavior. A suicide attempt may or may not result in injury.
Suicide attempter	An individual who has attempted suicide.
Suicide	Death caused by self-directed injurious behavior with any intent to die as a result of the behavior.
Suicide survivor	Someone who has lost a loved one to suicide. Suicide survivors are the ones left behind after a suicide loss (not someone who attempted).
Non-suicidal morbid ideation	Thoughts about one's death without suicidal or self-enacted injurious content.
Non-suicidal self-injury	Deliberate direct destruction or alteration of body tissue without a conscious suicidal intent.

about youth mental illness or suicide risk. In 1989, few school districts had any formalized procedures for suicide prevention, few school staff were trained to look for warning signs or how to intervene with a suicidal student, and very few lawsuits had been filed against schools after the suicide of a student. No states had legislative mandates requiring training for school personnel in suicide prevention, intervention, or postvention. The Centers for Disease Control would not start collecting data on suicide risk in high school for another two years through the Youth Risk Behavior Surveillance Survey. Poland describes his book this way:

> It was about what I learned and believed schools needed to know and has been described as me telling a story about my experiences with suicide in the schools. As I look back on forces and factors in youth suicide outlined in that book, there was a focus on music as several lawsuits were brought against musicians such as Ozzy Osborne by parents who believed that music lyrics contributed to the suicide of their children. There was also concern that playing the game Dungeons and Dragons contributed to the problem of youth suicide. There seemed to be almost a mystic quality associated with youth suicide and a concern that it could not be prevented.

There have been a number of significant changes in suicide prevention over the past 25 years. Perhaps the most significant development has been the demystification of youth suicide, as we now understand that youth considering suicide often have undertreated or untreated mental health problems. States such as Alaska, Kentucky, Louisiana, Tennessee, and Texas have passed legislation clarifying the important role that schools play in suicide prevention and outlining what schools need to do with regard to training, planning, and linking with community resources. Screening programs such as Signs of Suicide (SOS) have broadened prevention efforts beyond adults to students, although such programs are offered in only a small percentage of secondary schools. Psychotherapies such as dialectical behavior therapy (DBT) and attachment-based family therapy (ABFT) are promising approaches to reducing suicide risk in youth. Bullying, which was rarely acknowledged to be a legitimate problem in 1989, is now understood to be a risk factor for youth STB. Numerous professional organizations now provide excellent resources for suicide prevention, intervention, and postvention in schools. The Suicide Prevention Resource Center (SPRC) (http://www.sprc.org) is a federally funded clearinghouse for information about suicide prevention. The Garrett Lee Smith Memorial Act has provided funding through the Substance Abuse and Mental Health Services Administration (SAMHSA) since 2007 for suicide prevention in K–12 schools, universities, and tribal nations, Survivor groups have become very active. National goals have been set for suicide prevention. In addition, guidelines have been developed for the media that discourage focusing on the specifics of the tragedy and encourage instead focusing on mental health and suicide prevention resources.

Despite the progress, Poland sees many challenges for school-based suicide prevention:

> Most schools are still reluctant to accept a leadership role in suicide prevention and school administrators remain largely uninformed about suicide. I have had the opportunity over the last thirty years to give more than 1,000 presentations for school personnel on suicide and am well aware that few administrators were in attendance. There is growing concern about youth suicide clusters, but it often takes multiple student deaths in the same school or district to prompt more focus on suicide prevention. The death of a student by suicide is like throwing a rock into a pond with ripple effects in the school and community. The impact may be greater than ever before with the advent of social networks and vulnerable youth finding each other online. Prevention efforts now need to involve social media and there are promising signs as Facebook and other social media networks work to address the problem of youth suicide. Prevention efforts have to include outreach to parents, who are often uninformed about the incidence of suicide. It can be very difficult to get parents to come to meetings that focus on suicide prevention. I have

learned to change the title of presentations to focus on broader topics such as *Safeguarding Your Child and Building Resiliency* or *Raising a Child in a Challenging World*. The parents who attend these sessions receive suicide prevention information, but they also gain knowledge on good parenting and the message that they need to be very involved in their child's life, involve the school, and promote positive mental health in their family.

Scope of the Problem

The number of people who die every year by suicide is so huge that it is hard to grasp. The most recent data available found that 39,518 people died by suicide in the United States in 2011 (Centers for Disease Control and Prevention [CDC], 2014b). This number is equivalent to the number of people who died in the 9/11 terror attacks dying nearly every month for a year *every* year.

> **Expert tip:** We are facing a public health problem that can only be addressed by working within a community-based systems response perspective. It takes a village, so to speak, as there is a need to integrate support across the life of a child.

Who in your school is most likely to die by suicide? The students, right? Wrong. The staff are more at risk for dying by suicide than the students. Yes, it's true. According to the most recent statistics available from the CDC (2014b), suicide rates are highest for Caucasian males aged 45–60 years and those over 80 years. While we primarily discuss student suicide in this text, we also relate information about the loss of a teacher or staff member due to suicide, as that is perhaps a greater possibility.

Figure 1.1 emphasizes consistent patterns in suicide rates that suggest our teachers have always been and continue to be the ones in our building most at risk for suicide. Suicide rates for those in the middle years (25–64 years) have been increasing greatly, and there is an upward trend among all age groups beginning in 2008.

Suicide is responsible for more deaths among 10- to 24-year-olds than all natural causes combined (Wyman et al., 2010). A 2013 study by the CDC examining the behavior of students in Grades 9 through 12 found that 1 in 6 reported seriously considering suicide in the past year, 1 in 8 reported that they made a plan about how they would attempt suicide, 1 in 13 reported that they had attempted suicide one or more times, and 1 in 38 reported that they had made a suicide attempt that required medical attention (CDC, 2014a). How many students are in your school building? How many in each classroom? In a typical high school classroom

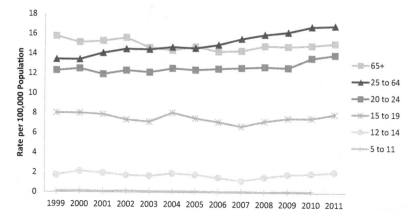

Figure 1.1 Trends in suicide rates among both sexes, by age group, United States, 1999–2011

Source: Centers for Disease Control and Prevention. Web-based Injury Statistics Query and Reporting System (WISQARS) [Online]. (2014). National Center for Injury Prevention and Control, Centers for Disease Control and Prevention (producer). Available from: URL: http://www.cdc.gov/injury/wisqars/index.html . [2014 Sept 25]. Note: 2011 rates not available for ages 5 – 11.

of 24 students three students would have made a suicide plan and two students would have attempted suicide at least once in the past year. That's in *each* classroom. The stakes are high.

A few more facts (CDC, 2014b):

- Suicide is the second leading cause of death among youth aged 15–24 years, only exceeded by accidents.
- We lost 4,822 youth aged 15–24 years in 2011 (that's nearly 13 young lives lost per day). In this age group, suicide accounts for 20% of all deaths annually.
- In youth aged 15–24 years, estimates indicate there are 100–200 suicide attempts for each suicide death.
- Suicide deaths result in an estimated $34 billion in medical costs and lost wages.
- Suicide attempts and non-fatal self-harm injuries cost an estimated $3 billion annually for medical care and an additional $5 billion for indirect costs.

Suicide Contagion

Suicide contagion is described as imitative behavior where one death by suicide is a contributing factor to another suicide death (American

Foundation for Suicide Prevention & Suicide Prevention Resource Center [AFSP & SPRC], 2011). Whereas suicide contagion is relatively rare and accounts for between 1% and 5% of all deaths by suicide annually (AFSP & SPRC, 2011), school personnel should know about it because it occurs almost exclusively among adolescents (Gould, Greenberg, Velting, & Shaffer, 2003). Contagion can lead to a suicide cluster, which is described as a group of suicides that have contributed to each other in some way. Between 100 and 200 students die each year in suicide clusters (Brock, 2011). Suggestions on how to prevent suicide contagion are presented in Chapter 8.

The Tipping Point

Suicide is complex. The cause of suicide is often presented as being a single event, such as a bad grade or an argument with a parent, when there are many factors that interplay for a student to potentially engage in suicidal behavior. We present below the risk and protective factors for suicide and warning signs that a student may be at risk for suicide. As represented in Figure 1.2, our ultimate goal is to tip the scale and decrease suicide risk by building on the protective factors a student already has in his or her life and developing others. School itself is a protective factor due to the positive supports inherent in school-based relationships.

Capacity for suicide is a term coined by Thomas Joiner (2007) in his interpersonal theory of suicide, a widely known and referenced theory. Joiner refers to capacity for suicide as an individual's *ability* to kill themselves. As humans are biologically wired for self-preservation, they must

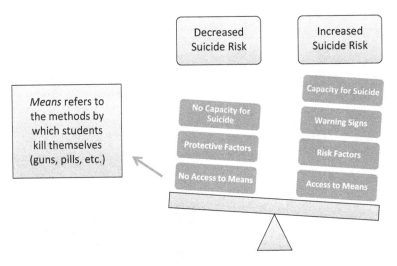

Figure 1.2 Factors That Increase or Decrease Suicide Risk

develop the capacity for suicide whereupon they no longer fear pain, self-mutilation, or death. Joiner's (2007) interpersonal theory of suicide suggests that even if a student has warning signs, risk factors, and access to means, they become at risk for suicide *only* if a capacity for suicide is also present. Students who injure or mutilate themselves may therefore be developing this capacity (see section below on NSSI for more information). Furthermore, Joiner's theory suggests that alongside capacity for suicide, suicidal individuals must have a desire to die. His belief is that a desire to die is created by two of the risk factors listed below being experienced immensely for extended periods of time: perceived burdensomeness and sense of low belongingness (Joiner, 2007). When desire to die and capacity for suicide are both present, the scale may be tipped and a suicide attempt may occur.

Risk Factors and Warning Signs

We must first understand what puts a student at risk for suicide and what the warning signs are that an adolescent may be contemplating suicide. Many people confuse these two terms. *Risk factors* refer to an individual's characteristics, circumstances, history, and experiences that raise the statistical risk for suicide. *Warning signs* are visible signs that a friend or loved one may show indicating that they may be in crisis and thinking about suicide. We can prevent suicide by learning to recognize the signs of someone at risk, taking those signs seriously, and knowing how to respond to them. The following are adapted from the extensive research published by AFSP (2014), the CDC (2014b), and SAMHSA (2012).

Risk Factors

Physiological/Behavioral Health

- Gender: Males are 4 times more likely to die by suicide than females (although females are 3 times more likely to attempt suicide)
- Age: People aged 45–60 years and over 80 years are at highest risk
- Race: Caucasians have the highest rates for all ages, followed by American Indians/Alaskan Natives
- Geography: Highest U.S. suicides rates are in the West; lowest rates are in the Northeast
- Gay, lesbian, bisexual, transgender (particularly if there is conflict, harassment, bullying, rejection, or lack of support)
- Chronic medical illness, such as HIV, lupus, or traumatic brain injury
- Psychiatric disorders: About 90% of those who die by suicide have a diagnosable and *treatable* mental illness, such as depression or bipolar disorder; personality disorders, particularly borderline or antisocial, and conduct disorders
- Anxiety or post-traumatic stress disorder (PTSD)

- Previous attempt: 20% of those who kill themselves previously attempted suicide
- Genetic predisposition: family history of mental illness or suicide
- Self-injurious behavior or self-destruction (e.g., cutting, eating disorders)
- Alcohol or drug dependence
- Impulsivity: Impulsive individuals are more likely to act on suicidal impulses
- Aggressiveness
- Low self-concept/esteem

Social/Environmental

- Isolation or lack of connectedness
- History of physical or sexual abuse
- Childhood trauma or witnessing trauma
- Pressure to be a good student/athlete/child
- Access to alcohol or illicit drugs
- Easy access to lethal methods, especially guns
- Exposure to a suicide loss (i.e., contagion)
- Trouble with the law
- Bullying
- Poor familial communications or parent/child discord
- Family stress/dysfunction
- Romantic difficulties in older adolescents
- Risk-taking or being reckless

Warning Signs

Suicide can be prevented. While some suicides occur without warning, 50%–75% of people who are suicidal give some warning of their intentions.

- Feelings of being a burden to others
- Lack of connection; withdrawing from friends and family
- Depressed, overwhelming sadness
- Loss of energy or extreme fatigue
- Loss of interest or pleasure in usual activities or sports
- No reason for living
- Discussing suicide in their writings
- Reference being dead, joking about it (referencing one's own funeral)
- Suicidal threats in the form of direct and indirect statements
- Suicide notes and plans
- Self-defeating statements or expressing a wish to die ("I'd be better off dead")

- Seeking suicide means, such as guns, pills, etc.
- Hopelessness about the future getting better; feeling trapped
- Feeling helpless or worthless
- Trouble concentrating or thinking quickly, indecisiveness
- Preoccupation with suicide/death in music, comics, movies, books, etc.
- Internet researching of methods or watching suicide/self-harm documentaries
- Increased hostility, agitation, defensiveness, anger, or rage (may be hostile if afraid you will uncover their suicide plan)
- Disinterest in making future plans ("I won't be here this weekend anyway")
- Euphoria, attitude becomes calm/certain (as they now have a plan to end the pain)
- Anxiety, psychic pain, and inner tension
- Deterioration of self-care: neglect of personal appearance or cleanliness
- Decreased school attendance or academic performance
- Change in eating habits (weight loss/gain)
- Change is sleeping routine
- Change in behavior or discipline
- Increased use of drugs, alcohol, sex
- Increased impulsiveness and taking unnecessary risks
- Feeling humiliated (e.g., problems with the law, recent psychiatric hospitalization)

Protective Factors

The presence of protective factors can lessen the potential of risk factors leading to STB. Protective factors are often the opposite of risk factors and can buffer the effects of risk. Students who possess multiple protective factors and are able to bounce back in the face of adversity are often said to have resiliency. Once a child or adolescent is considered at risk, schools, families, and friends should work to help the youth build social connections and other social and environmental supports. The following protective factors are adapted from *Preventing Suicide: A Toolkit for High Schools* (SAMHSA, 2012).

Physiological/Behavioral Health

- Positive self-esteem and emotional wellness
- Physical health
- Hope for the future
- Willingness to obtain and stay in treatment
- Easy access to effective mental health support/care
- Cognitive flexibility (ability to integrate and think through new information)

- Internal locus of control (feeling as if one has the power to create change)
- Effective coping strategies
- Effective problem-solving skills in the face of conflict or adversity
- Cultural and religious beliefs that affirm life and discourage suicide
- Resilience and trust that things will get better
- General life satisfaction, sense of purpose

Social/Environmental

- Sense of connectedness: having social supports such as family, friends, teammates
- Having at least one caring adult to which a student can turn
- Feeling connected to school and feeling safe there
- Connections within the community such as strong spiritual or religious ties
- Restricted access to alcohol or illicit drugs
- Restricted access to suicide means, such as guns, medications, etc.

Recommendations for Schools

Now that you have a framework for understanding the warning signs, risk factors, and protective factors for suicide, action steps can begin. First, designate or develop a suicide prevention expert within your building or district who will be the go-to person in the event of a suicide crisis. Ensure this staff member receives adequate training in suicide prevention programs, intervening in a suicidal crisis, and effective response in the aftermath of a suicide loss. The American Association of Suicidology offers a school suicide prevention accreditation, one way to ensure standardization in developing expertise as a school suicide prevention specialist; information can be found on its website: http://www.suicidology. org/training-accreditation/school-professionals.

Next, assess the teachers, administrators, and school staff in your building or district for knowledge of the warning signs and risk factors for suicide by using *A Suicide Quiz: Assessing Staff Knowledge*, included in your eResources. We suggest that you have your staff take this brief quiz at the next faculty meeting, staff retreat, or professional development day. If your staff does not appear to have adequate knowledge on suicide risk factors and warning signs, there are several options:

1. Do nothing and hope for the best! (Not recommended.)
2. Have your newly established suicide prevention expert or SMHP show staff the PowerPoint presentation provided as an eResource, which provides information to answer the quiz questions and much more.
3. Send staff for additional training or invite experts in the field of youth suicide into your school for in-service training.

4.   View online webinar trainings on suicide awareness and prevention chosen from the resources presented in Chapter 12.

Next, consider the importance of connecting and building relationships with families, community organizations, and other stakeholders, for these are integral in helping prevent suicide and coming together as a team in the aftermath of a suicide tragedy.

Expert tip: Engage parents who are sometimes too frightened to discuss suicide by conducting meetings and educational events to teach the warning signs of suicide and let them know about your school's suicide prevention efforts.

Most importantly, schools should continue to build relationships with the students and emphasize that help is available. Just as a school nurse will help a student's stomach pain, SMHPs are there to help with emotional pain. No student should have to suffer alone or in silence. Communication is key—begin the conversations about suicide prevention and getting help when needed and keep the conversations going.

Take a moment now to review your own school's crisis plan and procedures. If you find that your current plan does not answer all of the questions asked at the beginning of this chapter, you should revise your plan as you continue to read this text. If the two scenarios at the beginning of this chapter have left you with more questions than answers, the remainder of this text will provide those answers.

Reducing Shame and Stigma

There was a time, not too long ago, when the stigma associated with cancer was so strong that the word could not be mentioned in public. Today, thanks in part to pink ribbons, public health campaigns, and celebrity testimonials, people can say, "I have cancer" and expect others to react with care and compassion rather than judgment and disdain. We have not yet gotten to the point where we can expect that sharing thoughts of suicide, disclosing a suicide attempt, or mentioning that a loved one has died by suicide will be met with care and compassion. This book is one way in which we are fighting the shame and stigma associated with youth STB. Another way is to acknowledge that two of the three authors of this book (Erbacher and Poland) have lost a father to suicide. Dr. Scott Poland says,

Many people dedicated to the field of suicide prevention have been personally impacted by suicide. My father, Don Poland, died by suicide when I was a graduate student. I had seen a few warning signs of suicide in a textbook before, but I certainly never thought that a suicide could happen in my family.

Dr. Terri A. Erbacher also lost her father to suicide while in graduate school, but more than 25 years after Scott suffered his loss. Here are her thoughts:

> It was interesting for me to read Scott's perspective that he could not have imagined losing a family member to suicide because that is exactly how I felt. It was unimaginable. As suicide was not something that ever entered my mind, I had no idea about the stigma I was about to face—people who turned away or stared blankly at even the mention of the word *suicide*. I kept thinking I had to whisper the word just as many decades ago the word *cancer* was whispered. I decided to face the world and tell my story. As I did, I began to meet more and more people who had experienced a suicide loss but never told anyone. I met people whose family members still hid the cause of a loved one's death. I met older adults who were lied to and discovered that a parent had died by suicide decades after the fact. I decided then to embark on a journey to help reduce the shame and stigma associated with suicide, to help people not feel so alone, and to try to use my tragic loss as a means through which to save lives—if I impact even one life during my career, that is success! This beginning has laid the foundation for the birth of this text.

As an educator and community member, you too can help fight the stigma associated with suicide, mental illness, and the need for professional help. The person sitting next to you on a plane, in an in-service, or at a faculty meeting may have lost a loved one to suicide, is a suicide attempt survivor, or perhaps is struggling with suicidal thoughts right now. Be an advocate, one who allows others to feel safe in sharing their grief or reaching out for help when needed. After all, if a loved one is dealing with cancer or a colleague dies by a heart attack, we can talk about it without judgment. It should be the same for suicide.

References

American Foundation for Suicide Prevention [AFSP]. (2014). Risk factors and warning signs. Retrieved from http://www.afsp.org/understanding-suicide/risk-factors-and-warning-signs

American Foundation for Suicide Prevention & Suicide Prevention Resource Center [AFSP & SPRC]. (2011). *After a suicide: A toolkit for schools*. Newton, MA: Education Development Center, Inc.

Bolnik, L., & Brock, S.E. (2005). The self-reported effects of crisis intervention work on school psychologist. *The California School Psychologist, 10*, 117–124.

Brock, S.E. (2011). *PREPaRE Workshop 2: Crisis intervention and recovery: The roles of school-based mental health professionals* (2nd ed.). Bethesda, MD: National Association of School Psychologists.

Bryan, C. J., & Rudd, M. D. (2011). *Managing suicide risk in primary care.* New York: Springer Publishing Company.

Centers for Disease Control and Prevention [CDC]. (2014a). 1991–2013 High School Youth Risk Behavior Survey Data. Available at http://nccd.cdc.gov/ youthonline/. Accessed on October 1, 2014.

Centers for Disease Control and Prevention [CDC]. (2014b) *Web-based Injury Statistics Query and Reporting System (WISQARS)* [Online]. National Center for Injury Prevention and Control. (Fatal Injury Reports, 1999–2011, for National, Regional, and States [RESTRICTED]). Retrieved from http://www. cdc.gov/injury/wisqars/index.html. Available at http://www.cdc.gov/injury/ wisqars/index.html. Accessed September 25, 2014.

Gould, M. S., Greenberg, T., Velting, D. M., & Shaffer, D. (2003). Youth suicide risk and preventative interventions: A review of the past 10 years. *Journal of the American Academy of Child and Adolescent Psychiatry, 42*(4), 386–405.

Joiner, T. E. (2007). *Why people die by suicide.* Cambridge, MA: Harvard University Press.

Knieper, A. J. (1999). The suicide survivor's grief and recovery. *Suicide and Life-Threatening Behavior, 29*(4), 353–364.

National Research Council. (2002). *Reducing suicide: A national imperative.* National Academies Press.

Poland, S. (1989). *Suicide intervention in the schools.* New York: The Guilford Press.

Stein-Erichsen, J. (2011). *School psychologists' confidence levels with suicide intervention and prevention in the schools.* Unpublished doctoral dissertation.

Substance Abuse and Mental Health Services Administration [SAMHSA]. (2012). *Preventing suicide: A toolkit for high schools.* HHS Publication No. SMA-12-4669. Rockville, MD: Center for Mental Health Services.

United States Department of Health and Human Services [U.S. DHHS]. (2012). *2012 National strategy for suicide prevention: Goals and objectives for action.* Washington, DC: U.S. Department of Health and Human Services Office of the Surgeon General and National Action Alliance for Suicide Prevention. Retrieved from http://www.surgeongeneral.gov/library/reports/national-strategy-sui cide-prevention/full-report.pdf

Whitlock, J., Wyman, P. A., & Barreira, P. (2013). *Connectedness: Suicide prevention in college settings: Directions and implications for practice.* Ithaca, NY: Brofenbrenner Center for Translational Research, Cornell University. Retrieved from http://www.sprc.org/library_resources/items/connectedness-suicide-prevention-college-settings

Wyman, P. A., Brown, C. H., LoMurray, M., Schmelk-Cone, K., Petrova, M., Yu, Q., . . . Wang, W. (2010). An outcome evaluation of the Sources of Strength suicide prevention program delivered by adolescent peer leaders in high schools. *American Journal of Public Health, 100*(9), 1653–1661.

2 Training Gatekeepers

Case Study: Suffering in Silence

We begin with the case of a female student, Jeanette, a junior in high school. One quiet morning, another student brought a printout of Jeanette's social media page on Facebook to her homeroom teacher, Ms. Snow. There were multiple immediate concerns, one being that Jeanette was a member of a group called "I don't care if I die." Another being that, on her profile, she admitted to being a cutter and to being suicidal at times. Jeanette's social media profile page included statements referring to her scars as well as the following comments:

> *"death>this pain"*
> *"I want to die. I'll just do it."*
> *"idk [I don't know] what to do anymore"*
> *"death>life"*
> *"I'd rather just end it than feel like this"*
> *"I can't live like this anymore"*

Ms. Snow was immediately concerned because of the content of the posts, but also because a well-known recent graduate had died by suicide the month before. What Ms. Snow did not know was that Jeanette was currently taking 10 mg of citalopram (Celexa) once a day for depression, and she had comorbid school phobia for which she was not on medication. She had a history of self-injurious behaviors, particularly cutting herself, carving words in her skin, and scratching her skin until it bled. Before the teacher had time to act, the fire alarm went off for a prescheduled drill. As the students exited to the nearby soccer field, Ms. Snow kept Jeanette by her side, ensuring she was not out of sight for even a moment. After the drill was over and everyone was permitted back inside, Ms. Snow found a vice principal and discreetly handed him the printout. The vice principal quickly reviewed the printout and agreed that the statements made by Jeanette on her Facebook page should be taken seriously and addressed by the school mental health professional

(SMHP). Thankfully, the students, staff, and faculty at this school had all received training on the importance of acting as gatekeepers and were all provided with wallet cards (as found in your eResources) listing steps on how to respond if concerned a student might be suicidal.

The school psychologist then interviewed Jeanette, who reported significant racing thoughts as well as school anxiety, particularly after a teacher embarrassed her by calling out her bad test grade in front of peers. Jeanette reported that the most recent trigger for her depressive episode was being forced to spend weekends with her estranged father. Jeanette's parents had separated when she was a toddler, and she had not seen her father very often until six months prior to this interview. Jeanette now spent every other weekend at her father's house as directed by the court, but she spent much of that time secluded in her room. She reported that her father made no attempt to interact with her and seemed indifferent when Jeanette made efforts to interact with him. Jeanette reported that her mother, with whom she had a very close relationship, was too afraid of her ex-husband to address the issue, "I feel like my mom is bailing on me when I need her the most, and my so-called dad could care less about me. If he didn't want to be my dad, why did he go to court to make me stay with him?" Her feelings of abandonment by her mother and rejection by her father resulted in her feeling increasingly isolated, frustrated, and suicidal. Jeanette reported that she cried herself to sleep every night "not knowing when this hell will end." After conducting a thorough suicide risk assessment (see Chapters 6 and 7), it was clear to the SMHP that Jeanette was at moderate risk for suicide: She reported frequent and intense thoughts of suicide that interfered with her ability to do her school work and socialize with friends. She reported having a plan, but was unclear about when or if she would follow through. She stated that she would prefer living with one of her friends over dying but that didn't seem likely. This information alone suggested that Jeanette should be assessed for hospitalization. Since her mother was listed as the emergency contact on the medical card, the school psychologist called her and explained the situation. Her mother was concerned and agreed to pick up Jeanette and transport her to the local psychiatric emergency department (ED).

The social worker at the ED determined that Jeanette was not at imminent risk for suicide, and therefore admission would not be appropriate. The ED psychiatrist consulted with her prescribing psychiatrist and both agreed to raise her dosage of Celexa from 10 mg to 30 mg once a day. The discharge worker referred Jeanette and her parents to family therapy in the community, the school psychologist started seeing her once a week for counseling, and a school psychology intern enrolled her in a "stress busters" group in school.

Who were the gatekeepers in this case? Jeanette was fortunate to have had many people on her side looking out for her, including the peer who brought a printout of Jeanette's Facebook page to school, her teacher,

Ms. Snow, the vice principal, and the school psychologist. Jeanette's mother was also very supportive; she came to school immediately and did not hesitate in taking Jeanette to the crisis center. Had any one of these gatekeepers not acted immediately, Jeanette could still be suffering in silence. Or worse. Months later, Jeanette told the school psychologist "this is the best she had felt in some time", saying she could "finally breathe, like I was free, from depression, from everything." Thankfully.

It Takes a Village

David Brent, in his excellent text on cognitive behavioral therapy with depressed and suicidal adolescents talks about something called the "social ecology of wellness" (Brent, Poling, & Goldstein, 2011, p. 246). We love that phrase. It captures the essence of how we think about working with suicidal youth effectively. Suicidal youth are not suicidal in isolation, although they often feel that way. There are potentially life-saving connections that youth make with family, friends, school, and intimate partners. The SMHP will be the staff member with the most training in identifying youth at risk but the least likely to interact with students who are not already identified as needing mental health services.

> **Expert tip:** Schools in which identification and referral of youth at risk for suicide is left to the SMHP assume that suicide prevention is solely one person's responsibility. However, this chapter discusses why and how identifying a child at risk for suicide is the responsibility of *every* adult in a school.

For example, when one of the authors of this text provided training in suicide prevention to all bus drivers in one district, there were several occasions where drivers detected a suicidal student and brought them to the SMHP for help and a suicide risk assessment.

Schools are unique environments for identification of suicide risk because there are many adults who interact with youth in different capacities to observe risk factors and warning signs in students. For example, the principal and the custodian see the same students but in very different contexts. The principal might see the student to administer disciplinary action for a conduct violation. The custodian might overhear a student talking about suicide to another student. Both situations are windows into the life of a suicidal youth. School nurses are in a particularly unique position to help suicidal youth as students are more apt to talk to a nurse, who is in neither a disciplinary or academic role in the school (Cooper, Clements, & Holt, 2012).

A Systems Perspective

Throughout this book we talk about suicide risk as a multi-systemic issue. As illustrated in Figure 2.1, risk and protective factors exist at the most broad societal levels (e.g., media portrayals of suicide and availability of health care) to the most individual levels (e.g., psychopathology, personal values).

According to this biopsychosocial model, school-based prevention and intervention addresses suicide risk at the *community* level and *individual* level. In Chapters 3 and 5, we discuss crisis teams and suicide prevention from a multi-tiered framework (i.e., universal/Tier 1, selective/Tier 2, and indicated/Tier 3). In Chapters 6 and 7, we explore *individual-level* assessment and intervention. However, our text has focused almost entirely on suicide prevention within a single system at the community level—the school.

If students are involved in multiple systems, then it follows that those systems would be activated when a student is suicidal. The systems that SMHPs are most likely to think of are the mental health and medical systems, because school personnel experience the suicidal crisis moving from the school toward community mental health and emergency medicine. If, however, the student has been adjudicated or removed from the home due to abuse or neglect, a suicidal crisis would also activate the juvenile justice system or child welfare system. As SMHPs, knowing the role you play in a multi-systemic response to youth suicidal thoughts and behaviors (STB) will make it easier for you to help a student and his or her family get the help they need. Further, as listed in Table 2.1, a recent Substance Abuse and Mental health Administration (SAMHSA) report of Garret Lee Smith suicide prevention grantees found that nearly half of

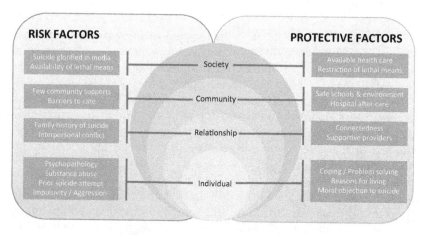

Figure 2.1 A Biopsychosocial Model of Suicide Risk and Protective Factors

Table 2.1 Setting Where Trained Gatekeepers Have Identified
At-Risk Youth (Sites = 368)

Identification Setting	Percentage of Youth Identified
School	49.2%
Mental Health Agency	15.8%
Juvenile Justice Agency	4.3%
Child Welfare Agency	2.7%
Emergency Room	2.2%
Law Enforcement Agency	1.9%
Physical Health Agency	1.1%
Substance Abuse Agency	0.0%
Other	15.8%

all youth were identified as at risk for suicide in the school setting, showing the need for school gatekeepers to be trained in suicide response.

What Is a Gatekeeper?

What (or who) is a gatekeeper in suicide prevention? A gatekeeper is someone
who identifies youth at risk for suicide and knows how to connect youth
with appropriate professional resources (Walsh, Hooven, & Kronick,
2013). As seen in Table 2.1, this is most often a school-based person and
can be anyone who regularly comes into contact with students, knows
the warning signs of suicide, and is willing to take action to ensure a
student has access to mental health services (Stiffman, Pescosolido, &
Cabassa, 2004).

Whether you are a school administrator, teacher or aide, nurse, counselor, hall monitor, or bus driver, you are in a pivotal position to notice
a distressed child through your daily contact. You are the one who may
notice that a child typically full of smiles now appears sad or tearful. You
may observe a child on the bus who is often boisterous but has become
reserved and withdrawn; now sitting alone. You might be the one to see
that a student's grades have dropped dramatically in the last month, that
another hasn't had lunch money recently, or that yet another has not
bathed or brushed her hair all week.

Expert tip: While teachers might have the most contact with students
and the most insight into their functioning, they often feel unable to
help as they report lacking the knowledge necessary to identify students at risk.

A study by King, Price, Telljohann, and Wahl (1999) found that only 9% of a national random sample of U.S. high school teachers believed they could recognize a student at risk for suicide. At the same time, teachers report feeling responsible for preventing potential suicides of their students (King et al., 1999). Education of these gatekeepers is therefore essential.

What Is Gatekeeper Training?

Gatekeeper training is just as it sounds—it is the training (or in-servicing) of school gatekeepers to increase their awareness and knowledge of the risk factors and warning signs of suicide and to provide skills to respond effectively to suicidal youth. It is a systematic approach designed to use the expertise of all school staff members to create an infrastructure of caring adults and to support youth in recognizing, talking about, and preventing suicide (Walsh et al., 2013). As most university educator programs do not adequately address suicide prevention, school administrators recognize the importance offering these trainings (Miller, Eckert, DuPaul, & White, 1999) that result in teachers reporting increased ability to recognize warning signs of suicidal youth and act accordingly (King et al., 1999) and that are shown to be promising (Robinson et al., 2013) with improvements in confidence, knowledge, attitudes, intervention skills, willingness to cope with a crisis, and referral practices (Wyman et al., 2008).

Some states are beginning to enact legislation requiring school districts to provide suicide prevention and awareness training to all credentialed school staff. According to a February 5, 2014 press release by four leading agencies supporting the mental health of youth (American Foundation for Suicide Prevention, American School Counselor Association, National Association of School Psychologists, and The Trevor Project), only four states currently require educators to receive annual suicide prevention training (Alaska, Kentucky, Louisiana, and Tennessee). These four organizations developed the 2014 Model School District Policy on Suicide Prevention, in which they stress the importance of not only having strong prevention policies but also mandating suicide prevention training programs in each state.

There are many practical barriers to staff gatekeeping, including concerns of funding and time for training, staff turnover and substitutes, and discomfort or fear of discussing issues of suicide and the related stigma. In addition, not all school personnel perceive suicide prevention as a part of their job role (e.g., bus drivers). Engaging all staff members in suicide prevention is a difficult but important challenge to undertake.

Identifying Students at Risk

We discussed the warning signs and risk factors for suicide in Chapter 1. In this chapter, we present some school-based examples of what these may actually look like in a school setting. In one example, a cafeteria worker brought disturbing artwork she found on the lunchroom floor to me (the school psychologist). It was a hand drawn cartoon about a pugnacious teen who was teased relentlessly by a criminal. At the end of the cartoon, the teen asked for the criminal's gun, and the last frames showed the teen with the gun to his own head and then blood spewing from his head. This was very disturbing, and I was glad this staff person had turned it in. I had never met this student before and did not know his history. I called him into my office, and we began a dialogue regarding the nature of his cartoon and an assessment of possible suicidal ideation. After some discussion, this student revealed that his cartoon was based on *South Park*, a television series in which, as the student described, a character named Kenny dies in nearly every episode by various methods. This student went on to show me his other cartoon series (he was quite talented!), one of which was about the innocent trials of a family of five living their daily lives under one roof. After further querying, it became evident that this student did not present with suicidal intent but rather was a creative artist. However, had it not been for our extensive dialogue and my risk assessment, we would not have known this. If he had been suicidal, this cafeteria worker may have saved his life by appropriately referring him.

What the Student May Say

There are many observable indications that a student may be experiencing STB. First, we give examples of things students might say in Table 2.2, then we delve deeper into examples of what suicidal indications may look like within a school environment. Thinking back to the example of Jeanette in the beginning of this chapter, she made many statements indicating suicidality. In a world of social media, Jeanette's communications were writings to her online world of friends. Students often make comments offhandedly and you may overhear them. Here are what these

Table 2.2 Suicidal Statements

What They Say	What It Means	Experience
"I feel hopeless."	Tomorrow will be no better than today.	Hopelessness
"I can't see any way out."	I cannot think of alternatives.	Cognitive constriction
"I'd be better off dead."	I have found the best solution.	Problem solving
"I'm so confused."	Part of me wants to live, part of me wants to die.	Ambivalence
"It isn't worth it."	My life is not worth keeping.	Differential value
"No one cares."	I'm all alone.	Social isolation

expressions sometimes mean and what students may be experiencing. These must be taken seriously as they may be indicative of a student who is feeling despair and does not know where to turn. Perhaps they even *hope* you overhear them and will help them.

Academic Indications

One indication that a student may be at risk for suicide is a change in academic performance. A student who was once on honor roll may suddenly no longer care about grades, saying something like "Who cares anymore?" or "I have no future anyway," to a teacher who queries about his or her dropping grades. Some of the most frequent gatekeeper referrers are English teachers because students often present suicidal thoughts or ideations in their creative writings. Imagine a student writes the following:

> *Rose went first. She put the gun to her head, pulled the trigger, though nothing happened. A look of relief flew over her as she passed the gun to Jamal. He slowly put the gun to his head, took a deep breath as he counted to three, and calmly said, "Good-bye" as we heard the loud BANG!*

The essay continued with Jamal's girlfriend being in shock that Jamal had died right next to her, and in the spirit of Romeo and Juliet, she killed herself as well. The teachers at this school were trained gatekeepers, and the English teacher took this writing seriously and turned it in to the counseling department for follow-up.

Behavioral Indications

Behavioral referrals frequently come from the discipline office. Students may have been written up in class for snapping at a teacher or fighting with a peer as an indication of distress. Adolescents who are upset, depressed, or suicidal often act out inappropriately because they do not realize the depth of their own pain, know how to deal with their emotions, know how to access supports, and do not feel that they can tell anyone. Teens frequently say that they do not want to burden their parents or "they thought they could handle it on their own." Gatekeepers are integral here in noticing through their daily contact when a student has a *change* in behavior or if a behavior is worsening. *Was a student in a fight who had previously never demonstrated aggressive behavior? Is an angry student becoming angrier or aggressive or showing increasingly negative behaviors?*

Self-Injurious Behavior

One behavioral indication frequently identified in schools is non-suicidal self-injury (NSSI). Also referred to as self-injurious behavior (SIB), NSSI is a complex behavior that despite its emotional and social regulatory functions increases risk of suicidal behavior (Joiner, Ribeiro, & Silva, 2012). NSSI can include a wide array of behaviors such as cutting or scraping oneself, burning or picking at skin, and banging one's head repeatedly. There are many myths surrounding NSSI, including the idea that individuals who engage in self-injury *are not* suicidal since they are finding a way, albeit an unhealthy one, to release their pain.

While NSSI does not involve thoughts of death in itself, Joiner's interpersonal theory of suicide suggests

> repeated exposure to a painful and provocative stimulus will result in a decrement of the original response (fear & pain) and an increase in the response of the opposite valence (relief & analgesia)—this is viewed as the process underlying the development of the capacity for suicide.
>
> (Joiner et al., 2012, p. 344)

NSSI can therefore be considered a potent risk factor for suicide as students are essentially practicing the act of harming themselves.

NSSI is clearly a strong predictor of suicidal behavior as 70% of adolescents aged 12–17 years who engaged in NSSI reported at least one suicide attempt, with 55% reporting two or more suicide attempts during their lifetime (Nock, Joiner, Gordon, Lloyd-Richardson, & Prinstein, 2006). The number of suicide attempts was correlated with the number of different NSSI methods used and the number of years the adolescent had been engaging in NSSI. Teachers and SMHPs should be aware that a history of NSSI might be a stronger predictor of attempted suicide than a suicide attempt history itself (Andover, Morris, Wren, & Bruzzese, 2012), particularly when the adolescent reports moderate to severe depressive symptoms and a history of alcohol use (Jenkins, Singer, Conner, Calhoun, & Diamond, 2014).

Teens who engage in NSSI sometimes describe how the physical pain experienced is much more manageable than the emotional pain they have been suffering. The self-injury takes their mind off the emotional pain, if for only a brief moment. One teenage female client describes her NSSI cycle to one of the authors. She reports being in a great deal of emotional pain. When this is at its most intense, she cuts herself in a place on her body she feels is least visible. She reports then feeling momentarily relieved from her emotional suffering. However, soon after, a rush of guilt overcomes her for the cutting she just did. More emotional pain is triggered by the guilt, she feels even worse, and cuts again. This becomes a cycle that only ceases when she becomes so exhausted that she just falls asleep. This is a difficult cycle to imagine a teenager living with. She eventually began to express suicidal ideation because she wanted all of her emotional pain to end and she couldn't see it getting better. Her

NSSI is a major risk factor for suicide, and if anything, she is rehearsing or developing the capacity for self-mutilation and bodily injury.

Cognitive Indications

Try to put yourself in a position where you were so upset that you had trouble thinking clearly and could not focus on anything other than the difficult situation you were facing. If you've never had a situation like this, you are extremely lucky. Many of us have experienced the death of a close family member, a job loss, or some other challenge that has consumed our thoughts. A child who is contemplating suicide may be unable to think clearly as well. Their depression and/or anxiety may be so overwhelming they cannot think about anything else in or out of the classroom. Cognitive indications include distorted thoughts, diminished attention span, weakened problem-solving skills, and confusion. For example, a gatekeeper may notice that a child who typically performs well in math suddenly makes errors when solving simple arithmetic problems.

Spiritual/Existential Indications

A common characteristic of a depressed individual is a spiritual or existential questioning. Spiritual questions such as "*Why me?*" "*Why do I deserve this?*" or "*How could God do this to me?*" are common and may include anger or bitterness at God or a sincere questioning of whether a spiritual deity they previously believed in even exists. Existential or philosophical questions may include "*Why am I even here?*" or "*What is my purpose in life?*" This lack of purposefulness can lead to feelings of defeat and suicidal thoughts such as "*Well, if I have no purpose here, why be on this earth?*" Gatekeepers should pay attention to these comments because a student may say them offhandedly.

Emotional Indications

As expected, common emotional indications suicidal youth exhibit include sadness or depression. They may appear tearful, down, or sullen, or they may present with anhedonia, not finding pleasure in activities they previously enjoyed. This may be a student who used to be involved in after-school sports and activities or used to love going to the mall but no longer has an interest in doing so. Younger children may express emotionality via somatic complaints, such as headaches or complaining of a "bad feeling in the pit of their belly." Gatekeepers should pay attention to an adolescent presenting with a labile mood, one that shifts quickly from depressed to angry to agitated; the child may be distressed, confused, and scared.

Social Indications

Withdrawing from others is a social indication that a student may be at risk for suicidal ideation or suicide. Students may withdraw because they are sad and want time alone to either cry or think things through. Or, depressed individuals may not have the energy to socialize and may feel like they are a burden to others. This is of great concern because those who feel they are a burden sometimes contemplate taking their life in order to relieve loved ones of that encumbrance (Joiner, Pettit, Walker, Voelz, & Cruz, 2002). These individuals may feel that they are acting out of love and care by taking their lives. Be wary of statements such as "*My parents would be better off without me*" or "*If I die, my friends won't have to worry about me anymore.*" Finally, individuals sometimes withdraw because once they have a suicide plan in mind, they may not want anyone to find out. Gatekeepers who know a child can more easily identify a change in socialization level.

Bullying/Cyberbullying

Tyler Clementi (18 years old) . . . Billy Lucas (15 years old) . . . Asher Brown (13 years old) . . . Phoebe Prince (15 years old) . . . Ryan Halligan (13 years old) . . . Amanda Cummings (15 years old) . . . Kenneth Weishunh (14 years old) . . . Hope Witsell (13 years old) . . . Rebecca Sedwick (12 years old) . . . Morgan Musson (13 years old) . . .

Do any of these names look familiar to you? They are just a few of the most highly publicized stories of adolescents taking their lives, many of whom were bullied online. While cyberbullying may not lead to a healthy child feeling suicidal, it can exacerbate the instability and hopelessness in vulnerable teens already dealing with stress and mental health issues (Hinduja & Patchin, 2010).

Expert tip: Bullying does not *cause* a person to attempt suicide, although it may increase the risk for an adolescent or teen who is already contemplating suicide.

Bullying of peers has always been a problem, but with technological bullying there is no escape. What was previously referred to as schoolyard bullying ended at 3:00 PM when the final school bell rang. As adolescents have phones on them at *all* times, there is potential for students to be subjected to 24/7 harassment, embarrassment, and abuse by peers. Between 20% to 35% of adolescents report experiencing some form of cyberbullying (Diamanduros, Downs, & Jenkins, 2008; Kowalski & Limber, 2007), which is defined as "an individual or a group willfully using information and communication involving electronic technologies to facilitate deliberate and repeated harassment or threat to another individual or group using technological means" (Mason, 2008). Cyberbullying can take many forms such as posting embarrassing pictures or harmful comments, spreading rumors, recording conversations, pretending to be someone else online to elicit gossip, sending harassing texts or emails, outing someone's sexual orientation online, or creating humiliating internet polls (i.e., who's hot, who's not?).

With all forms of bulling, suicide risk and depression are increased for both victims and bullies (Hindaju & Patchin, 2010), for both males and females, as well as for students in elementary, middle, and high school (Klomek, Sourander, & Gould, 2011). However, cyberbullying victims report more depressive symptoms, suicidal ideation, self-injury, and suicide attempts than victims of traditional school bullying (Schneider, O'Donnell, Stueve, & Coulter, 2012). The risk of psychological distress was most marked for those victims who experienced both forms of bullying as they were four times more likely to experience depressive symptoms and five times more likely to attempt suicide (Schneider, O'Donnell, Stueve, & Coulter, 2012). Females are particularly susceptible to victimization (Schneider et al., 2012) as are students who are among the lesbian, gay, bisexual, transgender, or questioning (LGBTQ) population (Lieberman, Poland, & Kornfeld, 2014).

While parents and school gatekeepers are encouraged to monitor children's online behavior, this presents with challenges as most online bullying is done either behind closed doors or on a smartphone, and 56% percent of teens report hiding their online activities from their parents (McAfee, 2010). We have included handouts on cyberbullying warning signs and tips for prevention in your eResources. Bullying programs must include both prevention efforts (e.g., cyberbullying should be included in a school's internet/computer acceptable use policy as an infringement of school code, allowing schools to take action in a cyberbullying incident) and intervention (e.g., students are taught how to intervene with distressed peers and how to report online harassment or teasing). In a world where social status is based upon how many Facebook friends or Twitter followers one has, adolescents should be taught when it is worth "unfriending" or blocking a peer who is causing more harm than good. Schools should also thwart bullying as it impacts academic performance and decreases school attachment. If that is not enough to convince your administration or school board of the importance of gatekeeper training, consider this: Parents have sued schools because they believed the school's failure to stop bullying led to their child's suicide. Examples of this litigation are presented in Chapter 4.

Social Media Gatekeepers

Social media sites are recognizing the importance of intervening with potentially suicidal individuals. Facebook, for example, has collaborated with Samaritans, a suicide prevention group, to extend help if someone is indicating suicidality (Castillo, 2011). When Facebook users are concerned about a friend posting possibly suicidal comments, they can alert authorities to contact the user for follow up. This function is to help individuals from falling through the cracks, such as the high-profile case of Tyler Clementi, who wrote on his Facebook profile "*Jumping off a bridge sorry*" prior to killing himself (Castillo, 2011). There have been many prominent cases featured in the media since, but perhaps with lessons learned, Facebook users will begin to take responsibility for their friends who are in crisis and report these concerns to authorities, thereby preventing another loss due to suicide.

Most recently, Apple's Siri (the application that allows users to complete tasks by talking into their phone) joined forces to be frontline prevention for users thinking about suicide. Prior to June 2013, if iPhone users told the electronic voice that they wanted to jump off a bridge, Siri would respond with locations of the nearest bridges (Stern, 2013). Now, however, Apple has programmed Siri to return with the phone number for the National Suicide Prevention Lifeline and ask if the user would like the number called or to provide a list of local suicide prevention centers on a map (Stern, 2013). Go ahead and pull out your iPhone if you have one . . . we know you want to test this.

Efficacy of Gatekeeper Programs

The National Registry of Evidence-Based Programs and Practices (SAMHSA, 2013) is an online resource supporting awareness, prevention, and treatment. Each intervention listed has been assessed to ensure requirement criteria has been met for both quality of research and readiness for dissemination (SAMHSA, 2013). Examples of gatekeeper trainings that have been widely used and are included in the Best Practices Registry include Signs of Suicide (SOS), Question, Persuade and Refer (QPR) and Linking Education and Awareness of Depression and Suicide (LEADS) for Youth (SAMHSA, 2013). While more extensive information on evidence-based programs is presented in Chapter 5, gatekeeper programs are introduced here. One study evaluating the efficacy of QPR found that teachers reported greater feelings of preparedness and commitment to perform a gatekeeper role and access services for suicidal students after training (Wyman et al., 2008). Interestingly, skills improved only for those adults who were already empathic but changed little for those who were not, suggesting those with the most empathy make the best gatekeepers.

The importance of peer education/gatekeeper programming lies in the fact that adolescents are more likely to share their suicidal thoughts or plans with a peer than with an adult (Kalafat & Elias, 1994), and adolescents should be trained in what to do. It is ingrained in children not to tattle and to be a good friend by keeping secrets, but it can be a deadly secret when it comes to suicide. Caregivers need to be clear to children about the importance of sharing information when someone's life could be at risk as peers shared their concern in the above case of Jeanette. Sources of Strength is a peer gatekeeper program designed to train youth leaders to change the norms and behaviors of their peers in order to increase positive coping behaviors. This program had positive effects on students' perceptions that adults in their school can help suicidal students, the acceptability of seeking help from adults, rejecting the codes of silence, and the likelihood of referring suicidal friends to adults (Wyman et al., 2010).

While the research mentioned above shows positive effects, research on the Yellow Ribbon Program, a nationally recognized program that includes student assemblies, training peer leaders and adult gatekeepers, outreach, and education, found little positive effect on students' help-seeking behaviors (Freedenthal, 2010). School personnel should realize the limitations of gatekeeper programs and use them with caution and only as part of a comprehensive school suicide prevention curriculum.

Referral Procedures

After two months, Jeanette reported significantly improved functioning due to increased supports. Gatekeepers should know that it is better to err on the side of caution when unsure if a student should be referred. It is not the role of the gatekeeper to assess *if* a student is at risk; a trained mental health professional will do the assessment. Following referral procedures is important because students who are at the highest risk for suicidal behavior are the ones least likely to seek help for themselves (Berman, Jobes, & Silverman, 2006). They may have a suicide plan that they do not want uncovered or they may be experiencing significant depression and unable to activate or take initiative, even with regard to their own well-being. Perhaps the student was already disenfranchised and does not feel connected enough to adult or peer support to seek assistance. Who knows what would have happened to Jeanette had her peers, teacher, vice principal not all been trained to know the warning signs and refer her.

Referral procedures vary in different schools, districts, and communities. Some schools have confidential boxes where students can anonymously write referrals. Other schools have school counselors assigned to each grade so rapport and relationships are built over time to promote sharing of concerns. School personnel should form strong bonds with students so they are more likely to perceive school personnel as approachable (Miller, 2011). School crisis responders often indicate that referrals always seem to come in at the end of a school day or on a Friday afternoon. The problem here lies in the fact that once a student leaves the school building, intervening becomes much more complex.

Expert tip: Students, teachers, school staff, and parents should be educated about the importance of referring students *immediately*.

A particular case comes to mind where a peer referral about a potentially suicidal teen was received on the day before Thanksgiving *after* all the students had already been dismissed. While parents were contacted on emergency numbers to communicate concerns, find the student, ensure safety, and seek treatment for the teen outside of school, this situation could have been dealt with much more readily if the SMHPs became aware of the situation earlier in the day while a SMHP could still access the student for an assessment. The sooner peers and teachers report concerns, the better able responding crisis personnel are to ensure the safety of the student.

What Do I Say?

Teachers often report not knowing what to say to a student who approaches them. Here are some examples of what to say if a child reports suicidal ideation to you:

> *I appreciate that you trusted me to tell me this. Now, I want to get you help.*
> *I can only imagine how scared you might feel.*
> *No one should have to be in this much pain, let's get you help.*
> *I am so sorry that you have had to suffer, please know there is help.*
> *I am honored that you felt you could come to me. Now we can get you the help you need so you don't continue hurting like this.*

What Not to Say

Despite our best intentions and training, sometimes we say things that unintentionally make a situation worse. The most common type of unhelpful response is what motivational interviewing calls the "righting reflex" (Miller & Rollnick, 2013), a knee-jerk impulse to offer a solution to a problem. Statements like, "What you should do is . . ." and "Something you might consider doing is . . ." are examples of the righting reflex. Another common response that is unhelpful is empathizing. While showing sympathy (concern for another's suffering) is indeed helpful ("I am sorry you are going through this"), empathy (sharing another's suffering) implies that you have experienced their same pain ("I know how you feel"). Regardless of your own thoughts, feelings, and experiences, it is important to practice unconditional acceptance with suicidal youth and ensure they feel no judgment from you. The following are some statements of the righting reflex, empathy, and others that are unhelpful, followed by the rationale why you shouldn't say them to a suicidal student:

> *I understand what you are going through.*
> *You should think of the positive.*
> *Your parents would be mad to hear you say these things.*
> *Consider all that you have to live for.*
> *I'll be right back.*

I Understand What You Are Going Through

We must be careful what we say to a suicidal youngster who has just shared his or her secret with us. If we tell them that we understand what they are going through, we may break our rapport, as their life is unique and they may have much more they are not telling us. Our intent may be to show the student compassion that they are not alone, but this may backfire as we never quite know the depth of their story or the intensity of their pain. If we tell them we understand, we may disenfranchise them as they feel that there is no way we could "get it."

You Should Think of the Positive

Our intent in this righting reflex may be to indicate that life will get better, there is help available, and that they should look on the bright side, but a student in a suicidal state cannot typically think clearly. They only hear your words and they may be defensive as this statement seems to be telling the student that they are wrong to think the way they do. The last thing they need is to feel as if they are being criticized, especially if they have just shared their deep, dark feelings with you.

Your Parents Would Be Mad to Hear You Say These Things

Similar to the previous example, the last thing a suicidal student needs is to feel as if they will be ostracized or disparaged further. A better statement is to tell them that their parents would not want them to hurt so much. Of course, this should only be said if you know that the parents are indeed caring and are not abusive in any fashion toward this child.

Consider All That You Have to Live For

A student in a suicidal state may feel at that moment as if they *do not* have *anything* to live for. They may feel alone, discouraged, that nobody cares about them, and that they are a burden to others. To tell them otherwise in the midst of a suicidal crisis can do more damage as this may only deepen the feeling that no one understands them and what they are going through. While they may have much to live for, it is important to remember that a depressed adolescent has blinders on and may only see those things that confirm their negative views. At these times, it is more helpful to demonstrate compassion, validate students' feelings, and reinforce these youth for their courage in sharing these difficult feelings.

I'll Be Right Back

Do not leave a student alone. Ever. After they have disclosed their secrets about suicide, many adolescents become weary and scared. They may fear what kind of "help" you will get them as movies often portray psychiatrists and psychologists as outrageous and irrational. (Have you ever seen the movie *What About Bob?*) Students may also fear what their parents will say. As a result, students may see this as their last opportunity to harm themselves before facing the wrath of having shared their secret. Fear of the unknown or anxiety over what will come next may prevail, with fight-or-flight mode kicking in. This becomes a time of heightened suicide risk as students may take an opportunity to flee and act impulsively out of this fear.

Conclusion

Protecting the lives of our children takes a village. Teachers, maintenance staff, SMHPs, administrators, school bus drivers, and cafeteria staff—we are all responsible. Those who see children and teens on a daily basis are in the best place to observe any changes in a student's behavior, academics, or general functioning. Many SMHPs and administrators rely on these reports, and it is essential that gatekeepers be trained to report concerns immediately. Students who are of suicidal concern should not be allowed to go home until concerns are addressed. As most teacher training programs do not address suicide or other crisis events, schools and school districts must take it upon themselves to do so. The lives of children are in our hands.

References

American Foundation for Suicide Prevention. (AFSP), American School Counselors Association (ASCA), National Association of School Psychologists (NASP), & The Trevor Project. (2014). Model school district policy on suicide prevention: Model language, commentary and resources. Retrieved from http://www.afsp.org/news-events/in-the-news/afsp-partners-with-trevor-project-and-others-on-model-school-policy-on-suicide-prevention

Andover, M. S., Morris, B. W., Wren, A., & Bruzzese, M. E. (2012). The co-occurrence of non-suicidal self-injury and attempted suicide among adolescents: Distinguishing risk factors and psychosocial correlates. *Child and*

Adolescent Psychiatry and Mental Health 6(11). Retrieved from http://www.capmh.com/6/1/11

Berman, A. L., Jobes, D. A., & Silverman, M. M. (2006). *Adolescent suicide: Assessment and intervention* (2nd ed.). Washington, DC: American Psychological Association.

Brent, D. A., Poling, K. D., & Goldstein, T. R. (2011). *Treating depressed and suicidal adolescents: A clinician's guide.* New York: The Guilford Press.

Castillo, M. (2011, March 8). Facebook teams up with Samaritans to prevent suicide. *Time.* Retrieved from http://www.techland.time.com/2011/03/08/facebook-teams-up-with-samaritans-to-prevent-suicide

Cooper, G. D., Clements, P. T., & Holt, K. E. (2012). Examining childhood bullying and adolescent suicide: Implications for school nurses. *The Journal of School Nursing, 28,* 275–283. doi:10.1177/1059840512438617

Diamanduros, T., Downs, T., & Jenkins, S. J. (2008). The role of school psychologists in the assessment, prevention, and intervention or cyberbullying. *Psychology in the Schools, 45,* 693–704.

Freedenthal, S. (2010). Adolescent help-seeking and the Yellow Ribbon Suicide Prevention Program: An evaluation. *Suicide and Life-Threatening Behavior, 40*(6), 628–639.

Hinduja, S., & Patchin, J. W. (2010). Bullying, cyberbullying and suicide. *Archives of Suicide Research, 14*(3), 206–221.

Jenkins, A. L., Singer, J. B., Conner, B. T., Calhoun, S., & Diamond, G. (2014). Risk for suicidal ideation and attempt among a primary care sample of adolescents engaging in non-suicidal self-injury. *Suicide and Life-Threatening Behavior.* doi:10.1111/sltb.12094

Joiner, T. E., Pettit, J. W., Walker, R. L., Voelz, Z. R., & Cruz, J. (2002). Perceived burdensomeness and suicidality: Two studies on the suicide notes of those attempting and those completing suicide. *Journal of Social and Clinical Psychology, 21*(5), 531–545.

Joiner, T. E., Ribeiro, J. D., & Silva, C. (2012). Nonsuicidal self-injury, suicidal behavior, and their co-occurrence as viewed through the lens of the interpersonal theory of suicide. *Current Directions in Psychological Science, 21,* 342–347. doi:10.1177/0963721412454873

Kalafat, J., & Elias, M. (1994). An evaluation of a school-based suicide awareness intervention. *Suicide and Life-Threatening Behavior, 24*(3), 224–233.

King, K. A., Price, J. H., Telljohann, S. K., & Wahl, J. (1999). High school health teachers' perceived self-efficacy in identifying students at risk for suicide. *Journal of School Health, 69*(5), 202–207.

Klomek, A. B., Sourander, A., & Gould, M. S. (2011, February). Bullying and suicide. *Psychiatric Times, 28*(2). Retrieved from http://www.psychiatrictimes.com/suicide/bullying-and-suicide

Kowalski, R., & Limber, S., (2007). Electronic bullying among middle school students. *Journal of Adolescent Health, 41,* S22–S30.

Lieberman, R., Poland, S., & Kornfeld, C. (2014). Suicide intervention in the schools. In A. Thomas & P. Harrison (Eds.), *Best practices in school psychology VI* (pp. 273–288). Bethesda, MD: National Association of School Psychologists.

Mason, K. L. (2008). Cyberbullying: A preliminary assessment for school personnel. *Psychology in the Schools, 45,* 323–348.

McAfee. (2010). *The secret online lives of teens.* Retrieved from http://us.mcafee.com/en-us/local/docs/lives_of_teens.pdf

Miller, D. N. (2011). *Child and adolescent suicidal behavior: School-based prevention, assessment and intervention.* New York, NY: Guilford Press.

Miller, D. N., Eckert, T. L., DuPaul, G. J., & White, G. P. (1999). Adolescent suicide prevention: Acceptability of school-based programs among secondary school principals. *Suicide and Life-Threatening Behavior, 29*(1), 72–85.

Miller, W. R., & Rollnick, S. (2013). *Motivational interviewing: Helping people change* (3rd ed.). New York: Guilford Press.

Nock, M. K., Joiner, T. E., Gordon, K. H., Lloyd-Richardson, E., & Prinstein, M. J. (2006). Non-suicidal self-injury among adolescents: Diagnostic correlates and relation to suicide attempts. *Psychiatry Research, 144,* 65–72.

Robinson, J., Cox, G., Malone, A., Williamson, M., Baldwin, G., Fletcher, K., & O'Brien, M. (2013). A systematic review of school-based interventions aimed at preventing, treating, and responding to suicide-related behavior in young people. *Crisis, 34*(3), 164–182. doi:10.1027/0227-5910/a000168

Schneider, S. K., O'Donnell, L, Stueve, A., & Coulter, R.W.S. (2012). Cyberbullying, school bullying, and psychological distress: A regional census of high school students. *American Journal of Public Health, 102*(1), 171–177.

Stern, J. (2013, June 24). *Apple's Siri can be first call for users thinking of suicide.* Retrieved from http://abcnews.go.com/Technology/apples-siri-now-prevent-suicides/sotry?id=19438495

Stiffman, A. R., Pescosolido, B., & Cabassa, L. J. (2004). Building a model to understand youth service access: The Gateway Provider Model. *Mental Health Services Research, 6*(4), 189–198.

Substance Abuse and Mental Health Services Administration (SAMHSA). (2013). *National Registry of Evidence-Based Programs and Practices.* Retrieved from http://www.SAMHSA.samhsa.gov

Walsh, E., Hooven, C., & Kronick, B. (2013). School-wide staff and faculty training in suicide risk awareness: Successes and challenges. *Journal of Child and Adolescent Psychiatric Nursing, 26*(1), 53–61. doi:10.1111/jcap.12011

Wyman, P. A., Brown, C. H., LoMurray, M., Schmeelk-Cone, K., Petrova, M., Yu, Q., . . . Wang, W. (2010). An outcome evaluation of the Sources of Strength suicide prevention program delivered by adolescent peer leaders in high schools. *American Journal of Public Health, 100*(9), 1653–1661.

Wyman, P. A., Inman, J., Guo, J., Brown, C. H., Cross, W., Schmeelk-Cone, K., & Pena, J. B. (2008). Randomized trial of a gatekeeper program for suicide prevention: 1-year impact on secondary school staff. *Journal of Counseling and Clinical Psychology, 76*(1), 104–115.

3   School Crisis Response Planning

A Planned Response

All school personnel have at times felt like their entire day was spent managing one crisis after another (we often refer to it as putting out fires). Students get into a fight; parents show up angry about statewide testing; administrators call emergency staff meetings about new policies; colleagues announce a divorce, death of a parent, not coming back the next year . . . They can be exhausting and taxing, but for the most part, they are over in a day or two. This chapter is not about those kinds of crises (which students might call drama and professionals might call personal crises or "really stressful parts of the job"). This chapter is about the kinds of crises that require a coordinated, planned response to an unusual event or series of events that cannot be successfully managed by one or two school personnel. Examples include death in the school by natural causes, suicide, or shooting; suicide attempt; terroristic threat (e.g., bomb threat, hate-crime graffiti); natural disaster (e.g., tornado or earthquake); or accident (e.g., school bus crash). These kinds of crises can be devastating for everyone, make the school seem like an unsafe environment, and significantly impact student and staff ability to focus on learning.

Following the Columbine High School shooting in 1999, numerous national organizations and agencies stressed the need for crisis planning in schools. While great strides have been made, Poland, in his 2009 U.S. Congressional testimony, noted that schools have since become complacent about crisis planning. In particular, schools have been reluctant to accept an active role in youth suicide prevention, focusing instead on school violence. This reluctance appears to be predicated on two false assumptions: There is no relationship between school violence and youth suicide and expanding the scope of crisis plans and teams to include suicide places an undue burden on school personnel's time and resources. Neither are true. In this chapter, we define *crisis* and define and describe the function and organization of crisis teams. We discuss the role of the crisis team in situations that affect the entire school (primary or universal response), a subset of people in a school (secondary or selective response), or specific individuals (tertiary or indicated response). We end with a review of the PREPaRE model of crisis prevention and response and the Incident Command System structure (ICS). Despite the great strides that have been made in school-based crisis response, there is more that needs to be done, particularly in the case of a suicide crisis.

What Is a Crisis?

A crisis encompasses the following criteria (Brock & Poland, 2002; Brock, Reeves, & Nickerson, 2014; Pitcher & Poland, 1992):

1. High levels of subjective discomfort
2. Individual(s) temporarily unable to act in a way to modify stress
3. Situation that overwhelms an individual's ability to cope/knowledge of coping strategies
4. Situation or event that an individual *perceives* as negative or threatening
5. Seemingly unsolvable problem

There are many different types of crises, such as developmental, environmental, existential, and situational (Gilliland & James, 2013). Situational crises are what schools deal with most frequently and have been defined as "events that are relatively rare, unexpected, unpredictable, have a sudden onset, and seem to strike from nowhere" (Brock & Poland, 2002, p. 273). Because the suicide death of a student is, thankfully, a relatively rare event, it can create a crisis for a school community. And yet, many schools do not consider suicide to be in the domain of the crisis team.

Crisis Plans

One of the authors of this text (Poland) has been advocating for and writing about crisis planning in schools since the late 1980s (Poland, 1989; Pitcher & Poland, 1992). His early writing stressed that an important factor in successful crisis planning is strong administrative support in crisis situations. One individual—no matter his or her position at the school—can make a difference if the person asserts himself or herself and refuses to give up in gaining administrative support for crisis teams (Pitcher & Poland, 1992). The crisis plan itself is a written document that is developed at either the district or school level. All school personnel are trained on the plan and each school staff member and stakeholder should have a copy. The plan defines different crises and details planned responses by school crisis teams.

Suicide prevention is a crucial piece to the school violence puzzle as the relationship between school shooters, often referred to in federal

> **Expert tip:** School crisis plans that are organized around school violence to the exclusion of suicide risk are misguided because they fail to consider the strong relationship between youth who commit acts of violence and youth who are at risk for suicide.

documents as "attackers," and suicide is very significant. The government report *Threat Assessment in Schools: A Guide to Managing Threatening Situations and to Creating Safe School Climates* (Fein et al., 2004) emphasized that most attackers (school shooters) had difficulty coping with significant losses or personal failures, and three-quarters of school shooters had a history of suicidal thoughts, threats, gestures, or attempts. This key finding illustrates how a focus on suicidal students also aids in the management of threatening situations and prevention of possible violence in schools. The information in the 2004 report will be helpful to school mental health professionals (SMHPs) when they lobby for improved and more regular suicide prevention training and initiatives. School personnel and individuals on school crisis teams should view the information in that booklet as a vital piece of their crisis planning and preparedness.

Crisis Teams

Pitcher and Poland (1992) initially outlined the elements of crisis teams, presenting their readers with examples of individuals and groups who can best serve on these teams. The members of the teams and key planning points have essentially not changed since their early work (Figure 3.1). Crisis teams should be assembled in a strategic manner to include the right mix of school personnel, outside agency employees, and community members. Team members should have requisite skills such as crisis knowledge and personal attributes such as calmness, good communication skills, and a team orientation.

A typical team structure as outlined by Poland (2004) might include the superintendent overseeing the crisis coordinator (manages the team—often a school principal), who is then in charge of the following: a counseling liaison (supports the emotional needs of staff and students—school psychologist, counselor, or social worker), law enforcement liaison (communicates with law enforcement—law enforcement member or school staff), media liaison (manages media correspondence following a crisis—communications specialist), student liaison (communicates with students), parent liaison (communicates with parents), campus liaison (communicates with campus staff), and a medical liaison (provides first aid—nurse or trained staff member) (Poland, 1997; Pitcher & Poland, 1992). Liaisons must know their responsibilities; each

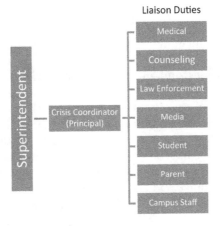

Figure 3.1 Organization of Crisis Teams for Prevention, Intervention, and Post-vention at the Building or District Level

position is essential in the management of the crisis. Poland and McCormick (1999) proposed that there are three waves that must be managed after a crisis: police and medical personnel, media, and parents.

To ensure competence and efficiency of team members, schools should facilitate team planning and development meetings, training programs, appropriate school policies, and crisis drills. Sample crisis drills and summaries of actual crisis events can be found in the literature and should be studied by individuals on crisis teams (Poland & McCormick, 1999; Pitcher & Poland, 1992). Schools are cautioned, however, not to have such realistic crisis drills that staff or students might become frightened. School personnel and students need to be prepared but not scared.

Organization of Teams

While the aforementioned sample crisis team is composed of individuals from the school *and* community, a crisis team can be developed on three different levels: (a) building level, (b) district level, or (c) community level (Poland, 1997; Pitcher & Poland, 1992). Levels are utilized depending on the nature and severity of the crisis, the size of the school and district, and the area in which it is located. A building team is the least restrictive in that it uses only school personnel who work in the same building. District teams engage more staff as additional school district personnel are called in to assist. Finally, community level response involves members of school staff as well as non-school staff in the community (e.g., police officers, medical personnel, mental health workers, and firefighters) (Pitcher & Poland, 1992). In this case, community personnel, such as law enforcement, may take over the role of the crisis coordinator, particularly if a suicide death occurs on campus.

A building team is easier to organize because members have higher levels of familiarity with each other and the students and have an easier time coordinating meetings. Building teams are also in the best position to develop and implement programs such as suicide prevention, school safety activities, and anger management. The downside of building level response is that smaller schools may not have needed personnel, especially school security, nurses, and counseling staff. District teams have the advantage that everyone works for the same school system and the district likely has law enforcement or security, a school nurse, and a counselor on staff. A disadvantage of a district level team is that staff may not be familiar with each other and meetings are harder to schedule to ensure good attendance. Finally, the community team has the advantage of including personnel in all needed areas but as these team members represent various agencies and entities and report to many different supervisors, scheduling meetings and developing close relationships between team members may be challenging (Poland, 2004).

Levels of Intervention

Caplan's (1964) theoretical model of primary, secondary, and tertiary prevention fits considerably well with the terms connected to suicide—prevention, intervention, and postvention. Remember that while we refer to it as a prevention model, these levels include all areas of prevention, intervention, and postvention. Crisis teams should be trained in prevention, intervention, and postvention and organize activities at each level to avert crises (Poland, 1997; Pitcher & Poland, 1992). These terms are similar but not synonymous with the current terms used in the field of education: universal, selective, and indicated interventions.

Universal interventions are very similar to primary prevention in that they are designed to reach the entire population; an example is depression screening for all students. *Selective interventions* are interventions provided for subgroups that may be at risk; an example is providing support and counseling for students who have experienced a crisis event and might be at risk for depression. *Indicated interventions* are tertiary postvention activities that include following up and providing support to staff and students affected by a tragedy, even months afterwards. You will find in Chapter 5 that this same model is applied within the public health approach to *solely* prevention strategies. Similarly, in Chapter 8, this model is adapted *specifically* to postvention strategies in the aftermath of a suicide.

Primary/Universal

Primary prevention efforts should include prevention programs for any possible crisis event. The leading causes of death for children are accidents, homicide, and suicide, and crisis teams members are encouraged to link with community efforts to prevent these tragic deaths. Primary prevention efforts should include coordinating crisis drills and crisis team prevention meetings, establishing a second-in-command in the event the crisis coordinator (school principal) is unavailable, and creating backup plans for possible obstacles (Poland 1997; Poland & Pitcher, 1992). Specifically with regard to suicide, primary prevention focuses not only on education about the warning signs of suicide and the importance of getting professional help but also increasing protective factors for students and reducing risk factors. These primary prevention efforts are recommended for all youth and are therefore universal.

Secondary/Selective

The individual on the crisis team in charge of secondary prevention efforts should be prepared to manage particular crises when they might occur with brief warning(s). Secondary prevention for a suicidal student includes providing support at school, notification to parents, and referral for community services that are outlined in great detail throughout this book. Secondary prevention after a suicide includes triaging students in need of additional support. Poland, Samuel-Barrett, and Waguespack (2014) outlined the following key questions to estimate the amount of potential emotionality following the death of a member of the school community: who was the person, what happened to them, where did the death occur, what other tragic losses has the school experienced, and was there a perpetrator or someone who caused the death.

Tertiary/Indicated

Tertiary prevention efforts regulate the long-term postvention strategies initiated in the aftermath of a crisis in an attempt to limit the distressing effects and avoid further crises. The authors' experience has been that many schools have underestimated the impact of the crisis and have not provided long-term follow-up and assistance for those most affected over a period of months or years. It is important to recognize that there can be an anniversary effect to suicide where the survivors might be suicidal on the anniversary of the loss or on the birthday of the deceased (Lieberman, Poland, and Kornfeld, 2014). Tertiary prevention efforts include providing long-term care, support, and assistance to affected personnel and individuals as needed. Poland, Samuel-Barrett, and Waguespack (2014) outlined circles of vulnerability to identify those who might be most likely to have long-term effects after the crisis. The three circles are geographical proximity, psychosocial proximity, and population at risk or those with trauma history. As can be seen in Figure 3.2, each area of vulnerability interacts with the others to create a combined impact on the youth.

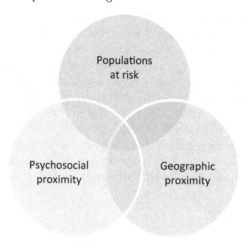

Figure 3.2 Circles of Vulnerability

1.   Geographical proximity identifies those individuals who were at the scene of the crisis.
2.   Psychosocial proximity identifies the family members and close friends of those who were injured or died.
3.   Population at risk/trauma history identifies those staff and students who had previous losses, perhaps to suicide, as well as those with a history of mental illness or previous suicidal ideation/attempts.

PREPaRE: National Incident Management System's Incident Command System (NIMS/ICS)

There is an evolution in crisis planning from the pioneer work of Pitcher and Poland (1992) and the early work of the National Emergency Assistance Team (NEAT) developed by National Association of School Psychologists (NASP). Additionally, NASP has cultivated the PREPaRE model as a newer means to preventing, preparing for, and acting in crisis situations (Brock, Nickerson, Reeves, & Jimerson, 2008; Brock et al., 2014):

P—**Prevent** and PREPaRE for psychological trauma
R—**Reaffirm** physical health and perceptions of security and safety
E—**Evaluate** psychological trauma risk
P—**Provide** interventions
a—**and**
R—**Respond** to psychological needs
E—**Examine** the effectiveness of crisis prevention and intervention

PREPaRE uses a combination of guidelines from the U.S. Department of Homeland Security and the U.S. Department of Education.

Like primary, secondary, and tertiary prevention methods, the PREP<u>a</u>RE method follows four stages of crisis management:

1. *Prevention:* implementation of activities in order to reduce the likelihood of a crisis
2. *Preparedness:* plan in advance steps to take in response to a possible crisis as well as protocols to implement following a crisis
3. *Response:* immediate reactions to crisis and the utilization of the ICS
4. *Recovery:* the implementation of protocols subsequent to a crisis event

PREP<u>a</u>RE operates these four steps through a multi-tiered approach to crisis prevention and response (Brock et al., 2014).

1. *Tier 1* includes universal crisis interventions that are used among the entire student population. This tier can also be seen as a means to prepare for and prevent crises as best as possible. The PREP<u>a</u>RE model stresses the development of crisis teams and crisis management plans such as the creation and coordination of the ICS (Brock et al., 2014). In addition to working to prevent and prepare for crises, Tier 1 under the PREP<u>a</u>RE model aids in keeping all students (and staff) in the affected school(s) physically and psychologically safe (Brock et al., 2014), ensuring social support systems are in place, training caregivers, and identifying students who might be in need of further psychological assistance.
2. *Tier 2* includes selective crisis interventions for those individuals who might be at moderate-to-severe risk for psychological distress. The PREP<u>a</u>RE model uses Tier 2 techniques for these individuals affected by a crisis at their school. The school psychologist and other crisis intervention specialists can and should provide psycho-education and, what PREP<u>a</u>RE calls "psychological first-aid" to those students at moderate-to-severe risk for psychological stress (Brock et al., 2014). Group interventions (i.e., debriefing) and other first-aid responses can be used in such a way that can help to identify those students who are in need of indicated crisis intervention (Tier 3).
3. *Tier 3* includes indicated crisis interventions for those individuals extremely traumatized or presenting with symptomology of extreme psychological disturbance following a crisis. While the former is likely a small percentage of the school population, the number of students tremendously affected is also dependent on the nature of a crisis. This tier emphasizes long-term psychological care for those in high psychological distress (Brock et al., 2014).

Incident Command System Structure (ICS)

The structure of the ICS within the PREP<u>a</u>RE model mirrors other community-based crisis teams. Brock et al. (2008) argue that this system provides an easier collaboration and coordination, particularly with law enforcement and first responders, through this explicit structure. We provide the elements of the ICS here as this collective approach will make certain that there are individuals being held accountable for all aspects of any and all possible types of crises. Under the control of the School Incident Commander are categories and subsequent subcategories in which personnel across disciplines are collaborating in order to efficiently respond to a crisis (Brock et al., 2008):

1. INTELLIGENCE (Thinkers)
2. OPERATIONS (Doers)

   a. *School security and safety coordinator*

      i. Facilities and grounds control specialist
      ii. Search, rescue, and accounting specialist
      iii. Crowd management specialist
      iv. Traffic safety specialist

   b. *School student care coordinator*

      i. Crisis intervention specialist
      ii. Student assembly and release specialist
      iii. Shelter, food, water, and supplies specialist

   c. *School emergency medical coordinator*

      i. First-aid specialist
      ii. Morgue specialist

   d. *School translation coordinator (liaison to the community)*

3. LOGISTICS (Getters)

   a. Facilities
   b. Supplies and equipment
   c. Staff and community volunteer assignment
   d. Communications (someone from the administration)

4. FINANCE (Payers)

Similar to other forms of organizing crisis teams, the number of individuals serving in the ICS depends on the size of the school district and area in which it is located (Brock et al., 2008). For instance, one individual may play multiple roles in the ICS in small school districts. Brock et al. (2008) provides much more detail for each role and responsibility in the ICS.

Conclusion

The authors are often asked what school personnel should do if they are interested in crisis intervention. While much of what school personnel learn about school crisis planning and response is learned on the job, training should come first. Training programs for counselors, school psychologists, social workers, and administrators are beginning to include coursework that attend to crisis intervention. But, training can also be obtained from these highly recognized training providers/programs: (a) National Organiation of Victim's Assistance (more information at http://www.trynova.org); (b) Critical Incident Stress Management (Mitchell, 1983; Mitchell & Everly, 1996); (c) Red Cross; or (d) PREPaRE. Each of these training programs has pros and cons for schools but it is important to note that PREPaRE was specifically designed for schools by NASP utilizing research based on children.

Expert tip: School personnel should carefully evaluate their training, consider the developmental ages of students, and stay current with the research on effectiveness for schools, implementing new findings into regular reevaluation of their crisis plans.

While one aspect of crisis that has received much attention is threat assessment, the main focus has been to assess the severity of violence against others, not against oneself as in the case of suicide. Threat assessment teams for schools and training in how to conduct threat assessment has been recommended by numerous national entities post-Columbine including the U.S. Department of Education and the U.S. Secret Service (Cornell, 2006). As the best decisions for threat assessments use a multidisciplinary approach (Poland, 2008), teams should ensure that they review all school records on the individual who reportedly made the threat and gather as much information as possible. Members of the crisis team should interview the individual reported to have made the threat, as well as the recipient of the threat and any witnesses. The threat of violence toward others is then evaluated based on information gathered from numerous sources and classified as substantial (i.e., one that has had planning, there might be a long-standing grudge, and the means to carry out the threat is available) or transient (i.e., one that is made in a moment of anger and less likely to be carried out) (Poland, 2008). While both types of threat deserve consequences, the consequence for a transient threat might not need to be as severe as suspension or expulsion. Notify and enlist the cooperation of the parents of both the individual reportedly making the threat and the recipient; providing strategies to reduce stressors as an important step toward threat reduction. This logical approach to threat assessment is similar to the suicide assessment procedures outlined in this book. However, there should never be consequences or punishment for a student who makes a suicidal threat; it is essential to focus on reducing stressors for the suicidal student and enlisting parental cooperation (see Chapter 7 for more details about communicating with parents following a suicide assessment).

Schools have become very familiar with assessing violent threats toward others, but may not place enough emphasis on assessing suicide threats because there have been no national initiatives or call to action with regard to suicide assessment. There is an obvious connection between suicide and violence, yet many fail to acknowledge this link. Individuals who serve on crisis teams are trained in crisis planning and intervention, and so it follows that they are also the logical ones to be trained in suicide prevention/warning signs of suicide. Increased understanding of suicide prevention, intervention, and postvention in a school environment may avert violence on school grounds. As the majority of school shooters experience suicidal ideation, threats, or attempts (and some engage in murder-suicide), the studying and training of suicide prevention techniques will help crisis teams be better equipped to identify and handle individuals who might pose a threat—either to self or others—in the school environment.

References

Brock, S. E., Nickerson, A. B., Reeves, M. A., & Jimerson, S. R. (2008). Best practices for school psychologists as members of crisis teams: The PREPaRE model. In A. Thomas & J. Grimes (Eds.), *Best practices in school psychology V* (pp. 1487–1504). Bethesda, MD: National Association of School Psychologists.

Brock, S., Reeves, M., & Nickerson, A. (2014). Best practices in school crisis intervention. In A. Thomas & P. Harris (Eds.), *Best practices in school psychology VI* (pp. 211–230). Bethesda, MD: National Association of School Psychologists.

Brock, S. E., & Poland, S. (2002). School crisis preparedness. In S. E. Brock, P. J. Lazarus, & S. R. Jimerson (Eds.), *Best practices in school crisis prevention and intervention* (pp. 273–288). Bethesda, MD: National Association of School Psychologists.

Caplan, G. (1964). *Principles of preventative psychiatry.* New York, NY: Basic Books.

Cornell, D. (2006). *School violence: Fear versus fact.* Hillsdale, NJ: Lawrence Erlbaum Associates.

Fein, R., Vossekuil, B., Pollack, W. S., Borum, R., Modzeleski, W., & Reddy, M. (2004). *Threat assessment in schools: A guide to managing threatening situations and to creating safe school climates.* Washington, DC: U.S. Department of Education, Office of Elementary and Secondary Education, Safe and Drug-Free Schools Program and U.S. Secret Service, National Threat Assessment Center.

Gilliland, B., & James, R. (2013). Crisis intervention strategies (7th ed.). Belmont, CA: Brooks/Cole, Cengage Learning.

Lieberman, R., Poland, S., & Kornfeld, C. (2014). Suicide intervention in the schools. In A. Thomas & P. Harris (Eds.), *Best practices in school psychology VI* (pp. 273–288). Bethesda, MD: National Association of School Psychologists.

Mitchell, J. (1983). When disaster strikes: The critical incident stress debriefing process. *Journal of Emergency Services, 8,* 36–39.

Mitchell, J.T., & Everly, G.S. (1996). *Critical incident stress management: The basic course workbook.* Ellicott City, MD: International Critical Incident Stress Foundation.

Pitcher, G.D., & Poland, S. (1992). *Crisis intervention in the schools.* New York: The Guilford Press.

Poland, S. (1989). *Suicide intervention in schools.* New York: The Guilford Press.

Poland, S. (1997). School crisis teams. In A.P. Goldstein & J.C. Conoley (Eds.), *School violence intervention* (pp. 127–159). New York: The Guilford Press.

Poland, S. (2004). School crisis teams. In A. Goldstein & J. Conoley (Eds.), *School violence intervention: A practical handbook* (2nd ed.). New York: The Guilford Press.

Poland, S. (2008, November). Threat assessments. *District Administration.* Retrieved from http://www.districtadministration.com/article/threat-assessments

Poland, S., (2009, July 8). Congressional testimony on strengthening school safety before the Joint hearing of the Subcommittees for Healthy Families and Communities and Elementary and Secondary Education, Washington, DC.

Poland, S. & McCormick, J. (1999). *Coping with crisis: Lessons learned. A complete and comprehensive guide to school crisis intervention.* Longmont, CO: Sopris West.

Poland, S., Samuel-Barrett, C. & Waguespack, A. (2014). Best practices in responding to deaths at school. In A. Thomas & P. Harris (Eds.), *Best practices in school psychology VI (pp. 303–320).* Bethesda, MD: National Association of School Psychologists.

4   School Liability and Implications for Best Practice

Liability for schools with regard to suicide is a complex issue with significant implications for all school staff but especially for administrators and school mental health professionals (SMHPs). There have been a number of court cases where schools were sued following the suicide of a student, and one of the authors of this text (Poland) has been an expert witness in a number of these cases. We go over court cases to review lessons learned and explain the meaning of the key legal terms of negligence, in loco parentis, duty to protect, immunity, state-created danger, intervening force, and foreseeability. One of the key issues in legal cases has also been failure to train school staff in suicide prevention, and questions around this issue are raised in the following example.

Recently one of the authors communicated with a school principal and offered to provide suicide prevention training for all staff at a local high school. The author volunteered to provide a workshop at no charge but did ask that the session be mandatory for all staff; the author believes it is essential for all staff members to know the warning signs of suicide, the importance of reporting suicidal thoughts and behaviors (STB), and how to work as a team to prevent a suicide. It has been over six months since the offer to bring the suicide training to the school, and nothing has come of it. The reason that the training has not been scheduled remains unclear. What do you think the barriers might be and the reasons for the principal's failure to schedule the training? One time of the year that the principal might be more likely to schedule the training would be during National Suicide Prevention Week, usually the second week of September. There are probably many reasons that the training has not been scheduled given all the demands on school personnel and perhaps the principal's lack of knowledge about the incidence of youth suicide. The key question is how does one go about getting the administration's attention, short of a student suicide followed by a potential lawsuit? Even if a school is not found liable subsequent to a suicide, a tragedy occurred and the school's name is associated with it. While it is difficult to find any one party accountable for the suicide of a student, a lawsuit can cost a school thousands (if not millions) of dollars in personal and legal costs, tremendous stress, time, and the placement of a stigma on the school/

school district. No precedent has yet been set regarding a school's liability in cases of suicide. While we may find one court that has upheld an action against a public school based on the duty to prevent suicide when school personnel were aware of such intent, we can find countless other courts that have not taken such action. The judges/jury must consider whether the student's death was a result of inadequate responses from school personnel; however, it is extremely hard to prove that a school's breach of duty to care *caused* the suicide while weighing other significant factors in the child's life.

Prior to the case of *Eisel v. Montgomery County Board of Education* (1991), courts consistently concluded that schools did not have a legal obligation to prevent suicide (Stone & Zirkel, 2012). It was not until this case that the courts concluded SMHPs might have a legal duty to attempt to prevent suicide due to the special relationship that these individuals have with the students. The outcome of this lawsuit attempted to set a new precedent for the duties of school counselors and personnel; however, this standard did not seem to persist over the years, and there have been many other court hearings since that did not come to the same conclusion (the Eisel case was, ultimately, found in favor of the school district). For instance, in *Scott v. Montgomery County Board of Education* (1997), the same school district that was initially found liable for a student's suicide death in 1991 was found not liable for a different student's suicide death in 1997. In the 1997 decision, the court decided that since there had been two months between the student's suicidal threat and the suicide that the threat did not indicate the near future and therefore did not predict imminent danger. Because there is a lack of consistency in litigation outcomes, schools often do not anticipate liability in such litigation and therefore may not adequately enact and/or enforce suicide prevention efforts. However, schools and school personnel should take all of the proper precautions in helping prevent student suicides, not only to protect themselves from the vulnerability of lawsuits, but also to save the life of a student.

Although it is imperative for the administration and key school personnel to know the past litigation involving schools and suicide prevention efforts, they might not be the ones who are reading this chapter. Therefore, it is the responsibility of the support staff, those who will have the knowledge and awareness of cases and other relevant information through this chapter, to call attention to such cases and liability issues to the administration of their respective schools. Obviously, there are many cases in which school districts are granted immunity; however, there are some cases that have found in favor of the plaintiff.

Expert tip: Rather than risking the time, money, stress, and stigma of being involved in a lawsuit, schools should do everything in their power to prevent a suicide from occurring.

Legal Terms and Key Legal Issues for Schools

Negligence

Negligence is a breach of duty owed to an individual involving injury or damage (suicide) that finds a causal connection between a lack of or absence of duty to care for the student and his or her subsequent suicide. There are four elements to a successful negligence case (Stone, 2003):

1. A duty is owed.
2. The duty owed was breached.
3. An injury has occurred (suicide).
4. There is a causal connection between breach of duty and injury.

Courts have required schools to produce records of staff training on suicide prevention. Schools should hold annual trainings and save documentation about when these trainings were held and who was in attendance.

Foreseeability

A school administration can be held liable if it is found that a reasonable person would have been able to recognize that a student was in an acute emotional state of distress and that self-harm or danger, in some way, could and should have been anticipated. Courts have allowed actions against school officials for such a cause, relating to the absence of appropriate supervision or the lack of appropriate policies/procedures used when a student's suicide was deemed foreseeable (a likely and imminent danger). This would potentially be found to violate the in loco parentis doctrine, as found initially with the case of *Eisel v. Board of Education* (1991), which is explained in more detail later in this chapter.

State-Created Danger

A school can be found to have been in violation of legal responsibility based on the constitutional rights of the victims. The argument states that through enacting or failing to enact/follow through with certain policies and procedures, the school caused danger to the student who attempted/died by suicide. To have a convincing argument, the plaintiff must establish there was foreseeable and direct harm, a state actor (school employee) acted with a degree of responsibility that shocks the conscience, there existed a relationship between the state actor and plaintiff such that the plaintiff was a foreseeable victim of the defendant's acts, and a state actor used authority to create danger for the citizen (*Sanford v. Stiles*, 2006).

Immunity

Government entities are granted immunity if their conduct does not clearly violate constitutional rights of which a reasonable person would have known. There is a constitutional right of a duty to protect students, and state laws require compulsory attendance for students; however legal cases have failed to find that a child's required attendance at school creates a relationship that would mandate a school's duty to protect students. Immunity is granted to school districts and entities because they are not held legally accountable for the unconstitutional actions of their employees. In other words, it is very difficult to sue a school or school district for the actions of its employees and have the district be found liable for their employees' violation of the constitutional rights of a duty to protect students. Unless the school board or administration is found to have enacted or failed to enact policies and procedures that violate their duty to protect (state-created danger) or a special relationship (to be defined shortly) existed, the entity maintains governmental immunity for the wrongful actions of the individual school employees. At the most basic level, this means that SMHPs can be sued for failing to protect students even if the school district has been determined to have immunity from such a lawsuit.

Courts have found that school districts have immunity even though they may hold special relationships with students. Special relationship is a legal term for the responsibility that a state entity (i.e., public school) has to protect individuals from harm from private actors. A special relationship, as explained in *Deshaney v. Winnebego County Department of Social Services* (1989), is very difficult to find unless the citizen is in the state's custody through prison, involuntary commitment into an institution, or foster care. It has been argued time and time again that public schools do hold a special relationship with their students, but the majority of courts find no substantial claims, continually affirming that public schools do not have a constitutional duty to protect their students from harm committed by private actors.

Doe v. Covington County School District (2012), although not related to youth suicide, provides a good example of how complicated the legal concept of special relationship is and how different courts can interpret it differently. Nine-year-old Jane Doe and her family brought litigation against the girl's school district for their failure to protect her due process rights through their deliberate indifference to her security. Jane Doe was repeatedly checked out of the school (six separate times) and sexually molested by a man who was not on her parents' approved list of individuals to release her to.

Her parents subsequently filed a lawsuit against the Covington County School District, claiming that the school had a special relationship with Jane in which they were to protect her from this private actor (i.e., the man who checked her out of school six times). Their argument stated that this special relationship existed due to Jane's young age, mandated school attendance through compulsory attendance laws, and the school's active, deliberately indifferent conduct of the school employees releasing Jane to this unauthorized man. Jane's parents argued that the school's failure to verify the identity of this man illustrated their deliberate indifference to Jane's safety. The federal court initially found that her parents did not bring a substantial argument for a special relationship to the courtroom. Upon appeal, the three judges on the Fifth Circuit panel found that there was indeed such a relationship between the school and Jane Doe; however, the panel's conclusions were later rejected when the case was heard *en banc* (in front of all judges of a court). The en banc opinions upheld the idea that schools have a legal right to protect their students' safety, but that in this case there was no constitutional violation to any such obligation. Jane Doe's individual liberty was not restricted because she was not incarcerated, involuntarily committed, or in foster care so no special relationship existed. The court found that Jane Doe's age was irrelevant as, no matter what the age, the parents have the primary responsibility for the food, shelter, safety, and welfare of their child. The court ruled that the school's failure to check the identity of the unauthorized adult did not violate her constitutional rights. And while this case does not involve a student's suicide, it does demonstrate failure of the courts to acknowledge a special relationship exists and how reluctant courts are to find schools liable.

Immunity is based on the state. If the state deems schools an arm of the state government, then schools within that state are granted sovereign immunity for negligence and/or state-created danger. However, if this is not the case, schools can often find ways to argue against the state-created danger violation because it is not clearly defined (i.e., how does one define "shocks the conscience?"). Often, courts grant summary judgment in favor of the defendants (schools and school boards) or dismiss cases because the actions or lack of actions taken by the school employee fail to be found to shock the conscience.

In the case of *Armijo v. Wagon Mound Public Schools* (1998), there was a small victory in favor of the plaintiffs (parents) when the Tenth Circuit Court of Appeals denied the school's effort for a summary judgment and allowed the case to proceed. A special education student was suspended, driven home by a school employee, and left unattended at the home where he killed himself by shooting himself in the chest. Prior to being driven home, school employees were aware of the child's suicidal threats and access to firearms in his home; however, the staff drove him home without parental consent and left him there unattended anyway. While the school was not ultimately found legally responsible, the fact that the lower courts permitted the case to go to trial allowed for the possibility of a jury to find the school liable for the suicide of a student under United

States Civil Rights Act Section 1983 (state-created danger). As stated above, the difficulty of defining "shocks the conscience" plays a large role in the dismissal of cases under this cause of action. *Armijo v. Wagon Mound Public Schools* is the only published case at this time recognizing the school's potential responsibility for state-created danger involving a student's suicide.

In Loco Parentis Doctrine

The name of the doctrine is Latin for "in the place of a parent" and refers to the legal responsibility of a school (or other organization) to function and perform the responsibilities of a parent for a student while at school. In other words, schools may be mandated by this doctrine (depending on the state) to look out for the student's best interest as they see fit. Schools assume the control and supervision of the children as stand-in parents while they are attending.

Intervening Force

Many school attorneys use the "intervening force" argument to defend the school and its personnel, stating that suicide is a superseding and intervening force that breaks the direct connection between the defendants' actions and the injury to another person. This concept is a difficult one to understand but to simplify it, think of any event that may occur between the original negligence of a school employee, such as failure to notify parents when they knew a student to be suicidal, and the actual suicide of the student. The intervening force is the real reason for the harm that resulted. The longer the timeframe between the negligence of the school and the suicide of a student, the more logical the intervening force argument.

Review of Legal Cases and Implications for Schools

We discuss a few cases in great detail throughout this chapter to highlight litigation issues involving suicide cases and schools.

Wyke v. Polk County School Board *(1997)*

In 1989, 13-year-old Shawn Wyke killed himself in his own home after two prior attempts on school property. He was living with his mother's ex-boyfriend's mother, Helen Schmidt, with whom both Carol Wyke (Shawn's mother) and Shawn were close. The court dismissed Ms. Wyke's federal claim after the defendants motioned many times to do so, citing *Deshaney v. Winnebago County Department of Social Services* (1989) mentioned earlier. However, the court did uphold the state claim against the

Polk County School Board. Carol Wyke claimed that the school board should be held liable under a failure to train theory, stating that the lack of training in suicide prevention/intervention demonstrates a direct indifference to their duty to care and protect. Additionally, she claimed the school was negligent, as it failed to notify Ms. Wyke or Ms. Schmidt of Shawn's two prior attempts on the school campus during school hours (school officials were aware of these attempts). Furthermore, another boy at the school had witnessed one of Shawn's attempts to hang himself in the school bathroom, and the boy informed his mother, Brenda Morton, what he saw. When Ms. Morton immediately called the school (as she reported not being close enough to Ms. Wyke to directly call her) to inform them of what her son had told her, the school's dean of students informed Ms. Morton that he would "take care of it." Ms. Morton felt as though she had done what she needed and that the dean of students would appropriately handle the situation.

When Ms. Wyke, after the death of her son, asked the dean of students how he had handled the suicide attempt, he reported to her that he called Shawn into his office and read bible verses to him after learning of the incident. He further stated that he thought he had it under control, that was the way he believed to handle such a situation, that he was not allowed to call parents, and that he did not expect Shawn would do something like attempt suicide again. A school custodian testified that after she had heard a boy discussing discord with his grandmother, she walked into the bathroom to find the same boy who told her he would have killed himself had she not walked in the door. After the boy left, she found a coat hanger and cord hanging from the ceiling, which she threw out. She then reported notifying the vice principal of this event without being asked to identify the boy and then being asked if she did not have anything else to be doing. The vice principal denied having this conversation. Two days later, Shawn died by suicide.

Carol Wyke and Helen Schmidt were not informed of either suicide attempt at school; however, they were aware of Shawn's behavioral and emotional issues. Ms. Schmidt had made an appointment for him to see a mental health counselor, but he killed himself prior to the appointment date. Ms. Wyke affirms that, had she known about her son's suicidality, she and/or Ms. Schmidt would have provided more care for and control over him in the home.

The jury felt as though Shawn's attempts (these were not just threats) on the school's campus would cause any sensible person to reasonably assume that he needed help/care or he would be in imminent danger to himself and attempt once more. As a result, the court determined that Shawn's suicide was *foreseeable*. While the school board argued that suicide is an intervening force, the jury found that the defendants had strong reason to anticipate this suicide. In the end, the school board was found liable for not offering suicide prevention programs (failure to train), for not providing adequate supervision of a student, and for failing to notify Ms. Wyke or Ms. Schmidt that Shawn was suicidal. The verdict was found to be in favor of Carol Wyke; it placed 33% of the fault on the school board, 32% of the fault on Carol Wyke, and 35% on Helen Schmidt. Although blame was also placed on Ms. Wyke and Ms. Schmidt, this was a victory for the plaintiffs, as the school board was found guilty.

> **Expert tip:** This case should have resulted in all schools increasing and documenting suicide prevention training for staff and developing guidelines to ensure that parents are promptly notified of the suicidal behavior of their child, but unfortunately few school administrators are aware of the important lessons from this case.

It also is puzzling that it did not set a precedent for future cases, but it occurred so long ago that courts seem to have forgotten about it. This case affirmed that the Polk County School Board was guilty in their negligence to take appropriate steps to prevent Shawn's suicide, and this litigation can be used as a reference in present and future lawsuits against schools for similar situations. Additionally, since this lawsuit occurred, much more research has been published regarding youth suicide, warning signs, and the steps schools should be taking to implement prevention programs/strategies.

Eisel v. Board of Education Montgomery County *(1991)*

Nicole Eisel was a 13-year-old student in Maryland. Upon hearing Nicole discuss her suicide plan, a few of her peers reported these statements to a school counselor. This counselor relayed these claims to Nicole's school counselor. The two counselors asked Nicole if she was planning to or thinking about attempting suicide, but Nicole denied making such statements. No call was made home nor did either counselor contact the school administration to inform any of the above parties of this conversation or of Nicole's possible suicidality. Shortly thereafter at a local park, Nicole completed an apparent murder-suicide pact with another 13-year-old student who attended a different school.

Following the suicide of his daughter, Stephen Eisel quickly brought litigation against the Board of Education of Montgomery County, Montgomery County Public Schools, the superintendent of the schools, and the school principal for negligence in their duty to intervene and protect a student's life. A mother of another child at the same middle school informed the school that she was aware that the school counselor was also informed of Nicole's suicide threats; therefore, he added her to the list of individuals as well. The defendants were granted a motion to dismiss the complaint with prejudice, one ruling stating that the allegations against the school's superintendent and principal were insufficient and that the Montgomery County Public Schools was not a separate entity from the school board. Following these rulings, the court ruled that public policies prevent the remaining defendants from any legal duty to intervene to prevent the suicide. Eisel quickly appealed.

Eisel did not argue that the defendant's action (or lack thereof) directly caused the suicide of his daughter; Eisel argued that due to the school's special relationship with his daughter, they had a duty to protect her from a foreseeable danger such as suicide. Eisel's argument was not that the school could and should have acted to physically prevent her suicide. Moreover, he attested that the school failed to inform him of the possibility of her STB and that such communication could have given him the opportunity to exercise his control as her parent to prevent her suicide. The school's relationship with its students, in loco parentis, suggests that the counselors have a duty to exercise reasonable care to the students, which these counselors did not do for Nicole. Furthermore, the counselors did not uphold their responsibility as SMHPs to take necessary steps to provide help for an identified student in need. The plaintiff's argument further demonstrated that the counselors did violate their duty to protect with foreseeable danger.

When deciding if a tort duty (legal duty to protect) is in place, there are several aspects of the events to consider. The plaintiff, Nicole's father, has obviously suffered a great deal of injury, and the suicide took place very close to when the counselors were made aware of this possibility (connection). Eisel argued that his daughter's suicide was foreseeable, as many of her peers had made it clear to the counselors that she was speaking about it. Additionally, the school had enacted a suicide prevention program prior to Nicole's death. One of the papers from this program gives steps that must be followed, and one of these steps for a suicidal crisis or when warning signs for a suicide are brought to a staff member's attention is to tell others as quickly as possible (which the counselors did not do). While the counselors argued that limits of confidentiality should not be breached by a duty to call a parent/guardian, it is well known that confidentiality is not a prime matter when suicide is the concern.

The appeal judgment was in favor of Eisel, making way for a trial to ensue. Due to the above evidence, the courts found that the counselors had a legal duty to protect, including making a phone call to Mr. Eisel. While Nicole denied making suicidal statements when questioned by the counselors, research demonstrates that adolescents are much more likely to confide in peers than an adult (Lieberman, Poland, & Kornfeld,

2014). With this information, counselors should take it very seriously when students bring the suicidal ideation of another student to their attention.

It is also important to note that the aforementioned sequence of events only occurred after the case went through several courts, but ultimately it was dismissed. This illustrates how difficult a task it is for one to bring about a lawsuit and even get it before a jury. The school had incurred legal fees, stress, and stigma throughout the whole process. In the end, the Board of Education of Montgomery County was exonerated, but the fact that this court case made it to trial without being dismissed demonstrates the possibility of legal duty on behalf of the school personnel. All they had to do was pick up the phone: "I was told that your daughter was discussing and thinking about suicide. While she is denying it to me, I wanted you to be aware that this was going on. If we see any other warning signs or gain any further information, we will notify you immediately." That is all it would have taken. One phone call not only could have prevented the entire lawsuit for the Board of Education of Montgomery County, but it also could have prevented the horrific tragedy for the Eisel family.

Fowler, Martin, Vick, and the Cypress-Fairbanks Independent School District v. Szostek and Szostek *(1995)*

In the aforementioned cases, suicidal threats and past suicide attempts preceded the student's actual completed suicide; however, it is also important to be aware of other instances that may be precipitating events to a student's suicide. For instance, undergoing extreme discipline (e.g., suspension or expulsion) could provoke a student's suicidal ideation/ attempt even with no prior warning signs. *Fowler v. Szostek* (1995) highlights the importance of handling school disciplinary situations appropriately to avoid litigation and/or a tragedy.

Fourteen-year-old Brandi Nelson showed no warning signs of suicidal tendencies. The school had found marijuana on another eighth-grade student who claimed that he and another boy had bought drugs from Brandi. After hearing this claim, the principal, Mr. Martin, searched Brandi's belongings for any evidence of drugs and had the nurse search Brandi's person to ensure no drugs were found on her; the principal's secretary witnessed this search. When nothing was found, Brandi was told that she was not under suspicion at that time because no evidence had been found during the search; Brandi denied any reason a peer would want to get her into trouble. However, the assistant principals were asked to receive written statements from the two boys who had supposedly bought the marijuana from Brandi. Both of these written statements (claiming Brandi sold them $25 worth of marijuana) were found to be sufficient evidence in order to recommend Brandi be expelled.

The following day, all three of the students' parents were brought in to the school. Both boys identified Brandi through a school photograph and were punished appropriately for possession of drugs.

Another assistant principal, Mr. Fowler, met with Mary Szostek, Brandi's mother, and Brandi. He explained the situation (without using the boys' names) and that the punishment for selling marijuana was expulsion according to the Texas Education Code. Mr. Fowler also explained that this was not a final decision and that Brandi was entitled to a hearing to review the recommendation. Brandi was tearful throughout the meeting, and Brandi and her mother left that day without speaking to the principal (although they were told he was available). Mr. Szostek, Brandi's stepfather, was notified by telephone of the situation by Mr. Fowler and was given the phone number for the associate superintendent, Mr. Goodson, who manages such disciplinary hearings. Immediately, Mr. Szostek telephoned Mr. Goodson to set up a hearing. After setting a date for two-and-a-half weeks later, Mr. Szostek informed Brandi that he had set a hearing and would clear up the situation.

On the same day of her emergency removal from school, Ms. and Mr. Szostek both left Brandi at home, alone, while doing their respective errands. During this time, Brandi shot herself with her stepfather's gun, leaving a note that read: "I lied—I love you."

The primary argument from the plaintiff's attorney was that the school should have realized that because Brandi Nelson was in a severe discipline sequence, she might be suicidal. Their argument was based on the facts that suicide is the third leading cause of death for teenagers and national surveys have found that 12%–14% of all teenagers admit to having suicidal thoughts. The plaintiffs argued that the school had a duty to further explore the possibility of Brandi's suicidal ideation.

The defendants' motion for summary judgment was ultimately granted after being initially denied, demonstrating that the doctrine of sovereign immunity impedes almost all claims made by plaintiffs. Furthermore, the judge who granted summary judgment also reported that the wrongful death claim by Mr. Szostek would be dismissed because Texas state law forbids stepparents from making such claims.

While no evidence would be needed due to the school officials and district maintaining sovereign immunity, the judge affirmed that substantial evidence of a constitutional violation was absent from the plaintiffs' claims. Although it is unknown whether the recommended expulsion is a direct cause of Brandi's suicide, it is apparent that it played a key role in her actions. School officials must handle disciplinary measures with compassion and care, because it is not uncommon for suspension or expulsion to provoke students into destructive and impulsive actions. It is recommended that the school officials (this might be an administrator, SMHP, disciplinarian, etc., depending upon the nature of the situation, school roles, and with whom the student has rapport) take some extra time with these students, as well as the students' parents, to ensure their safety and avoid litigation. Some examples and recommendations of what to say/do to provide care for the disciplined student are provided below.

1. Ask the student: "Are you going to be okay?" and "Do you need or want to see a counselor before you leave school?"
2. Tell the student: "We still care about you."
3. To the parent/guardian: "Do you think you could stay home with your child today? He or she might need a little extra supervision and care today."
4. Discuss with the SMHP if he or she may know about any additional warning signs for that student. Also ask the SMHP to question the student about self-harm thoughts and suicidal ideation.

Professional Ethical Standards for Key School Personnel

No Maleficence/Do No Harm

For a SMHP to uphold his or her ethical standards, that person must do no harm. A school administration may be hesitant to have official requisites in suicide prevention due to the legal implications of not carrying them out; however, SMHPs should ensure that their responsibility to do no harm encompasses suicide prevention efforts. With the grave statistics of youth suicide in mind, suicide prevention efforts seem to be common sense to those who wish to do no harm to the student population.

Expert tip: Although there is inconsistency in the outcomes of previous court hearings on the extent of SMHPs legal obligation to prevent a student's suicide, their ethical obligation to "*do no harm*" is not in question.

SMHPs are ethically bound to make every attempt to prevent harm to the student and protect that student from potential danger.

Competence

SMHPs must be competent and up to date on the risk factors and warning signs of suicide. This can be ensured through mandating trainings on suicide prevention, assessment, and intervention. Based on statistics, there is no explanation for a SMHP not being familiar with such information and how to handle these situations. For example, the state of Washington recently passed new legislation titled "K–12—Troubled

Youth" mandating that school nurses, school social workers, school psychologists, and school counselors attend a training (at least three hours in length) on youth suicide screening and referral as a requirement for both initial and continuing certification.

Confidentiality/Confidentiality Exceptions

It is important to note that while SMHPs are to always uphold confidentiality, there are exceptions to this rule. The suspicion of STB is one of those exceptions. All students should be aware of the limits of confidentiality and that school staff may have to break silence if it is under one of those limits. While it may upset the student that you are divulging private information to his or her parents or other necessary school staff, it will be less difficult to repair rapport with a student who is alive than to deal with the potential outcomes if he or she does attempt or die by suicide without parent notification.

Notifying Parents

Importance of Making the Call

Failure of the school to notify a student's parent or guardian when there is reason to suspect that the student is suicidal is the most common source for lawsuits (Berman et al., 2009). As noted prior, when there is reason to believe that a student is contemplating suicide, the confidentiality is broken and the parents should immediately be notified. School personnel have an obligation to report any child who is suspected to be at risk for suicide based on foreseeability. In other words, even if a student denies suicidal ideation or intent, it is the duty of the school to notify the parents if information available implies that the student may be suicidal, and it is considered negligence for school personnel to refrain from doing so (*Eisel v. Board of Education of Montgomery County*, 1991).

When it comes time to warn parents that their child might be suicidal, some issues may arise. First, if the team decides that it is more of a risk to inform the parents based on suspected neglect or abuse in the home, school staff should call local child protective services instead. Second, some parents may be uncooperative and refuse to come to the school to talk or personally pick up their children to bring them home safely. To avoid a negligence lawsuit, school staff should not allow children to walk or take the bus home alone, no matter what the parents suggest. If a parent or guardian refuses to ensure the safety of their child, refuses to seek additional mental health services for the child, or does not take the suicide risk seriously, the school psychologist or other school personnel should call local child protective services.

Transfer of Responsibilities to Parents Through Notification

Once parental notification is accomplished and properly documented, school personnel have fulfilled their legal duty to transfer responsibility to the parents through notification. Throughout this process, school staff should use an *emergency notification form* for documentation. An *emergency notification form* asks parents to sign and acknowledge that they have been notified of the suicidal emergency with their child and have been informed about needed treatment and supervision. If a parent refuses to sign, a second school employee should note their refusal on the form and protective services should be called. The school should keep the form to document that it notified the parents and made appropriate recommendations in case any legal action is taken against the school by the parents. A sample of an *emergency notification form* is in your eResources.

The authors recommend school personnel continue to monitor the student in school (see Chapter 7 for information and tools to do this) to ensure he or she is receiving the support needed. SMHPs should follow up with the family to inquire if outside services are being rendered.

Providing Appropriate Postvention Response

The term *postvention* refers to events and activities that are planned for schools to put into action following a suicide as a means to assess the overall impact, identify at-risk individuals, prevent a contagion effect from occurring, and support survivors who are emotionally affected by the death. These strategies for postvention and more are covered in Chapters 8 and 9. While schools are often unprepared to handle the aftermath of a suicide, what is implemented following a suicide is just as essential as the prevention efforts. For a nicely packaged postvention resource, please refer to the U.S. Department of Health and Human Services' *Preventing Suicide: a Toolkit for High Schools* (Substance Abuse and Mental Health Services Administration, 2012).

Mares v. Shawnee Mission School District *(2007)*

The authors are only aware of one legal case that involves how a school's handling of a student suicide contributed to another suicide, the case of *Mares v. Shawnee Mission School District* (2007). In this suit, Barbara Mares sued the school district for negligence in its duty to protect her sons who both died by suicide in 2003 (Chartrand, 2007). The courts ruled that the statute of limitations had expired on the first suicide, 16-year-old Jason Mares. The allegations involving the subsequent suicide of Mrs. Mares's 18-year-old son, Justin, went through a lengthy legal process that is outlined below. Mrs. Mares declared that the school district failed to implement postvention procedures at West High School following her younger son's suicide and claimed that such an implementation could have prevented her older son's suicide just seven months later.

On February 21, 2003, Barbara Mares' 16-year-old son, Jason, hung himself to death on a tree in a local park near the school, leaving a note expressing his hatred for school and specific teachers and insisting that his family was not the problem. Justin had been living in Michigan to attend a different school near relatives for his senior year due to his dislike for West High School (Chartrand, 2007). Following Jason's death, his older brother, Justin, moved home to grieve with his family and he was re-enrolled at West High by the end of March 2003. West High School informed Justin in May that his out-of-state transcript from his previous school did not provide him a sufficient amount of hours to graduate that year with his class. Throughout these months, Justin had been taking trips to the park where Jason hung himself and asking the local park rangers which tree Jason used (never getting an answer). On September 12, 2003, just over six months after his brother hung himself from a tree in Shawnee Mission Park, Justin Mares did the same.

Mrs. Mares attests that she was naïve as to how she and her family should appropriately cope with the death of her son, Jason (Chartrand, 2010). She also claims that she and other family members attempted to get in touch with the principal of West High School to discuss the tragedy, but he had refused to answer. (It is interesting to note that the principal had experience in this situation; he had been the principal at a nearby school where there were a number of student suicides.) The school staff also refrained from reaching out to Justin Mares except to tell him that he could not graduate. The school itself did not present any sort of postvention response or offer counseling to Justin. The school did not reach out to Mrs. Mares to make suggestions as to how she should handle the aftermath of her son's suicide with her other children (Chartrand, 2007). Was it the school's responsibility? Mrs. Mares attempted to file a lawsuit for the wrongful death of both of her sons, stating that Jason's death was a result of bullying from students and teachers and that the school failed to properly protect Justin through postvention procedures following Jason's suicide. The school district filed for a summary dismissal, but this motion was denied. As noted above, the judge affirmed that the statute of limitations had passed to file a lawsuit regarding Jason's suicide, but the litigation for the wrongful death of Justin Mares against the school district proceeded. Not only did Mrs. Mares seek monetary damages, she also sought the implementation of up-to-date suicide training for prevention, intervention, and postvention.

One aspect in question here is if a sensible person would have reason to anticipate Justin Mares' depressive and suicidal thoughts. Further, should West High School's trained professionals have anticipated this?

If so, did they have a duty to do something about it? Was Justin Mares' suicide preventable with school intervention?

Throughout the legal proceedings, it was apparent that the judge was honoring the in loco parentis doctrine, making it clear that the defendants had the duty to intervene in some way, to reach out to Mrs. Mares to discuss the emotional difficulties her children were having. The judge even noted the incongruence of the fact that the school would be more apt to call home if a child was failing a class than if he or she were experiencing obvious emotional troubles (Chartrand, 2007). The defendants maintained that because the suicide(s) occurred off campus, they no longer had the in loco parentis control. Furthermore, the defense argued that it was the Mares family, not the school district, who was in the best position to witness Justin's emotional turmoil and intervene appropriately.

The defendants filed another petition for a summary judgment; however, the judge again rejected it (Chartrand, 2007). The school district was reportedly planning to file an appeal in order to overturn the rejection ruling when it approached the Mares family to attempt to reach a settlement outside of court. As a settlement was occurring, the judge reversed his two earlier rulings and granted a summary judgment in favor of the defendants.

The Shawnee Mission School District settled with Mrs. Mares out of court, but the specifics of the settlement are sealed (Poland & Chartrand, 2008). One lesson that can be learned from this exhaustive process is that any school postvention response to a youth suicide is better than doing nothing. While the Mares' case did not go to trial, the amount of time, energy, and money that the Shawnee Mission School District spent on this case (as well as the stigma placed on school district and principal) could have been prevented had the district implemented an appropriate postvention program.

Bullying and Suicide: Legal Issues

Implications of "Bullycide" Lawsuits

The media has coined the term *bullycide* to describe a suicide that occurs in the aftermath of and is caused by bullying. As discussed in Chapter 2, students involved in bullying as a victim or bully are at a significantly higher risk for depression and suicide. The more frequently an adolescent is involved in bullying, the more likely it is that he or she has feelings of hopelessness, has serious suicidal ideation, or has attempted suicide (Gould & Kramer, 2011). Knowing the frequency of bullying that occurs in schools and the statistics illustrating the connection between bullying and suicide, it makes sense for schools to thoroughly screen for suicidal thoughts/behaviors when addressing bullying incidents and/

or through bullying prevention programs (Suicide Prevention Resource Center, 2011).

While we discussed in Chapter 2 that there is no clinical evidence supporting the idea that bullying *causes* suicide, there have been a number of lawsuits filed by parents against school personnel, citing the school's failure to stop bullying as a proximal cause of their child's suicide. The Blue Springs School District in Missouri settled with the parents out of court following the suicide of Brandon Myers (Evenson, 2012), a 12-year-old student whose parents alleged had been a victim of continuous bullying. In addition to the monetary settlement of a half million dollars, the settlement included the school holding an annual bullying awareness day as well as having two additional school administrators undergo off-site bullying awareness training (Evenson, 2012; Morris & Burnes, 2012). With the increase in student suicides being linked to bullying, school districts should implement both *bullying* and *suicide prevention programs* within their population.

Witsell et al. v. the School Board of Hillsborough County *(2011)*

Hope Witsell, a 13-year-old student, was sent to the principal's office following her teacher's noticing of "shallow cuts" to Miss Witsell's thigh. It was known by both the teacher and principal that Hope was experiencing tremendous teasing, bullying, and harassment following her sending a suggestive image via text the previous school year. On the same afternoon that the teacher sent Hope to the principal's office, Hope met with the school social worker for counseling. This was Hope's first encounter with the social worker and her first experience with mental health counseling. The school social worker spent the afternoon with Hope in isolation but failed to consult with other school staff and did not notify any administrative staff or Hope's parents of the counseling, the shallow cuts, or the need for continued care. It is likely that had the social worker consulted with other school staff, the decision would have been made to notify Hope's parent immediately. The following day, Hope died by suicide in her home. In her bedroom, Mr. and Mrs. Witsell found a no-harm contract signed by Hope and the social worker. This contract stated that Hope would not kill herself and that she would call the social worker before making a suicide attempt. The existence of this contract suggested that the social worker believed Hope was at risk for killing herself. As is discussed in Chapter 7, having a student sign a no-harm or no-suicide contract is considered poor practice; it neither protects the SMHP nor provides quality clinical care to the student. In Hope's case, the school professional had a duty to address the bullying and the suicide risk. Basic professional standards for social work, counseling, and psychology require communication with parents and providing more than a no-suicide contract to address suicide risk.

Hope Witsell's case is a cautionary tale for school districts and SMHPs. Hope's parents sued the School Board of Hillsborough County, Florida, with allegations of negligence and a violation of its duty to protect a student's life. While the court dismissed the case after the defendant's arguments, the parents have the option of filing a wrongful death lawsuit against the school board in a local circuit court. Hope Witsell's suicide occurred in September 2009, and the school board still has to manage the litigation (along with the stress, time, money, and stigma that accompanies it) years later. In addition, the school board argued that it was not responsible for an employee who did not follow policy and left the social worker to defend herself. This is a good argument as to why all mental health providers should carry their own liability insurance.

The Estate of Montana Lance et al. v. Kyer et al. *(2011)*

In another bullying instance, Mr. and Mrs. Lance filed a lawsuit against the Lewisville Independent School District following their nine-year-old son's suicide. Montana Lance was a special education student in the fourth grade, having been diagnosed with both an emotional disturbance and a learning disability with speech impairment (a strong lisp). Montana and his parents had complained to the school on many occasions of bullying incidents involving Montana as the victim; however, there is no documentation that any action was taken to alleviate Montana's distress at school. Based on a psychological assessment conducted by the school psychologist, Montana endorsed depressive symptoms and suicidal ideation. Montana stated that he felt as though his life was continually getting worse, that he hated himself, and endorsed "almost always" on questions involving his thoughts regarding death/dying. The school had developed an individualized education plan (IEP) and a behavioral intervention plan (BIP) for Montana.

Although it is documented that Montana continued to be involved in numerous physical and verbal altercations with other students, there is no documentation that his parents were contacted or that school personnel used the interventions in the BIP (nor was there proof that the school staff/teachers were trained in such interventions). Upon one confrontation, Montana had pulled out a small pocketknife (without opening it) as a defense while being tormented by other students. After this incident, the school decided to send Montana to a disciplinary alternative education program (DAEP). The plaintiffs argued that under Texas law (and the Individuals with Disabilities Education Act [IDEA] of 2004), a child with special needs who is placed in an alternative school must have a special hearing to ensure that his or her behavioral issues are not a manifestation of his or her disabilities (manifestation determination review), but Montana was not granted this hearing. Mrs. Lance appealed the school's decision to place Montana in the DAEP, but it was not granted.

In fact, there is no written evidence that the DAEP was aware that Montana Lance was a child with special needs and of the special interventions that were supposed to be put in place for him. During his time at the DAEP, Montana divulged to a school counselor that he was suicidal. While the counselor informed Montana's father, there is no documentation that the school counselor further assessed Montana's suicidal ideation/plan/intent, put interventions in place, or made other recommendations. Furthermore, there is no written proof that Montana's home elementary school was informed of his suicidal statements upon Montana's return.

Following Montana's return, he continued to be verbally and physically harassed by the same students. Montana reacted in a manner that caused him to be disciplined and sent to the principal's office. Again, there is no documentation that the BIP interventions were being used. Montana was with school staff until he went to use the restroom in the nurse's office. He had previously locked himself in the nurse's bathroom (although his parents were not aware of this), and did so again on this day. The nurse found the bathroom locked and Montana not answering, and she did not have the key. When a custodian unlocked the door to the bathroom, Montana was found. He had hung himself using his belt and was pronounced dead after unsuccessful attempts at reviving him.

Mr. and Mrs. Lance filed a lawsuit against the Lewisville Independent School District, arguing that the school failed in their duty to protect Montana. They claimed the school failed to provide a safe environment for Montana, a suicidal special education student, by not having in place policies, procedures, and trainings on how school staff should work with Montana and protect him from the bullying. The parents further argued that the school held a special relationship with their son because he was a student with a disability, and it had a legal obligation to protect him. Furthermore, he was in a setting (the principal's office) in which he was being held involuntarily, creating a special relationship. The plaintiffs also made the claim of state-created danger (allowing a suicidal student to lock himself in a restroom). According to the Lances, Montana was discriminated against as evidenced by the school's negligence to address Montana and his family's complaints of the bullying and harassing, which led to Montana's suicide. The judge dismissed the case, claiming that the plaintiffs did not provide sufficient evidence to demonstrate that Montana Lance was discriminated against. He further claimed that no special relationship existed as Montana Lance was not imprisoned, involuntary committed in an institution, or in foster care. While the case was dismissed, the implications of this tragedy are widespread. This case demonstrates the necessity of comprehensive suicide screenings for children who are obvious targets for bullying.

How School Personnel Can Best Protect Themselves From Suicide Liability Issues

1. Maintain liability insurance: Nurses, social workers, psychologists, and counselors in schools should carry individual malpractice insurance.
2. Seek supervision from colleagues: While SMHPs should be competent and informed on proper ways to handle suicidality in students, it is important to always consult with others to gain another perspective and ensure the best care is being taken of the student.
3. Keep good records: Prioritize thorough documentation as without records, there is no evidence. (See Chapter 7 for a detailed discussion on documentation.) These documents can save a school from an unfavorable ruling in a courtroom.
4. Document crisis training: Provide mandatory crisis training to all personnel and document the dates and those in attendance.
5. Provide best practice response: A school should be implementing suicide prevention tools (Chapter 5), appropriate intervention response (Chapters 6 and 7), and appropriate postvention actions (Chapters 8 and 9) should a suicide occur within their district. In order to limit the potential to be found liable in a suicide, a school should follow the steps in the Table 4.1.

Table 4.1 Summary: Lessons Learned From Legal Proceedings Involving Schools Regarding Suicide

---

1) *Bullying:*
   a. Perform suicide risk assessment on victim and bully (as well as those students at high risk to be a victim/bully)
   b. Notify parent or guardian immediately
   c. Discuss with parent or guardian the importance of increased supervision
   d. Obtain ROI to student's outside therapist*
   e. Discuss bullying situation at school with student's outside therapist (if no outside therapist, provide referral)
   f. Document
   g. Follow-up
   h. Document
2) *Suspected suicidal ideation (even with student's denial):*
   a. Notify parent or guardian immediately (face-to-face if possible)
   b. Do not allow student to be alone (even in bathroom) and ensure a parent comes to pick student up
   c. Discuss with guardian the importance of increased supervision

---

(Continued)

Table 4.1 (Continued)

     d. Obtain ROI to student's outside therapist*

     e. Consult with student's outside therapist if at all possible (if no outside therapist, provide referral)

     f. Document

     g. Follow-up

     h. Document

3) *Suicidal ideation with plan/intent:*

     a. Notify parent or guardian immediately (face-to-face if possible)

     b. Do not allow student to be alone (even in bathroom) and ensure a parent comes to pick student up

     c. Follow state's policies regarding involuntary admission to psychiatric care if student is at imminent risk to himself or herself

     d. If returning home, discuss with guardian the importance of increased supervision

     e. Obtain ROI to student's outside therapist*

     f. Consult with student's outside therapist if at all possible (if no outside therapist, provide referral and insist student and parents follow through with appointment)

     g. Document

     h. Follow-up

     i. Document

4) *Following a suicide attempt:*

     a. Notify parent or guardian immediately (face-to-face if possible)

     b. Follow state's policies regarding involuntary admission to psychiatric care if student is at imminent risk to himself or herself

     c. If returning home, discuss with guardian the importance of increased supervision

     d. Obtain ROI to student's outside therapist*

     e. Consult with student's outside therapist if at all possible (if no outside therapist, provide referral and insist student and parents follow through with appointment).

     f. Document

     g. Follow-up

     h. Ensure student sees SMHP

     i. Document

5) *After extreme disciplinary action taken against student:*

     a. Notify parent or guardian

     b. Discuss face-to-face

     c. Take time with the student (do not rush through punishment)

     d. Follow school district's disciplinary procedures

     e. Discuss with SMHP any potential warning signs or risk factors that he or she should assess for or is already aware of

     f. Discuss with guardian the importance of increasing supervision

     g. Obtain ROI to student's outside therapist*

     h. Consult with student's outside therapist if at all possible (if no outside therapist, provide referral and insist student and parents follow through with appointment).

     i. Document

     j. Follow-up

     k. Document

---

* While there may be some resistance by parents to sign an ROI (release of information) to the student's outside therapist, be persistent and persuasive in following through with this step. Communication between school psychologist and outside therapist regarding a suicidal student's emotional state may assist in a school's legal argument as well as help to save the student's life.

6. Use all the resources of the school system and involve SMHPs: Accept responsibility and recognize that a student at your school could die by suicide and that some students are thinking about it now. Schools that implement solid suicide prevention programs and procedures greatly reduce risk of liability, follow the legal duty to care for the students, and just might save a life.

Conclusion

Schools have a responsibility to identify suicidal students and respond to such situations appropriately and as mandated by their respective county and state laws. Does your district have a policy in place? Do you know what is being done to enforce the policy? Make sure your district has current and appropriate policies in place. Know those policies. If policies are inconsistent with research or the actuality of practice on the ground level, provide this feedback to administrators. After all, the common goal is to prevent a student death involving negligence or a failed duty to protect and to be able to prove in court that the district and its employees did everything they could to prevent a suicide according to generally accepted best practices.

References

Armijo v. Wagon Mound School District, 159 F.3d 1253 (10th Cir. 1998).

Berman, L., Eastgard, S., Gutierrez, P., Mazza, J., Poland, S., Roggenbaum, S., Singer, J., & Smith, J. (2009). *School suicide prevention accreditation resource guide* (2nd ed.). Washington, DC: American Association of Suicidology.

Chartrand, D. (2007). *A duty to act: Mares v. Shawnee Mission Schools.* Retrieved from http://www.davidchartrand.com/DavidChartrand/Mares_v.SMSD.html

Chartrand, D. (2010). *Angels in the Park.* Manuscript submitted for publication.

Deshaney v. Winnebego County Department of Social Services, 489 U.S. 189 (1989).

Doe v. Covington County School District, 675 F.3d 849 (5th Cir. 2012).

Eisel v. Board of Education of Montgomery County. 324 Md. 376, 597 A. 2d 447 (Md Ct. App. 1991).

Evenson, K. (2012, October 3). Bullying suicide lawsuit settled. *The Examiner.* Retrieved from http://www.examiner.net/news/x354107888/Bullying-suicide-lawsuit-settled

Fowler v. Szostek, 905 S.W. 2d 336 (Tex. App.—Houston [1st Dist.] 1995).

Gould, M., & Kramer, R.A. (2011). Youth suicide prevention. *Suicide and Life—Threatening Behavior, 31,* 6–31. doi:10.1521/suli.31.1.5.6.24219

Lieberman, R., Poland, S., & Kornfeld, C. (2014). Suicide intervention in the schools. In A. Thomas & P. Harrison (Eds.), *Best practices in school psychology VI* (pp. 273–288). Bethesda, MD: National Association of School Psychologists.

Mares v. Shawnee Mission School District, No. 06CV00160 (2007).

Morris, M., & Burnes, B. (2012, October 16). Blue Springs bullying case settled for $500,000. *Lee's Summit Journal.* Retrieved from http://www.lsjournal.com/2012/10/17/90343/blue-springs-bullying-case-settled.html

Poland, S., & Chartrand, D. (2008). Suicide prevention and schools. *District Administration.* Retrieved from http://www.districtadministration.com/article/suicide-prevention-and-schools

Sanford v. Stiles, 456 F.3d 298 (3rd Cir. 2006).

Scott v. Montgomery County Board of Education, No. 96–2455 U.S. App LEXIS 21258 (4th Cir. 1997).

Stone, C. (2003, May 3). Suicide: A duty owed. From http://www.ascaschool counselor.org/article_content.asp?edition=91&section=140&article=780

Stone, C., & Zirkel, P. A. (2012). Student suicide: Legal and ethical implications. *ASCA School Counselor, 49*(5), 24–30.

Substance Abuse and Mental Health Services Administration. (2012). *Preventing suicide: A toolkit for high schools.* HHS Publication No. SMA-12-4669. Rockville, MD: Center for Mental Health Services, Substance Abuse and Mental Health Services Administration.

Suicide Prevention Resource Center. (2011). *Suicide and Bullying Issue Brief.* Newton, MA: Author.

The Estate of Montana Lance et al. v. Kyer et al. No. 4:2011cv00032 (E.D. Texas 2011).

Witsell et al. v. The School Board of Hillsborough County, No. 8:11-cv-00781 (M.D. Florida 2011).

Wyke v. Polk County School Board, 137 F.3d 1292 (11th Cir. 1997).

5   Evidence-Based Suicide Prevention Programs

Between January and May 2007, four students from a school district in Kentucky died by suicide. A few months later, the schools in that district were among 150 across the state of Kentucky to deliver a universal suicide prevention program, Signs of Suicide (SOS). The SOS program screens students for depression and suicide risk and teaches students how to recognize signs that a friend might be in crisis and the importance of not keeping any suicidal communication or concerns regarding a friend a secret (Aseltine, James, Schilling, & Glanovsky, 2007). In the wake of such enormous tragedy, the speed of the response is impressive. You might be asking yourself, "How did the school administrators come up with a suicide prevention strategy so quickly? How did they know that SOS was the right program for their school? Can a school implement a single program and prevent suicide? Did school mental health professionals (SMHPs) deliver the program? If so, where did they get the training? Where did the funds come from to purchase, train, and implement SOS? How were school personnel able to accomplish all of this over summer vacation?" These are great questions, and we'll answer all of them in this chapter. For now, just know that delivering the SOS program was not a spur-of-the-moment decision. The groundwork for implementing school-based suicide prevention in Kentucky was started by a statewide coalition, the Kentucky Suicide Prevention Group (KSPG), five years earlier in 2002.

In this chapter, we provide a review of empirically supported programs that take a universal (i.e., all students, regardless of risk), selective (i.e., students at risk but not suicidal), and indicated (i.e., students who are suicidal) approach to suicide prevention. We review strategies for getting administrative buy-in, developing community supports, and deploying schoolwide prevention efforts. Because suicide prevention programing sometimes comes to individual schools and districts through statewide initiatives, we share the story of Kentucky's statewide suicide prevention efforts (hereafter referred to as the Kentucky experience). The Kentucky experience is a valuable illustration for several reasons: Suicide prevention in Kentucky started at the district level, but after a series of suicide contagions in school districts around the state (including the district mentioned above), it became clear that Kentucky needed to expand suicide prevention efforts statewide. The process of planning and implementing school-based suicide prevention is complicated and needs to consider student characteristics, school environment and culture, administrative support, finances, and politics. The Kentucky experience provides practical, on-the-ground insights into the challenges involved in planning and implementation. The information about the Kentucky experience comes from two of the principle players, Jan Ulrich and Patti Clark. In 2006, Jan was the technical coordinator for the Kentucky Department for Behavioral Health, Developmental and Intellectual Disabilities (KDBHDID)'s "Suicide Prevention in Youth: A Collaborative Effort (SPYCE)" project funded by a three-year Garrett Lee Smith (GLS) Memorial Act Youth Suicide Prevention grant through the federal Substance Abuse and Mental Health Services Administration (SAMHSA). Jan is currently the state suicide prevention coordinator. Patti joined the effort in 2011, as part of a second Garrett Lee Smith grant received by KDBHDID called SPEAK (Suicide Prevention Efforts for Adolescents in Kentucky) to address suicide prevention in the state.

Defining Suicide Prevention

Suicide prevention is any effort to reduce suicidal ideation, suicide attempt, and death by suicide. Because there is no single cause of suicide and no group of people is immune to suicide, prevention efforts target factors that have been shown to contribute to the development of suicidal thoughts and behaviors (STB). Some prevention efforts do not have an explicit focus on STB but address factors that increase risk for suicide such as depression, substance use, parent-child conflict, unsafe school environment, and access to guns. Other prevention efforts look more like interventions. For example, hospital-based programs to reduce parent-child conflict (Wharff, Ginnis, & Ross, 2012) or improve follow-up with discharge appointments in the community (Asarnow, Baraff, Berk, Grob, & Devich-Navarro, 2011) and the psychotherapies that have been developed to work with suicidal youth and their families (Brent, Poling, & Goldstein, 2011; Diamond et al., 2010; Linehan, 1993; Stanley et al., 2009) all have the ultimate goal of preventing death by suicide.

Other examples of suicide prevention are the following:

- Screening all students (in a grade or school) for depression, thoughts of suicide and attempts, anxiety, and substance use (e.g. SOS; Aseltine et al., 2007).
- Identifying community mental health agencies that can provide intervention and management of suicidal youth.
- Training adults (such as school staff, parents, church leaders) to recognize warning signs of suicide and make appropriate and timely

referrals (e.g., Question, Persuade, and Refer [QPR]; Wyman et al., 2008; Applied Suicide Intervention Skills Training, ASIST; Rodgers, 2010).

- Increasing student awareness of suicide risk behaviors, risk factors, and warning signs of suicide (e.g., "More Than Sad" http://www.morethansad. org/abouttd.html).
- Conducting a suicide risk assessment (explained in detail in Chapter 6).
- Participating in a public arts project that seeks to reduce the shame and stigma associated with suicide by painting a mural (Mohatt et al., 2013).

How is painting a mural in the same category as screening youth for suicide risk? They are both suicide prevention efforts because they ulti-mately seek to reduce death by suicide, albeit through radically different approaches. The "Finding the Light Within" suicide prevention mural (muralarts.org/findingthelight) was an arts-based, community suicide prevention effort that engaged more than 1,000 people over a 15-month period with the intention of sparking dialogue and creating a public mural to address suicide risk and loss. Stakeholders, including survivors, consumers, mental health practitioners, local agencies, and commu-nity members, not only participated in community paint days for the mural itself but also engaged in the writing programs, workshops, and collage-art that surrounded the mural activities, allowing for a climate of expression and sharing where voices could be heard.

Prevention efforts are most commonly categorized into a three-level or tier system. The landmark 2002 report *Reducing Suicide: A National Impera-tive* (National Research Council, 1994, 2002) used the public health model categories of universal, selective, and indicated. In contrast, school-based prevention efforts are described as Tier 1, Tier 2, and Tier 3 following the tiered framework of the response to intervention (RTI) education model (for a comprehensive review please see Brown-Chidsey & Steege, 2010). While the terminology is different, the concepts are the same. You might remember in Chapter 3 we discussed how the PREPaRE model for school-based crisis prevention and intervention uses the universal/ Tier 1, selective/Tier 2, and indicated/Tier 3 model (Brock et al., 2009). We most often use the terms universal, selective, and indicated (see Fig-ure 5.1) because that is how suicide prevention programs are categorized and described in the literature.

1. *Universal prevention/Tier 1* programs target everyone, whether the people involved have any risk for, or are currently exhibiting, the behavior. Schoolwide screening programs are the most common universal prevention programs. There is no quick and easy way to screen all students for suicide risk. Resources must be in place to complete suicide risk assessments and make appropriate referrals for

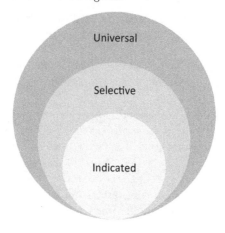

Figure 5.1 The Public Health Model of Suicide Prevention

youth identified as at risk following a universal screen. Other examples of universal suicide prevention programs are the SOS program mentioned in the beginning of the chapter, and the gatekeeper training QPR.

2. *Selective prevention* programs target people who are at risk for a certain behavior. Examples of selective prevention might be support groups for children whose parents are in jail, divorced, or deceased. The purpose of these groups is not simply to bring these children together but to reduce the risk that these children will develop specific problems such as suicidal ideation or depression in the future. *Reconnecting Youth* (RY; W. V. Eggert, McNamara, Eggert, & Nicholas, 2009) is an example of a program that targets youth at risk for dropping out of school or exhibiting other characteristics that are known risk factors for suicide. Kentucky used RY as a selective prevention program, but it has also been used as an indicated prevention program for those who have already dropped out.

3. *Indicated prevention* programs target people who are showing symptoms of a specific problem. In the world of suicide, this includes students who are reporting suicidal thoughts, attempts, or plans. For example, SOS programs use the CDC's (Centers for Disease Control and Prevention) Youth Risk Behavior Survey to screen students for signs of depression and suicide risk. Students found to be at risk are referred to a professional (Aseltine et al., 2007). The screening component of SOS is universal, but the referrals are an indicated prevention effort because the students who are referred to a professional after the surveys have been administered are at risk for depression and/or suicide.

Evaluating the effectiveness of suicide prevention programs is challenging for a number of reasons (Klimes-Dugan, Kingbeil & Meller, 2013). The most obvious way to see if a suicide prevention program is working is to measure whether it has prevented any deaths by suicide, but this is almost impossible. Suicide is a low base rate behavior, meaning that it rarely happens. Because it is a rare event, it is hard to establish causation. Let's imagine your school district implements a comprehensive suicide prevention program that provides universal and selective intervention services for all 100,000 students. In the year before the suicide prevention effort was implemented, 11 students died by suicide. If 9 students died by suicide the year following implementation, would your prevention program be considered effective? What if 13 students died by suicide? Statistically, it is impossible to demonstrate that your suicide prevention program was the cause of the +2/-2 variation in suicide deaths. Politically, it is impossible to celebrate 9 student deaths instead of 11. Further, you will never know how many lives were saved because of the program. Perhaps there would have been 23 suicides that year had no programming been implemented. There is no way to measure what *could* have happened. Because of this, most suicide prevention programs are not evaluated based on reductions in deaths by suicide or even reduced STB (although some, such as SOS and QPR, have that objective). Instead, they are evaluated on outcomes such as whether youth report increased knowledge of suicide warning signs or adults report increased knowledge of how to identify and refer suicidal youth.

Setting the Stage for Implementing School-Based Suicide Prevention

The Substance Abuse and Mental Health Services Association (SAMHSA, 2012) recommended a four-step process for developing suicide prevention programs in high schools.

Step 1. Engage administrators, school boards, and other key players. The importance of getting buy-in from school administrators, superintendents, and school board members cannot be overemphasized. Administrators need to endorse programmatic changes in the school and justify the significant amount of time and money it takes to train school personnel and students, deploy screening, and engage in follow-up, referral, and intervention for students identified as at risk. Key players need to understand the scope of the problem and need to know that asking students about suicidal thoughts and attempts will not increase risk (for a thorough review of this issue, please see Gould et al., 2005). They also need to know that doing nothing provides less legal protection than doing something. As discussed in Chapter 4, *Wyke v. Polk County School Board* (1997) set the precedent that schools must train personnel in suicide prevention and intervention. For some administrators and school boards, however, the most persuasive argument you can make is that suicide prevention will improve educational outcomes. Patti Clark explained it like this:

> When students are thinking about suicide, they are not thinking about their school work. When school officials understand that by putting appropriate policies and procedures in place and delivering appropriate evidence-based prevention programming, they will in effect increase the academic performance of their students by help-ing them reach out sooner for the help they need.

Step 2. Bring people together to start the planning process. There are two groups that need to be engaged throughout the planning process: school staff and community partners. Various school staff members will have different understandings of the problem and different perceptions of the need for suicide prevention programs. Getting their buy-in from the start will go a long way to ensure the success of the program. Com-munity partners include mental health service agencies to whom you might refer students or call on to provide crisis intervention, members of citywide or statewide suicide prevention coalitions, county child fatal-ity review teams, clergy, cultural leaders, and parent groups. Later in the chapter, we share Kentucky's experience in training school and commu-nity providers.

Step 3. Provide key players with basic information about youth suicide and suicide prevention. Provide information about risk factors, warning signs, and protective factors such as the comprehensive list provided in Chap-ter 1. It is likely that you will need to address myths of suicide in order for some people to believe that suicide prevention is a worthy effort. A more detailed list with deeper explanations of the corresponding facts is avail-able in the online eResources:

Myth #1: If I ask a student about suicidal ideation, I will put the idea in his or her head.
Fact #1: Asking someone about suicide will not make him or her suicidal (Gould et al., 2005).
Myth #2: If a student really wants to die by suicide, there is nothing I can do about it.
Fact #2: Suicide is preventable. Even students at the highest risk for suicide still have part of them that wants to live.
Myth #3: Students who talk about suicide all of the time are not actually sui-cidal, therefore you don't need to take the statements seriously.
Fact #3: Youth who make suicidal statements typically have some risk for sui-cide. All suicidal statements should be taken seriously.

In order to convince key players that this is a problem worth invest-ing in, you'll need local statistics on youth suicide, suicidal ideation, and suicide attempts. Providing these statistics on the rates of STB in your state or district (provided below) is a basic way of establishing the scope of the problem and can be a powerful way of emphasizing the need for suicide prevention programs (see eResources for state and local data on STB from 2013). The approach can be either, "look—we're doing well, let's make sure our rates don't increase," or "these rates are higher than the national average—we need to do something about it." Suicide rates by race, gender, and age group since 1999 can be found in the CDC Web-based Injury Statistics Query and Reporting System, WISQARS™ (http://www.cdc.gov/injury/wisqars/fatal.html). Table 5.1 lists the suicide rates by state for 2010, the most current year available at the time of publication, for all youth ages 0–19 (83.2 million), 11–14 (16.5 million youth), and 15–19 (22 million). Note: There are no statistics for elementary-aged youth because, thankfully, there were not enough deaths to establish a rate. In 2010, out of 44,722,560 youth age 10 and under, there were a total of 14 reported suicide deaths. Suicidal ideation and attempt, however, is a significant problem among elementary-aged youth (Singer & Slovak, 2011).

The second resource is the Youth Risk Behavior Survey (YRBS) (http://www.cdc.gov/HealthyYouth/yrbs/index.htm), also through the CDC, which gathers data on the risky behaviors reported by youth in middle school and high school and is administered by 43 states (Figure 5.2) and 21 districts (Figure 5.3). The YRBS is the best source for statewide and districtwide (where available) information on past-year reports by youth of having had a serious thought of killing themselves, making a plan, making an attempt, or making an attempt that was serious enough to require the attention of a doctor or nurse. We are not aware of data available for states that do not participate in the YRBS. According the YRBS, rates of suicidal ideation, making a plan, and making an attempt increased between 2009 and 2013, but making an attempt requiring medical attention did not change (CDC, 2014).

Step 4: Develop your overall strategy. The SAMHSA suicide prevention toolkit recommends assessing current policies, programs, and school culture prior to selecting and implementing a prevention program. This includes taking an inventory of existing behavioral health programs and suicide prevention programs, some of which might be community based. Suicide prevention strategies must consider issues of race, class, gender, and culture.

We recognize that each school and district has a unique governance, structure, and leadership. Duties vary by title, different titles have different roles, and the degree to which school administrators recognize the relationship between mental health and educational outcomes varies. SAMHSA offered this four-step plan as a jumping-off point to start a suicide prevention effort that is right for your district. The need to make it site-specific is part of your challenge, but it ensures that your program fits the needs of your students, staff, and community.

Table 5.1 USA Suicide Injury Deaths and Rates per 100,000, All Races, Both Sexes

State	0–19 years				11–14 years		15–19 years	
	Total Deaths	Population	Crude Rate	Age-Adjusted Rate	Deaths	Crude Rate	Deaths	Crude Rate
Alabama	36	1,276,312	2.82	2.68	—	—	29	8.44
Alaska	21	207,840	10.10	10.17	—	—	19*	36.44*
Arizona	49	1,819,641	2.69	2.69	—	—	40	8.67
Arkansas	21	795,930	2.64	2.61	—	—	18*	8.83*
California	180	10,452,042	1.72	1.63	27	1.30	152	5.38
Colorado	49	1,364,692	3.59	3.66	—	—	39	11.49
Connecticut	12	915,776	1.31	1.20	—	—	12*	4.78*
Delaware	—	233,803	—	—	—	—	—	—
District of Columbia	—	123,720	—	—	—	—	—	—
Florida	70	4,512,990	1.55	1.46	14*	1.55*	56	4.56
Georgia	57	2,781,629	2.05	2.04	12*	2.19*	45	6.34
Hawaii	10	338,301	2.96	2.95	—	—	—	—
Idaho	22	475,281	4.63	4.79	—	—	19*	16.47*
Illinois	77	3,496,522	2.20	2.11	—	—	69	7.48
Indiana	43	1,806,582	2.38	2.29	—	—	38	7.99
Iowa	28	820,510	3.41	3.28	—	—	25	11.53
Kansas	30	810,644	3.70	3.71	—	—	27	13.25
Kentucky	26	1,146,204	2.27	2.22	—	—	22	7.41
Louisiana	26	1,254,237	2.07	2.02	—	—	23	7.04
Maine	11	310,959	3.54	3.17	—	—	10*	11.32*
Maryland	22	1,516,626	1.45	1.37	—	—	20	4.92
Massachusetts	32	1,621,143	1.97	1.76	—	—	29	6.27
Michigan	84	2,648,885	3.17	2.90	11*	2.03*	73	9.87
Minnesota	45	1,431,211	3.14	3.10	—	—	39	10.6
Mississippi	20	849,495	2.35	2.26	—	—	18*	8.01*

Missouri	44	1,601,411	2.75	2.65	—	—	35	8.26
Montana	18	251,036	7.17	6.98	—	—	13*	19.48*
Nebraska	—	512,472	—	—	—	—	—	—
Nevada	13	736,328	1.77	1.79	—	—	12*	6.57*
New Hampshire	10	325,802	3.07	2.72	—	—	—	—
New Jersey	38	2,291,204	1.66	1.60	—	—	34	5.68
New Mexico	29	579,841	5.00	4.89	—	—	27	18.02
New York	70	4,897,511	1.43	1.30	—	—	64	4.68
North Carolina	50	2,558,680	1.95	1.92	—	—	46	6.97
North Dakota	15	171,935	8.72	7.95	—	—	15*	31.6*
Ohio	70	3,067,126	2.28	2.15	—	—	64	7.77
Oklahoma	32	1,041,610	3.07	3.08	—	—	25	9.45
Oregon	17	972,183	1.75	1.68	—	—	17*	6.67*
Pennsylvania	90	3,179,390	2.83	2.59	17*	2.68*	71	7.84
Rhode Island	—	261,758	—	—	—	—	—	—
South Carolina	29	1,224,425	2.37	2.26	—	—	24	7.3
South Dakota	22	226,740	9.70	9.75	—	—	18*	31.23*
Tennessee	37	1,676,121	2.21	2.15	—	—	30	6.86
Texas	164	7,621,714	2.15	2.19	21	1.41	141	7.49
Utah	35	962,537	3.64	3.95	—	—	26	11.76
Vermont	—	150,255	—	—	—	—	—	—
Virginia	40	2,083,685	1.92	1.84	—	—	36	6.53
Washington	45	1,769,895	2.54	2.48	—	—	38	8.22
West Virginia	10	439,213	2.28	2.12	—	—	—	—
Wisconsin	48	1,502,196	3.20	3.05	—	—	42	10.52
Wyoming	—	151,513	—	—	—	—	—	—
Total	1,933	83,267,556	2.32	—	260	1.58	1,659	7.53

Note. State-level counts and rates based on fewer than 10 deaths have been suppressed (—). Rates based on 20 or fewer deaths may be unstable (*). Use with caution (http://webappa.cdc.gov/sasweb/ncipc/dataRestriction_inj.html).

Age-adjusted rate takes into account variations in the state's age distribution. Specific age groups cannot have age-adjusted rates (http://www.cdc.gov/cancer/npcr/uscs/technical_notes/stat_methods/rates.htm).

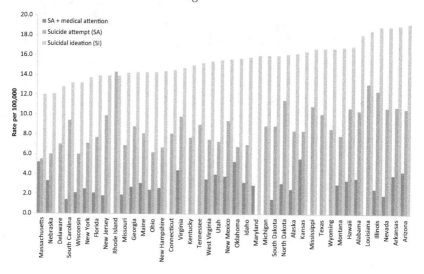

Figure 5.2. Rates of suicidal ideation, plan, attempt, and attempt with medical attention (defined as seen by a doctor or a nurse) in states that participated in the 2013 Youth Risk Behavior Surveillance Survey.

The Kentucky Experience: Assessing School Readiness and Capacity

In summer 2013, the SPEAK grant delivered 14 regional two-day "train-the-trainer" workshops across the state. The training module was based on SAMHSA's *Preventing Suicide: A Toolkit for High Schools.* The goals included:

- Provide trainings in each of the 14 community mental health agency regions in the state.
- Train at least 35 people per region.
- Create a cadre of trainers who could teach the staff in their school districts or regions to meet the requirements of the 2010 Kentucky law mandating two hours of suicide prevention training for administrators, SMHPs, and teachers in all public middle and high schools.
- Provide overviews of evidence-based suicide prevention programming and train staff to develop implementation plans for suicide prevention delivery to students at the middle and high school level by September 1 of the school year, as mandated by state law.
- Introduce school and community staff to appropriate early identification, referral, and follow-up plans for students identified as at risk for suicidal crises.

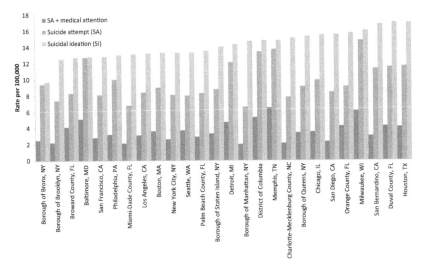

Figure 5.3 Rates of suicidal ideation, plan, attempt, and attempt with medical attention (defined as seen by a doctor or a nurse) in districts that participated in the 2013 Youth Risk Behavior Surveillance Survey.

- Introduce appropriate postvention procedures to increase safety for students and staff after a suicide death connected to the school (see Chapters 8 and 9 for a thorough discussion of postvention).
- Use public domain products as much as possible in order to increase sustainability of efforts beyond the life cycle of the grant funding.

Nearly 600 school and community members who attended the workshops went into the communities to train the school staff members in their districts in a variety of evidence-based curricula including Lifelines, More than Sad, SOS, and QPR.

With such a well-constructed plan, what could go wrong? According to Patti Clark, the SPEAK grant coordinator,

As we rolled out the trainings during the summer of 2013, we learned that despite earlier trainings and nearly four years of implementation of the state mandates [for suicide prevention education], not all schools had the capacity or the readiness to implement all suggested components of a comprehensive plan in their district. We had some schools that were much farther along the implementation continuum than others. The implementation plan they left with looked much different from that of a school district that was just beginning to identify its need for policies, procedures and protocols.

Lessons learned for successful systemwide or statewide trainings:

1. Start where the school is. Use the tools in the SAMHSA Toolkit (2012) to assess readiness and capacity of schools.
2. Have schools complete "readiness" assessments to help determine the level of expertise of the school personnel that will attend the training.
3. Use the information from the readiness assessment to group trainees by level of expertise.
4. Conduct small group trainings in which participants have similar skill levels.

    a. A basic level training, for example, would offer more risk factors, warning signs, statistics, and basics of implementation.
    b. A more advanced group might review and update their own policies while receiving guidance on the best strategies to include and/or eliminate.

5. Monitor participants' levels of distress. Establish a care person who will be on the lookout for participants in distress and can address issues of grief, trauma, or loss that might come up for participants. Participants will be more relaxed and able to focus on participating if they know someone is looking out for their emotional well-being.

School-Based Suicide Prevention Programs

Sy Sims, the discount clothing store magnate, famously said, "An educated consumer is our best customer." Just as there are many different types of clothes that one could buy, there are many different types of suicide prevention programs that one could buy (conceptually and literally). A successful wardrobe will include different clothes for different occasions, and a successful suicide prevention strategy will tailor universal, selective, and indicated programs to meet the needs of the school district. While we have already introduced you to the concepts of universal, selective, and indicated prevention, the next few pages review the three types of prevention efforts most commonly implemented in schools (see the online eResources for detailed descriptions of each program). By the end of this chapter, you will have a better idea of not only the purpose of the three levels of prevention, but also what evidence exists for these programs. To paraphrase Sy Sims, you will be an educated customer of suicide prevention programs.

Universal Prevention

Universal suicide prevention efforts target all students, regardless of their risk for suicide. The American Indian Life Skills Development (formerly Zuni Life Skills Development) curriculum (AILSD; Lafromboise & Lewis, 2008); Lifelines; QPR (Question, Persuade, and Refer) Gatekeeper Training for Suicide Prevention (QPR; Wyman et al., 2008); Good Behavior Game (Katz et al., 2013); and Signs of Suicide® Prevention Program (SOS; Aseltine et al., 2007) are examples; they can be found on SAMHSA's National Registry of Evidence-Based Programs and Practices (NREPP) (http://www.nrepp.samhsa.gov/) and the Suicide Prevention Resource Center Best Practice Registry (SPRC-BPR) (http://www.sprc.org/bpr).

Selective Prevention

Selective suicide prevention programs target students at risk for suicide who have not yet reported suicidal thoughts or behaviors. Examples include Reconnecting Youth (RY; W. V. Eggert et al., 2009) and Coping and Support Training (CAST; L. L. Eggert, Thompson, Randell, & Pike, 2002), both of which target youth who demonstrate poor school achievement and an increased potential for dropout. CAST is an abbreviated version of RY that targets youth ages 14–18 in Grades 9–12 at risk for suicide, depression, substance use, and school problems and has three main goals: increase mood management (i.e., depression and anger), improve school performance, and decrease drug involvement. Both programs are listed on the NREPP and SPRC-BPR.

Indicated Prevention

Indicated suicide prevention programs exist only as part of multi-tiered programs. SOS (Aseltine et al., 2007) targets youth who have already expressed STB; another, unrelated program with the same initials, Sources of Strength (Wyman et al., 2010), tries to reduce individual risk factors by increasing identification and referral of students at high risk for suicide. Al Roberts and colleagues (Roberts, Knox, & Tesh, 2013) discussed the Sources of Strength program as an example of how the RTI framework is applied:

> Tier 1 involves direct screening of school populations for mood, substance abuse, and suicide problems; Tier 2 involves training school staff to increase identification and referral of suicidal student; and Tier 3 is a hybrid program combining psychoeducational curricula with screening to increase student self-referrals.
>
> (p. 558)

In Chapter 6 and 7, we walk you through the levels of assessing suicide risk: *screening* (for anyone that you come into contact with), *assessment* (for youth who screen positive for suicide risk, whether you have used a formal screening form or not), and *monitoring* (for ongoing interaction with youth who have been assessed as at risk for suicide).

POPULATION-BASED SUICIDE PREVENTION

Suicide prevention is not the exclusive domain of schools. The most successful population-, or community-based prevention effort is restricting people's access to lethal means of suicide. In the United Kingdom, after acetaminophen was made available only in bubble packs, suicide by acetaminophen was reduced by 20% (Hawton et al., 2004). In Switzerland, the military restricted access to firearms, significantly reducing the number of suicides by gun as well as the overall suicide rate (Reisch, Steffen, Habenstein, & Tschacher, 2013). In countries around the world, barriers installed on popular bridges have reduced suicides from those sites (Beautrais, 2007; Gunnell & Miller, 2010). The reason why means restriction works is that when people cannot use their method of choice (e.g., jumping, taking pills, using a gun), they are not likely to look for another method (Hawton, 2005). In suicide prevention, we call that "means substitution." Decades of research shows that when a common method of suicide is restricted or eliminated, the suicide rate decreases. The most controversial population-based means restriction effort, and undoubtedly the one that would be the most significant in reducing the suicide rate, is restricting access to guns. The statistics are sobering. A youth with access to a loaded gun is 32 times more likely to die by suicide than a youth without access to a loaded gun (Brent et al., 1993).

Case Study: Development and Implementation of Statewide Suicide Prevention in Kentucky

Throughout this chapter, we have illustrated various aspects of suicide prevention with examples from the statewide suicide prevention efforts in Kentucky. While those illustrations are useful, they fail to tell the larger story, including how suicide prevention began in Kentucky, what the legislative initiatives were, and the development of school-community partnerships. Again, the information for this case study was provided by Jan Ulrich and Patti Clark.

In the spring of 2002, the KDBHDID launched a statewide effort to reduce suicide in the commonwealth because Kentucky's suicide rate had consistently been above the national average (e.g., in 2000, the suicide rate for youth 0–24 years of age was 5.16 per 100,000, while the national average was 4.33 per 100,000). The KSPG began as an advisory group open to the public that included mental health practitioners and advocates as well as suicide loss survivors. One of the key figures in the development of the KSPG program, Jan Ulrich, was motivated to participate in suicide prevention after the death of her son by suicide in 2002. She attended one of KDBHDID's statewide suicide prevention meetings two weeks after his death and worked as an advocate and later became a QPR (Question, Persuade, Refer) trainer. She is now the state suicide prevention coordinator and a QPR Master Trainer. The formation of the KSPG coincided with the release of the *National Strategy for Suicide Prevention* (U.S. Department of Health and Human Services, 2001). The KSPG included a variety of community partners in an effort to create a statewide planning document. The combination of efforts would prove to be beneficial as the programs grew.

Getting the First Programs off the Ground

The first efforts of the SPYCE grant were to implement empirically supported universal suicide prevention programs in the SPYCE grant districts. One hundred and fifty middle and high schools delivered the Signs of Suicide (SOS) program to their students. Much needed support came from KDBHDID, which sponsored evidence-based training for certain school personnel to become Reconnecting Youth (RY—12 weeks) and Coping and Support Training (CAST—6 weeks) facilitators. Kentucky school districts found these selective prevention programs extremely helpful in increasing positive coping skills and reducing risk factors, therefore continuing use of the curricula today. Later, as part of the 2013 SAMHSA grant, the school districts were also required to do the EIRF, which is the Early Intervention, Referral and Follow-Up form with students identified as at risk.

Because life and policy change are not simple, all of what was previously mentioned did not happen without some stumbling blocks. Unfortunately, the KDBHDID lacked the funding or personnel to install CAST, RY, and SOS in all school districts across the state. As a response to the lack of funding, in 2009, Ulrich produced a video called "School-Based Suicide Prevention: A Matter of Life and Death," featuring three Kentucky school principals who had lost students to suicide as an effective and persuasive tool within schools, the Kentucky Department of Education, and the Kentucky School Board Association. This video is mentioned in the SAMHSA Preventing Suicide toolkit as a resource for other schools and programs. When a Kentucky Department of Education representative was asked what it would take to get suicide prevention programs statewide after hearing more about suicide contagion, her reply was that such action would have to be legislatively mandated. Legislation proposing that public middle and high school staff receive suicide prevention training was first introduced in 2009, but was defeated.

With the help of survivors of suicide loss and suicide prevention advocates who had built a strong relationship with Senator Gordon Smith, a legislator who had lost his son to suicide, two laws were passed in 2010 around school-based suicide prevention. (The laws are based on the Jason Flatt Act, which first passed in Tennessee in 2007. Kentucky's laws are similar to but not identical to the Jason Flatt Act). One law mandated annual training for middle and high school staff, and the second required that all middle and high school students must receive suicide prevention information or materials by September 1 annually. The Kentucky Department of Education could have fought the passage of these laws, but instead requested that the KDBHDID become a resource to the schools once the laws took effect. This allowed the KDBHDID to stay involved with the fulfillment of these laws and to promote the use of safe and effective programs and trainings. The result of the these laws passing was that as part of their 2010 annual training requirements, 16,000 school middle and high school teachers received QPR training: approximately half received face-to-face QPR training with the rest taking online QPR training.

Jan became the State Suicide Prevention Coordinator in 2011, the same year the SPEAK initiative began, with the primary goal of focusing on two regions with a higher military population. With the grant award, SPEAK now needed to use a curriculum that would work with their populations of interest. Again a new curriculum needed to be found. According to Jan, "We chose the Lifelines curricula because it promoted help-seeking behavior, and because it was the only curricula available at the time the grant was written." Maureen Underwood, the primary author of the Lifelines series came to Kentucky to train school personnel and others who work with the schools in those two regions in the prevention, intervention, and postvention components of the curricula.

Jan's November 2011 hiring of Patti Clark as the SPEAK project coordinator was an important connection because Patti had a background in substance abuse prevention and newspaper publishing. Her efforts were focused on disseminating the work that had been done in the first grant in a strategic, intentional manner. Approximately 400 trained certified QPR instructors were already in place as a result of the first grant. Building upon those trainers while building the capacity of other resources to address suicide prevention efforts across the state was the grant team's intention. It also dovetailed with the primary goal of KDBHDID: to build a complete network of trained gatekeepers across the state, while also focusing on improving policies and procedures in schools and other organizations serving youth. And so began the quest for a connection with outside resources.

Improving School-Based Identification and Referral: Reaching out to
Community Mental Health Centers

The SPEAK program began to tap into the regional prevention center (RPC) structure in the state (connected to all Kentucky community mental health centers). All of these prevention centers have multiple prevention specialists in place, many of which already have relationships with school staff and community organizations and coalitions. Tapping into this existing network allowed the program to increase its reach and begin to establish a statewide safety net for its youth. Although much progress has already been made in connecting community mental health centers (CMHCs) and schools, there is much work to be done. Helping both schools and CMHCs talk to each other and understand the importance each plays in keeping our students safe is imperative.

While CMHCs are connected to the state as a funding source, each is autonomous in its operation and each has its own relationship with community partners. Some are functioning in a strongly proactive manner and others are not. In some communities, these connections are strong. For example, mental health professionals from the CMHCs may provide services within the school setting, and prevention specialists may be consulted when it is time to choose and deliver prevention curriculum. In some cases, additional funding has aided in building these relationships (in addition to regular block grant dollars appropriated to the CMHCs). In others, personalities and close community connections create stronger partnerships.

If suicide prevention coalitions and projects start with the assumption that grants will end, but the connections and relationships that are developed during a suicide prevention project do not have to end, then it is more likely that projects will be sustained over time. For those reasons, grant staff work hard to develop relationships with not only the CMHC staff, but also school staff, intentionally offering connection points and increased opportunities for building partnerships at the grassroots level. For example, during delivery of 14 summer trainings designed to educate school staff and regional prevention staff in order to deliver state mandated school trainings in the districts, regional prevention centers were the main community contact point and served as the hub of the trainings. While they were funded by state grant monies, the CMHC and RPC received credit and earned "social capital" for offering a much-needed training and expertise to school staff. At the same time, school staff who may not have realized the resources of their regional prevention center—for whatever reason—were introduced to these services and given an opportunity to understand this resource as a valuable partner in their prevention process.

With all the good that was happening with the SPEAK program in 2011, an unexpected logistical setback took place when the Kentucky

Department of Education interpreted the school law to mean that schools could not use their standard two-day summer professional development days for suicide prevention training. Suddenly, it was necessary to expand options in order to meet the demands for all eligible school districts. In year one, there were three months to deliver staff trainings across the state. But in year two, there was one week or less each year to accomplish all of the trainings, which was close to impossible under the current plan, since this would necessitate the training of nearly 600 middle and high schools in Kentucky by state staff. As a result of the time limit, they had to create a system to build the capacity of the communities to deliver the required school trainings. This effort was the "train-the-trainer" sessions described earlier in the chapter.

Conclusion

We are in the early years of evaluating the success of school-based suicide prevention programs. A recent systematic review of school-based suicide prevention programs found that the only programs that demonstrated success in reducing actual suicide attempts were Signs of Suicide (Aseltine et al., 2007) and the Good Behavior Game (Katz et al., 2013), and the only program to demonstrate success in reducing suicidal ideation was the Good Behavior Game. However, neither program alone is sufficient to prevent suicide. The Kentucky experience illustrates the complexities of identifying and implementing school-based suicide prevention and intervention strategies at the district, community, and state levels. It has taken over a decade to create a system to address the issues that have routinely put Kentucky at the top of the rankings when it comes to youth suicide. Kentucky did not reinvent the wheel; it deliberately used available resources and existing information to plan and implement its suicide prevention strategy. From the early rollouts of CAST, Reconnecting Youth, and QPR to Signs of Suicide, More Than Sad, and Lifelines, Kentucky's successes are based on the passion behind the coordination of suicide prevention, intervention, and treatment strategies across all phases of the prevention continuum. As you develop your suicide prevention program, we urge you not to reinvent the wheel. SAMHSA publications and the insights gleaned from their GLS grantees are a treasure trove of information about school-based suicide prevention programs. Pioneers like Jan Ulrich are available to discuss the programming needs in your community.

References

Asarnow, J. R., Baraff, L. J., Berk, M. S., Grob, C., & Devich-Navarro, M. (2011). An emergency department intervention for linking pediatric suicidal patients to follow-up mental health treatment. *Psychiatric Services, 62*(11), 1303. doi:10.1176/appi.ps.62.11.1303

Aseltine, R. H., Jr., James, A., Schilling, E. A., & Glanovsky, J. (2007). Evaluating the SOS suicide prevention program: A replication and extension. *BMC Public Health, 7,* 161. doi:10.1186/1471-2458-7-161

Beautrais, A. (2007). Suicide by jumping: A review of research and prevention strategies. *Crisis: The Journal of Crisis Intervention and Suicide Prevention, 28*(Suppl 1), 58–63. doi:10.1027/0227-5910.28.S1.58

Brent, D. A., Perper, J. A., Moritz, G., Baugher, M., Schweers, J., & Roth, C. (1993). Firearms and adolescent suicide: A community case-control study. *American Journal of Diseases of Children, 147*(10), 1066–1071. doi:10.1001/archpedi.1993.02160340052013

Brent, D. A., Poling, K. D., & Goldstein, T. R. (2011). *Treating depressed and suicidal adolescents: A clinician's guide.* New York: The Guilford Press.

Brock, S. E., Nickerson, A. B., Reeves, M. A., Jimerson, S. R., Lieberman, R. A., & Feinberg, T. A. (2009). *School crisis prevention and intervention: The PREPaRE model.* Bethesda, MD: National Association of School Psychologists.

Brown-Chidsey, R., & Steege, M. W. (2010). *Response to intervention: principles and strategies for effective practice.* New York: The Guilford Press.

Centers for Disease Control and Prevention [CDC]. (2014). 1991–2013 High School Youth Risk Behavior Survey Data. Available at http://nccd.cdc.gov/youthonline/. Accessed on October 1, 2014.

Diamond, G. S., Wintersteen, M. B., Brown, G. K., Diamond, G. M., Gallop, R., Shelef, K., & Levy, S. (2010). Attachment-based family therapy for adolescents with suicidal ideation: A randomized controlled trial. *Journal of the American Academy of Child and Adolescent Psychiatry, 49*(2), 122–131.

Eggert, L. L., Thompson, E. A., Randell, B. P., & Pike, K. C. (2002). Preliminary effects of brief school-based prevention approaches for reducing youth suicide—risk behaviors, depression, and drug involvement. *Journal of Child and Adolescent Psychiatric Nursing: Official Publication of the Association of Child and Adolescent Psychiatric Nurses, Inc., 15*(2), 48–64.

Eggert, W. V., McNamara, B. E., Eggert, L. L., & Nicholas, L. J. (Eds.). (2009). *Reconnecting youth: A peer group approach to building life skills. Administrator's handbook.* Redmond, WA: RY Publications. Retrieved from http://www.reconnectingyouth.com/pdfs/RY_Admin_Handbook_FINAL.pdf

Gould, M. S., Marrocco, F. A., Kleinman, M., Thomas, J. G., Mostkoff, K., Cote, J., & Davies, M. (2005). Evaluating iatrogenic risk of youth suicide screening programs: A randomized controlled trial. *JAMA: The Journal of the American Medical Association, 293*(13), 1635–1643. doi:10.1001/jama.293.13.1635

Gunnell, D., & Miller, M. (2010). Strategies to prevent suicide. *BMJ, 341*(jul06 1), c3054–c3054. doi:10.1136/bmj.c3054

Hawton, K. (2005). Restriction of access to methods of suicide as a means of suicide prevention. In K. Hawton (Ed.), *Prevention and treatment of suicidal behaviour: From science to practice* (pp. 279–291). Oxford/New York: Oxford University Press.

Hawton, K., Simkin, S., Deeks, J., Cooper, J., Johnston, A., Waters, K., . . . Simpson, K. (2004). UK legislation on analgesic packs: Before and after study of long term effect on poisonings. *BMJ (Clinical Research Ed.), 329*(7474), 1076. doi:10.1136/bmj.38253.572581.7C

Katz, C., Bolton, S.-L., Katz, L. Y., Isaak, C., Tilston-Jones, T., Sareen, J., & Swampy Cree Suicide Prevention Team. (2013). A systematic review of school-based suicide prevention programs. *Depression and Anxiety*, 30, 1030–1045. doi:10.1002/da.22114

Klimes-Dougan, B., Klingbeil, D. A., & Meller, S. J. (2013). The impact of universal suicide-prevention programs on the help-seeking attitudes and behaviors of youths. *Crisis*, *34*(2), 82–97. doi:10.1027/0227-5910/a000178

Lafromboise, T. D., & Lewis, H. A. (2008). The Zuni Life Skills Development Program: A school/community-based suicide prevention intervention. *Suicide and Life-Threatening Behavior*, *38*(3), 343–353. doi:10.1521/suli.2008.38.3.343

Linehan, M. M. (1993). *Cognitive-behavioral treatment of borderline personality disorder*. New York: The Guilford Press.

Mohatt, N. V., Singer, J. B., Evans, A. C., Jr, Matlin, S. L., Golden, J., Harris, C., . . . Tebes, J. K. (2013). A community's response to suicide through public art: Stakeholder perspectives from the Finding the Light Within Project. *American Journal of Community Psychology*, *52*(1–2), 197–209. doi:10.1007/s10464-013-9581-7

National Research Council. (1994). *Reducing risks for mental disorders: Frontiers for preventive intervention research*. Washington, DC: The National Academies Press. Retrieved from http://www.nap.edu/catalog.php?record_id=2139

National Research Council. (2002). *Reducing suicide: A national imperative*. Washington, DC: The National Academies Press.

Reisch, T., Steffen, T., Habenstein, A., & Tschacher, W. (2013). Change in suicide rates in Switzerland before and after firearm restriction resulting from the 2003 "Army XXI" reform. *American Journal of Psychiatry*, *170*(9), 977. doi:10.1176/appi.ajp.2013.12091256

Roberts, A. R., Knox, K. S., & Tesh, M. (2013). School-based adolescent suicidality: Lethality assessments and crisis intervention. In C. Franklin, M. B. Harris, & P. Allen-Meares (Eds.), *The school services sourcebook* (2nd ed., pp. 553–568). New York: Oxford University Press.

Rodgers, P. (2010). *Review of the Applied Suicide Intervention Skills Training Program (ASIST): Rationale, Evaluation Results, and Directions for future Research*. Calgary, Canada: LivingWorks Education. Retrieved from https://www.livingworks.net/assets/Assets/Programs/ASIST/ASIST-review2010.pdf

Singer, J. B., & Slovak, K. (2011). School social workers' experiences with youth suicidal behavior: An exploratory study. *Children & Schools*, *33*, 215–228. doi:10.1093/cs/33.4.215

Stanley, B., Brown, G., Brent, D. A., Wells, K., Poling, K., Curry, J., ... Hughes, J. (2009). Cognitive-behavioral therapy for suicide prevention (CBT-SP): Treatment model, feasibility, and acceptability. *Journal of the American Academy of Child and Adolescent Psychiatry*, *48*(10), 1005–1013. doi:10.1097/CHI.0b013e3181b5dbfe

Substance Abuse and Mental Health Services Administration. (2012). *Preventing suicide: A toolkit for high schools*. HHS Publication No. SMA-12-4669. Rockville, MD: Center for Mental Health Services, Substance Abuse and Mental Health Services Administration. Retrieved from http://store.samhsa.gov/product/Preventing-Suicide-A-Toolkit-for-High-Schools/SMA12-4669

U.S. Department of Health and Human Services. (2001). *National Strategy for Suicide Prevention: Goals and Objectives for Action*. Rockville, MD: Author. Retrieved from http://www.ncbi.nlm.nih.gov/books/NBK44281/

Wharff, E. A., Ginnis, K. M., & Ross, A. M. (2012). Family-based crisis intervention with suicidal adolescents in the emergency room: A pilot study. *Social Work, 57*(2), 133–143. doi:10.1093/sw/sws017

Wyman, P. A., Brown, C. H., Inman, J., Cross, W., Schmeelk-Cone, K., Guo, J., & Pena, J. B. (2008). Randomized trial of a gatekeeper program for suicide prevention: 1-year impact on secondary school staff. *Journal of Consulting and Clinical Psychology, 76*(1), 104–115. doi:10.1037/0022–006X.76.1.104

Wyman, P. A., Brown, C. H., LoMurray, M., Schmeelk-Cone, K., Petrova, M., Yu, Q., . . . Wang, W. (2010). An outcome evaluation of the Sources of Strength suicide prevention program delivered by adolescent peer leaders in high schools. *American Journal of Public Health, 100*(9), 1653–1661. doi:10.2105/AJPH.2009.190025

6 Guidelines for Suicide Risk Assessment

What Is a Suicide Risk Assessment?

As a school mental health professional (SMHP), you should be prepared to conduct a thorough suicide risk assessment (SRA) when a student is identified as at risk during screening, when a school staff member or student makes a referral, or when a student discloses suicide risk to you. We wish your hard work setting up and deploying a multi-level comprehensive all suicide prevention program (reviewed in Chapter 5) were enough to prevent all suicidal thoughts and behaviors (STB). Realistically, however, some students exposed to even the best suicide prevention programs will still have thoughts of wanting to die, see suicide as the best way to end their emotional pain, and possibly have detailed suicide plans. And tragically, some will die by suicide. The SRAs is used to identify the presence of suicidal ideation, intent, and plans and determine if a student is at risk for doing something to end his or her life in the near future (usually within 24–48 hours; see the court cases of *Szostek* and *Wyke* discussed in Chapter 4 for more details).

We have written this chapter for the school personnel identified in the school's crisis plan as being responsible for conducting SRAs (see Chapter 3). This chapter provides you with a detailed, practical explanation of an SRA (a *Suicide Risk Assessment Form* and an audio recording of the authors walking you through the SRA are available in the online eResources). We begin by distinguishing between the SRA, a suicide screen, and suicide risk monitoring. We introduce levels of risk and the components of a risk assessment and discuss techniques for uncovering suicidal ideation and intent as well as modifications of the suicide assessment protocol for youth in elementary, middle, and high school.

Suicide Screen Versus Risk Monitoring Versus Assessment

Suicide Screens

Suicide screens can be as simple as a single question, "Have you had thoughts of killing yourself in the past two weeks?" As part of a comprehensive suicide prevention program, schoolwide suicide risk screenings are used to identify students who need more in-depth assessments to determine whether they are suicidal, and if so, at what level of severity (Gutierrez & Osman, 2009). Outside of a schoolwide screening initiative, should SMHPs screen for suicide risk? Yes, SMHPs should use a suicide screen whenever they meet with students who present with any of the risk factors identified in Chapter 1. Does this happen? Yes, all the time. Unfortunately, some mental health professionals think they are doing an SRA when in fact, they are doing a suicide screen. A suicide screen is simply a way to identify someone who might benefit from more in-depth assessment. We have developed a five-question *Suicide Risk Screening Form* based on existing suicide screens (a formatted version is available on the eResources website) (see Horowitz et al., 2012; Posner et al., 2011). The five questions are the following:

1. Have you wished you were dead?
2. Have you felt that you, your friends, or your family would be better off if you were dead?
3. Have you had thoughts about killing yourself?
4. Do you intend to kill yourself?
5. Have you tried to kill yourself?

Suicide Risk Monitoring

Students who have previously been assessed and found to have low, moderate, or high suicide risk need to be monitored regularly for changes in suicide risk. Suicidal ideation is episodic; it weakens and intensifies, and at times it goes away completely. Among teenagers, the episodes tend to be more frequent than among adults. Regular monitoring will increase the likelihood that variations in the student's suicide risk are being identified and addressed. We have found that the suicide screening questions listed above are insufficient to monitor students already identified as having STB. In addition to assessing for ideation, intent, plan, and attempts, we look for warning signs, protective factors, reasons for living, and interpersonal connections. Although this information is gathered during the SRA discussed in this chapter, we find it unreasonable for SMHPs to do a thorough SRA on a regular basis. We have created a *Suicide Risk Monitoring Form* (available online in your eResources), which you can use to monitor the suicide risk of students who have previously had a thorough SRA. For the rest of the chapter, we describe and unpack a thorough suicide risk assessment.

Typology of Suicidal Youth

As SMHPs, you are more likely to be familiar with a student who presents with suicide risk than someone who works in an emergency department or an outpatient mental health clinic. Berman, Jobes, and Silverman (2006) identify eight typologies of suicidal youth. We offer these typologies as helpful ways to quickly conceptualize which diagnostic criteria might be more prevalent in the suicidal youth with whom you work:

1. *Depressed:* experiences overwhelming hopelessness, irritability, and/ or sadness even when things are going well.
2. *Substance abusing:* self-medicates with substances or engages in increasingly risky behavior while under the influence.
3. *Borderline or schizotypal:* has difficulties maintaining healthy interpersonal relationships and expressing emotions in healthy ways.
4. *Antisocial, acting out, or conduct-disordered adolescent:* rejects socially sanctioned notions of health, well-being, and pro-social activities.
5. *Marginal, isolated loner:* disconnected from peers and parents; associates mostly with other marginalized youth (e.g., homeless youth).
6. *Rigid perfectionist:* experiences any type of failure (either other-or self-defined) as fatal.
7. *In-crisis:* lives in a state of perpetual stress-related overwhelm; responds in impulsive and irrational ways; unable to engage in creative productive problem solving.
8. *Psychotic:* experiences delusions or hallucinations or lives in fear of decompensation.

Standard of care: Students who present with command hallucinations (e.g., the voices in their head tell them to kill themselves) are automatically considered at high risk for suicide. In one case example, a student heard voices telling him to kill himself by throwing himself out of a window at school.

Levels of Risk

Have you ever read a weather report and thought to yourself, "What does it mean that there is a 30% chance of rain? Does that mean there is a 30% chance that it might rain at all, or does it mean that there is 100% chance that it will rain 30% of the time?" If you work indoors, this might be a question of idle curiosity. If you work outdoors, knowing the chance of rain could be among the most important pieces of information you can have. Although very few people expect meteorologists to accurately predict the weather, the general public expects mental health professionals to predict behavior, especially when there is risk that our clients might harm themselves or others. While mental health professionals cannot accurately predict the future, what we can do, and what we are expected to do by the courts, is to conduct a thorough assessment of risk in order to prevent a *foreseeable* suicide in the very near, or imminent, future (Berman, 2009; Bongar & Sullivan, 2013). After conducting an SRA, the most basic question you must answer is, "Is this student at imminent risk for death by suicide?"

According to Berman and Silverman (2013), the concept of imminent risk is the basis for all involuntary psychiatric commitment statutes. They summarize the basic language of these statutes and comment on the subjective nature of establishing imminent risk:

1. Real and present threat of substantial harm to self or others
2. Likely to injure if not thwarted
3. Unable to care for self
4. . . . in the reasonable future

> As the reader may note, these statutory provisions offer language that leaves the determination of imminent risk entirely up to the clinician's best judgment applied to a subjectively determined timeline (i.e., some undefined number of hours into the future; e.g., 24, 48, or 72 hours). Hence, imminent risk determinations are clinical and temporally related predictions of behavior in the near future (with no agreed-upon operational definition of what is meant by the near future).
>
> (Berman & Silverman, 2006, p. 4)

In order to determine what qualifies as imminent risk, we have to determine what does not qualify as imminent risk. David Rudd and colleagues described a five-level system of suicide risk that ranges from no risk to mild, moderate, severe, and extreme risk (Rudd, Joiner, & Rajab, 2001). A person who meets criteria for severe or extreme risk is considered to be at imminent risk for suicide. We believe their description of what constitutes different levels of risk and the corresponding actions one should take is thorough and practical. We have modified it to fit the three levels of risk most commonly used in school and community mental health: low, moderate, and high risk. This three-tier system is adequate to communicate risk with administrators, other mental health professionals in the community or hospitals, and parents. Before we present the criteria for low, moderate, and high risk, however, we briefly discuss how you can tell when a student presents with no risk for suicide.

No Risk

Most of the youth you come in contact with will have never thought about, planned, or attempted suicide. Estimates of suicide risk vary, but the most reliable surveys of suicide risk in the United States suggest that approximately 85% of students report never having seriously thought about killing themselves (CDC, 2013; Nock et al., 2013). The question is, how do you determine if a student is part of the 85%? The only way to answer that question with any certainty is to conduct an SRA. You can safely conclude that the student has no risk for suicide if, by the end of your SRA, the youth reports no suicidal ideation, intent, or plan; you have uncovered no evidence to contradict the student's statements (e.g., indicators from the student that he or she is misrepresenting suicide risk); and there is no third-party information (e.g., reports from adults or documentation such as a suicide note) that presents evidence to the contrary.

You might be asking yourself, "If someone is referred to me for a suicide assessment, wouldn't I find some risk?" Great question. The answer is not necessarily "yes". School personnel might assume that all students who exhibit symptoms of depression, anxiety, or trauma, or who make verbal or written statements referring to death, are at risk for suicide. While it is totally appropriate to refer these students for services, only a fraction will present with suicide risk. Alternately, a student might be referred to you because an adult observed self-injurious behavior (e.g., self-inflicted cutting, scratching, burn marks, or bruises) and assumed that self-injury is the same as a desire to die. It is not (as described in Chapter 2). If the student reports that the cuts were not made with the intention of dying and he or she denies suicidal ideation, intent, or plan, you can feel more confident that the self-injury was indeed without suicidal intent. If you have assessed a student and determined that he or she is at no risk for suicide, you would contact the parents and your administrator, document the SRA, implement strategies and interventions if needed for other concerns (i.e., non-suicidal self-injury [NSSI]), and send the student back to class.

What if it turns out that these students present with suicide risk? How do you distinguish between youth with low-, moderate-, and high-risk for suicide? What follows is our synthesis of the best information from school professionals and suicidologists on determining levels of suicide risk in youth (Berman et al., 2006; Lieberman, Poland, & Cassel, 2008; Rudd et al., 2001).

Low Risk

Characteristics of youth at low risk for suicide: Youth who report passing ideation that does not interfere with their activities of daily living, no desire to die (i.e., intent), no specific plan, few risk factors, and identifiable protective factors qualify as low risk for suicide. (Both risk and protective factors are described in detail in Chapter 1.)

What to do: (In Chapter 7 we include the action steps to take for each level of risk. For now, we've provided the basic outline.)

- Notify parents.
- Create a safety plan with youth and parents (unless parents are a trigger for suicide risk).
- Identify school-based supports for youth. These could be a teacher, coach, or counselor but often will be support staff.
- Coordinate (with parents) to connect youth with community mental health services.

Moderate Risk

Characteristics of youth at moderate risk for suicide: These youth report frequent suicidal ideation with limited intensity and duration. They may report some specific plans to kill themselves but report no intent. Moderate risk youth will demonstrate good self-control, some risk factors, and be able to identify reasons for living and other protective factors.

What to do: Same as low-risk *and*:

In school:

1. Increase frequency and duration of visits with the SMHP or another school staff member who has been identified as an accepting, non-judgmental adult with whom the student feels safe and comfortable.
2. Reevaluate for suicide risk at every meeting and identify if youth is moving into low-risk or high-risk category.
3. Keep regular phone contact with student's parent(s) and the community mental health provider to provide updates on how the student has been doing in school and what changes the parents and therapist are seeing in the community.

In the community:

1. Psychiatric consultation to review for the appropriateness of medication.
2. Family therapy (e.g., attachment-based family therapy).
3. Access to 24-hour availability of crisis services/hospital/hotline.

High Risk

Characteristics of youth at high risk for suicide: These are the youth that everyone imagines when you mention that you work with suicidal youth. Youth at the highest risk present frequent, intense, and enduring suicidal ideation. They report specific plans, including choice of lethal means and availability/accessibility of the method. They will present with multiple risk factors and identify few if any protective factors. This risk level requires the most interaction between various systems: parents, school professionals, the community, and mental health services outside of the school.

What to do:

1. Following the SRA, contact parents immediately. In Chapter 7, we review some of the challenges SMHPs experience telling parents that their child is at high risk for suicide and needs to be evaluated for hospitalization. We discuss engagement strategies that SMHPs can use to improve the likelihood that parents will be involved in the crisis plan and longer-term treatment.
2. Arrange with parents, law enforcement, or other professionals to transport the student to a hospital or outpatient community mental health agency responsible for evaluating youth for hospitalization. Some schools or districts may have a mobile support team available. This is another option to call where available.
3. Discuss the entire process with parents so they have a better understanding of what will occur at the hospital as well as what will happen if the student is hospitalized (e.g., homework, classes) and once he or she is reintegrated into school (see Chapter 7 for a discussion of re-entry).

Expert tip: Conducting a thorough risk assessment is difficult, even for the most seasoned professionals. I find it helpful to remember that you can reach three distinct conclusions following a suicide risk assessment: (a) The student is not suicidal (none or low risk); (b) The student is somewhere in between (moderate risk); (c) The student is at imminent risk for suicide. Your response to students at either end of the continuum (no risk or imminent risk) is clear. None/ low suicide risk: call the parent, administrator, document the suicide assessment, and send the student back to class. Imminent risk: consult an administrator, call the parent, document, coordinate, and refer for hospitalization. I find that the most challenging management situation is with students who present with moderate risk. Monitoring and managing a student's fluctuating risk requires me to regularly assess suicide risk (using the *Suicide Risk Monitoring Form*); coordinate with parents, outpatient mental health providers, administrators, teachers; consult and document . . . the list goes on and on. The youth with moderate suicide risk is always on my mind. That said, one of the most satisfying (and relieving) professional moments is when I see a student's suicide risk decrease from moderate to low to none.

The Assessment of Elementary, Middle, and High School Students

Most people who die by suicide are adults (Centers for Disease Control and Prevention, National Center for Injury Prevention and Control, 2013). Consequently, most research has tried to understand why adults die by suicide (Joiner, 2007), and how we can best assess for suicide risk in adults (Ribeiro, Bodell, Hames, Hagan, & Joiner, 2013). There is a small body of research that has looked into suicide risk among adolescents and an even smaller body of research that has investigated suicide risk among elementary-aged youth. But, the basics of the suicide assessment are the same, regardless of the individual's age.

Elementary school-aged youth. Although elementary aged youth rarely die by suicide (e.g., there were 34 suicide deaths among youth ages 0–11 in the United States in 2010), SMHPs routinely work to address suicide risk in this age group (Centers for Disease Control and Prevention, National Center for Injury Prevention and Control, 2013; Singer & Slovak, 2011). A recent study found that SMHPs conducted approximately the same number of suicide assessments with students in Grades K through 6 (31.2%) as with students in Grades 7 and 8 (31.2%) and with students in Grades 9–12 (36.4%) (Ribeiro et al., 2013). Among school social workers in elementary school settings, 75% reported working with at least one student who reported serious suicidal ideation, and 40% reported working with at least one student who had been hospitalized for suicide risk in the previous two years (Singer & Slovak, 2011). Although older adolescents report more frequency and duration of suicidal ideation, even transient suicidal ideation among elementary-aged children is predictive of poorer outcomes in adulthood (Steinhausen & Metzke, 2004). As a result, suicidal ideation in elementary school-aged youth should be taken seriously. Some approaches for assessing suicide risk in elementary-aged youth include:

- Consider using drawings or play therapy techniques to uncover suicidal ideation or intent. If a child is having a hard time finding words to describe their pain, have him or her draw a picture of what they feel like. Have hand puppets or toys available for the student to use to act out details.
- If children struggle with numerical rating scales, use the "How are you feeling" faces scale as a substitute (see online eResources for example).
- Use short sentences, avoid passive voice, and check in frequently to make sure the student understands (Barrio, 2007).
- Ask about triggering events, but avoid asking why or trying to get at the meaning behind events. The exception is asking about what it means to die. It is important to gauge what a young child understands

about death. You could ask a child, "if you were to [suicide method of choice; strangle stab, shoot] yourself, what would happen?" or "What would happen after you died?" The latter is not an assessment of conceptions of an afterlife. If a student answers, "I will wake up and everyone will be happy to see me," then you know the student does not understand what it means to die.

- Use the behavioral incident technique discussed later in this chapter to get a clear picture of the chain of events. If the student appears to have difficulty sequencing, then make sure to verify events with teachers, parents, or other adults.
- If a child becomes upset and unable to focus, use breathing exercises to help calm them down. "I'd like you to take a deep breath in through your nose—like you are smelling the most delicious pizza you've ever eaten, and then breathe it out through your mouth—like you are cooling off a hot piece of pizza." Of course, substitute pizza for whatever hot food item would be most appealing.

Middle school-aged youth. Middle school-aged youth report the highest rates of suicidal ideation, plan, and attempt of any age group, although the death rate is lower than older adolescents and young adults. Youth in this age range have just transitioned from having the highest self-esteem of their lives to the lowest. Youth enter a phase of all-or-nothing thinking, increased impulsivity, and self-criticism. They move away from parents and school personnel as confidants and sounding boards. Traditional bullying peaks in middle school, although cyberbullying appears to plateau in middle school and high school (Singer & Slovak, 2011). Be sure to ask questions on these issues during your SRA.

High school-aged youth. These students are most similar to the adults who are the subjects of most suicide research. They have the greatest access to means and are more likely to report long-term suicidal ideation and possibly a prior attempt. Although the ages vary, most states consider 14-year-olds to be adults when it comes to consenting for treatment outside of school. This means that suicide assessments, safety planning, and interventions are more likely to require involuntary commitment to hospitals in case of high risk. Low-to-moderate risk youth cannot be forced into treatment, which can be frustrating to both the SMHP and the parents. Therefore, addressing with the high school student "What's in it for me" will be much more important when developing a treatment plan than for younger students for whom treatment is not so much a choice, but a requirement on the part of their parents and on occasion, the school.

Components of a Suicide Risk Assessment

Before you can establish levels of risk and determine the appropriate intervention, you must conduct a thorough SRA. In order to keep the assessment manageable, Shea (2002) recommends a three-stage process for assessing suicide risk: assessing risk and protective factors; identifying suicidal ideation, intent, and plan; and combining the information into a clinical, or risk, formulation (King, Foster, & Rogalski, 2013; Shea, 2002). In 2003, the American Association of Suicidology (AAS) published a mnemonic to help people remember signs and assess suicide risk, IS PATH WARM (Ideation, Substance abuse, Purposelessness, Anxiety, Trapped, Hopelessness, Withdrawal, Anger, Recklessness, Mood changes) (http://www.suicidology.org/c/document_library/get_file?folderId=231&name=DLFE-598.pdf). The items are not specific to youth, however, and there has yet to be a study that demonstrates that learning the mnemonic improves SRA skills. The following warning signs were recently developed specifically for youth (see http://www.suicidology.org/ncpys/warning-signs-risk-factors for more details):

1. Talking about or making plans for suicide.
2. Expressing hopelessness about the future.
3. Displaying severe/overwhelming emotional pain or distress.
4. Showing worrisome behavioral cues or marked changes in behavior, particularly in the presence of the warning signs above. Specifically, this includes *significant*

    *   Withdrawal from or change in social connections/situations.
    *   Recent increased agitation or irritability.
    *   Anger or hostility that seems out of character or out of context.
    *   Changes in sleep (increased or decreased).

In the following sections of this chapter, we take you through the *Suicide Risk Assessment Form* created to assess risk areas as suggested by Shea (2002). We take you through each of the ten sections of the form in detail and within the context of the case of Trinity. But we must first ensure our SRA is valid by establishing rapport with and ensuring honesty from the person we are assessing.

Establishing Rapport

It sounds cliché, but establishing rapport is essential to conducting a thorough SRA (Singer, 2005). If you are talking with a student who might be or is known to be at risk for suicide, you have limited time to establish rapport. If you know the student and already have a certain level of rapport established, your job is to activate the rapport you already have. If you don't know the person and have to establish rapport from scratch, you have to sell yourself a little more to gain trust and honesty quickly. For all scenarios, it is helpful to set expectations for your conversation, including confidentiality and what you will do with the information you get. For example, you might say something like this:

> I know your teacher was really worried about you because of the essay you wrote. My job is to hear from you what is going on and figure out what I can do to help you. Your job is to be honest with me. I'm going to ask very specific questions along the way. I will probably take some notes because what you tell me is important and I want to remember it. Before we are done, I will talk with someone else to make sure I have not missed something important. Most things you tell me will stay between me and you. But there are three things that I have to tell another adult, and they all have to do with your safety: that you will do something to hurt yourself, that you are thinking of hurting someone else, or that someone else is planning on doing, or has done, you harm (i.e., child abuse). Anything you tell me that is not related to safety will stay between us. At the end of our conversation we will talk about how to tell your parent(s). If we can figure out a way to do it, my preference would be for you to be the one to tell your parent(s) about any thoughts of suicide you may have. My bottom line is that I want you to be safe and happy. By the time you leave, we will have a plan to figure out how we can work toward both.

Throughout your conversation with the student, use as many encouraging and affirming phrases as possible without sounding fake. The wording of the affirmation is often less important than the tone with which it is delivered. That said, people in a suicidal crisis often appreciate hearing things like, "It takes courage to share what you are sharing," and "While being a sensitive person is a great quality, it can be hard to feel as deeply about things as you do."

Assessment Validation Techniques

Were you reading the last section and asking yourself, "How do I know if the student will tell me the truth?" If so, nicely done! Assessing for suicide risk is complicated in part because there are many reasons why students might misrepresent or obfuscate their suicidal thoughts and behaviors. Some might feel ashamed, embarrassed, or humiliated about their STB. Some might fear the consequences at school—missing days of school and falling behind in academics, being kicked off a sports team, losing a position in a school organization, or suffering embarrassment if the word gets out among peers. Some might fear the consequences at home—increased restrictions (either because the parent is angry or protective) or having to be emotionally intimate with parents (e.g., talk with parents about what has been going on in the student's life). Depending on the severity of the STB, students might fear being hospitalized.

There are many more reasons why it might be hard to gather accurate information regarding suicide risk. The good news is that Shawn Shea (2002), one of the pioneers in the field of suicide assessment, has identified and described six validation techniques to increase the likelihood that you will uncover suicidal ideation and intent: behavioral incident, shame attenuation, gentle assumption, symptom amplification, denial of the specific, and normalization. We briefly describe them and illustrate their use in the dialogue below.

Behavioral incidents are very specific trains of thoughts or actions. One of the ways you can be sure you are doing a thorough risk assessment is if you can visualize what a person was doing or thinking at the time of their suicidal crisis. Examples of eliciting behavioral incidents include, "How many pills did you take?" and "What were you thinking when you opened the bottle? What happened next?"

Shame attenuation is a way to gently and respectfully uncover shameful content. You are giving the student the benefit of the doubt. For example,

> Sometimes when people experience their first break up, they feel so sad and confused that they find themselves thinking things they never imagined they'd think, such as "I might as well kill myself." I know you have recently been through a really rough break up and I'm wondering if you've ever surprised yourself by having thoughts of suicide?

Your previous knowledge of the student will help you know what the student might see as shameful. For example, you might know that a student feels shame because of his or her religious beliefs, because of the status he or she has in school, or because of particular family expectations.

Gentle assumption is when you frame questions as if a behavior is occurring. By gently assuming a behavior is occurring you increase the likelihood that the student will be honest. For example, if the student in your office is a known troublemaker, instead of asking "Have you had any conflict with teachers this week?" you can say, "Which teacher did you have the most conflict with this week?" Instead of asking, "Have you thought of other ways to kill yourself?" gently assume that she has and ask, "What other ways have you thought about killing yourself?"

Symptom amplification addresses the phenomena of people downplaying bad or shameful behavior. When a police officer pulls you over for speeding and asks, "Do you know how fast you were going?" you knowingly give a lower speed than you were actually driving. Symptom amplification sets the bar high so that even if someone downplays the behavior, it is likely to be closer to the truth. For example, if you ask, "How many times have you thought about killing yourself this week?" the answer might be, "Once or twice." If you amplify the symptom (suicidal ideation) and ask, "How many times have you thought about killing yourself this week? Ten, fifteen, twenty times?" even a downplayed response will often be higher than "Once or twice." The student is more likely to give the actual number because he or she now thinks that it is not so bad.

Denial of the specific works on the assumption that it is harder to deny a request for specific information than a request for general information. If you ask, "Have you ever thought about killing yourself?" you might get a no. If, however, you ask, "Have you ever thought about hanging yourself?" you are more likely to get the truth, simply because it is harder for people to lie.

Normalization is a technique where you let the student know they are not alone in their experience. Normalization should not be confused with normalizing suicide risk. This was a message that first generation suicide prevention programs pushed: "Don't feel bad about having thoughts of suicide—everyone does!" This message was both incorrect and counterproductive. You can convey the message that the student is not alone without telling him or her that everyone else feels the same way. For example, "Every day I talk with kids who feel their lives are so awful that they think about killing themselves. Have you ever had thoughts like that?"

To hear Shawn Shea use these techniques in a role play of a suicide assessment with a 17-year-old male student, please see Singer (2012).

Assessing for Suicidal Ideation, Intent, Plan, and Means

- *Ideation* refers to thoughts of killing oneself.
- *Intent* reflects the level of motivation and ability to follow through with a suicide plan.
- *Plan* and *Means* describes when and how the person will kill him or herself.

Imagine that you have a 13-year-old student, Trinity, in your office. Trinity was referred by her teacher because of an essay she wrote in which she described a girl her age dying by suicide. Sitting in your waiting area, she appears sullen and withdrawn. Her textbook is open and she is studying for an exam she tells you she has next class. You're thinking to yourself, "Okay, she seems in a bad mood—maybe she is having a bad day. Her assignment in English class was to write an emotionally compelling piece; suicide is an easy way to tug at the heartstrings so maybe she was just taking her assignment seriously. She's studying for her exam, which suggests that she's thinking about the future and cares about doing well. None of these things suggest that she's going to kill herself." These are excellent thoughts, and right on the money too. But that doesn't mean the student in your office isn't at risk for suicide. How do you distinguish a suicidal teen from a teen in a bad mood or a teen whose creative project was suicide themed? The answer is to conduct a thorough SRA.

No one has created the definitive way to assess for suicide risk. Most professionals (e.g., school psychologists, social workers, counselors, nurses, or professionals in hospitals, partial hospitalization, residential, or outpatient mental health) use whichever SRA protocol has been approved by their organization. If your school or district does not have an SRA protocol, we have provided the *Suicide Risk Assessment Form* as part of your online eResources that has been created based upon a multitude of suicidology research. If you have an SRA protocol already, great—keep using it. We suspect that ours will look similar but not identical to the one your district has approved. That's okay. What is important is that the essential content is covered. If you find that there is content covered in our assessment that is not covered by your district's approved assessment protocol, and you believe that it would be an important addition for your colleagues to have, please contact your central office and recommend the change. The next several pages talk you through how to use our *Suicide Risk Assessment Form.*

Section I: Assessing Ideation

The first piece of information to gather in any suicide assessment is whether the student has thoughts of suicide. Why? For most youth, suicide risk appears to increase along a continuum from ideation to plan to attempt to death. The average time between first thought and first attempt is one year (Nock et al., 2013). When you assess for ideation, you want to find out when the student had the ideation. Shea (2002) recommends assessing for ideation in the past two weeks, past two months, ever, and then return to the present. "Have you had thoughts of killing yourself in the past couple of weeks? How about the past couple of months? When was the first time you thought about killing yourself? Right now, as we're talking about it, are you having thoughts of killing yourself?"

A quick word about language: It is important to use the phrases "kill yourself," "suicide," and "take your own life" when assessing for suicidal ideation. Students who have no desire to die by suicide but who engage in NSSI to cope with overwhelming emotions or the absence of emotions can answer yes to "Have you had thoughts of hurting yourself?" Most adolescents will say yes to "Have you had thoughts of dying?" because it is developmentally appropriate to consider mortality. "Have you ever wanted to be dead?" Again, youth can say yes to this question without having thoughts about killing themselves. Not only does asking, "Have you had thoughts of killing yourself?" ensure that the yes or no will be related to suicide, it can also provide the student with reassurance that you are not afraid to talk about suicide. That said, we acknowledge that the shame, stigma, and embarrassment associated with suicide might inhibit people from answering yes to a direct question. One way of building up to asking about suicide is simply to start out with more general terms and end with the specific:

You: Have you had thoughts of hurting yourself? *[Self-harm]*
Trinity: Yes. *[Possibly is in emotional pain, only wants to end the pain]*

Y: Have you had thoughts of wanting to die? *[Non-suicidal morbid ideation]*

T: Yes.

Y: Have you had thoughts of wanting to end your life? *[Suicidal ideation]*

T: Yes.

Any time you get the sense that the student is hesitant, ashamed, or embarrassed, you can use Shawn Shea's validity technique shame attenuation, described above.

Once you get a yes, ask the student what specific thoughts she or he has? Get their exact words so you can use them for the duration of the assessment. Using their words lets them know you're listening, and sometimes hearing their own words replayed back can be a reality check. During the student's description, ask clarifying questions about the nature of their suicidal ideation. Do they have thoughts every hour, once a day, once a week (i.e., *frequency*)? How long do they last? Do the thoughts go in and out, or do they last for most of the day (i.e., *duration*)? When they have thoughts, are they able to go about their business, or are they paralyzed by them (i.e., *intensity*)? You also want to find out when and where they have the thoughts: morning, noon, or night; in school, home, work, social situations; with others, or alone? There are many other questions you can ask using basic behavioral analysis concepts, but frequency, duration, intensity, and when and where are the basic questions. Here's an example of how to use them in an assessment:

You: I know you've really been struggling lately to adjust to the new school. Sometimes people are so overwhelmed by the new situation that they find themselves having thoughts they ordinarily wouldn't have, such as thoughts of suicide. Have you found yourself having thoughts of killing yourself?

Trinity: Sometimes.

Y: Can you tell me about them?

T: I mean, I just have them.

Y: When was the most recent time that you had thoughts of ending your life?

T: This morning.

Y: What went through your head?

T: All the kids are right, I should just kill myself. The world would be a better place with me gone.

Y: That sounds like a really hopeless place. How often have you had that thought? *[Frequency]*

T: A couple of times.

Y: A couple of times today, in the past week, past month? *[Frequency]*

T: A couple of times in the past hour.

Y: The past hour. . . . you're really dealing with a lot right now. I'm impressed you're talking with me about this. When you've had these thoughts this past hour, how long have they lasted?

T: What do you mean?

Y: I mean, has the thought "I should just kill myself" popped into your mind for a split second and then you've thought about something else or has the thought hung out for a while? *[Duration]*

T: It hangs out for a while.

Y: Like 10 minutes, 15 minutes, 20 minutes? *[Symptom amplification since she already mentioned she thinks about it several times within ONE hour]*

T: Like 10 minutes.

Y: So when this thought, "I should just kill myself" comes into your mind, it hangs out for about 10 minutes and then leaves, but then it comes back a couple times an hour. Did I get that right?

T: Yeah, I guess that's about right.

Y: When you're having these thoughts, do they keep you from concentrating on your school work or even conversations you're having with people? *[Intensity]*

T: No. I can usually ignore them.

Y: How do you do that?

T: I dunno. I just do.

Y: Are there any specific places or times when you have these thoughts, have them more often, or they are more disruptive? *[Context]*

T: Yeah. When I'm at school. When I'm at home I can hang out in my room and text my friends. But when I'm at school, particularly in math and science—because that's where Shoshana and all them are—that's when they are the worst.

Y: So, you don't experience thoughts of suicide when you're at home or when you're otherwise distracted?

T: Yeah, not really. It is mostly at school.

At this point you know that Trinity is having current and frequent suicidal ideation. Her suicidal thoughts last about 10 minutes at a time, but are not distressing and do not appear to interfere with her ability to do school work. Her ideation is context specific, in part because she is able to distract herself when she's at home. We still don't know if she can stop the thoughts herself. That's important. If she can, we can use that in our safety plan, which we'll discuss in detail in chapter 7.

Y: I'm so glad that you get a break from these thoughts of suicide when you're at home. Can you remember a time when you were at school and you were able to stop the thoughts?

T:	If we're doing something interesting in class they usually don't pop up.
Y:	That makes sense. I'm wondering if you've ever been able to stop the thoughts as they were happening?
T:	No. I don't think so.
Y:	How do you feel when you are having these thoughts?
T:	Scared. Sad.

Upon hearing Trinity's fear and sadness, your instinct to intervene might kick in. "Trinity, you sound like a really thoughtful young woman with so much to live for. Let's figure out a way for you to not feel so sad and scared. What do you say?" Our advice: Hold off on intervention until after the assessment is over as Trinity may feel as if you are discounting her feelings of despair, instead telling her what to do. You can certainly "plant seeds" in the student's mind during an assessment with phrases like, "that was a creative way to solve that problem," or "it sounds like you're really excited to be at your sister's five-year-old birthday party next month." Further, there is so much information to gather when conducting a risk assessment for suicide (or homicide or psychosis) that assessment and intervention should remain separate.

Section II: Assessing Intent

Trinity's essay has been shown to have some truth behind it: She has suicidal ideation. The next step is to assess her intent: How much she wants to die. We assess intent on a 3-point scale where 1 = I don't want to die, 2 = Part of me wants to live and part of me wants to die, and 3 = Nearly all of me wants to die. The 3-point scale is better for younger children, those that are cognitively constricted, and those that have high emotionality than a 5- or 10-point scale because there is no question what it means to be a 1, 2, or 3; and the ratings mirror the general risk levels (low, moderate, and high). For the sake of instruction, we present two dialogues, one demonstrating low intent and the other demonstrating high intent.

Low intent:

Y:	When you have these thoughts, how much of you wants to die?
T:	I don't know.
Y:	On a scale of one to three, where one means that you don't want to die—no part of you wants to die, three means that nearly all of you wants to die, and two means that part of you wants to live and part of you wants to die, on that 3-point scale, where are you?
T:	I'm like a 1.5.
Y:	How would you describe it?

T:	Like I don't really want to die, but sometimes I think it would be better for everyone. But I don't really want to do it.

High intent:

Y:	When you have these thoughts, how much of you wants to die?
T:	I don't know.
Y:	Would you say that 80% of you wants to die, 90%, 99%? *[Symptom amplification]*
T:	Ninety-nine percent? Really? If I wanted to kill myself that badly I wouldn't be here talking to you [note: that is actually a myth—see myth handout in your eResources]. Not that much. Probably like 75% of me wants to die.
Y:	So most of you wishes you were dead?
T:	Yeah.

Section III: Assessing Plan

More so than any other part of the suicide assessment, assessing for plan is like putting on your journalist hat. When you assess for plan, you want to figure out the what, when, how, who, and why. *What* are the details of the plan: Is it vague or specific? *When* will it occur: at some unknown point in the future, or is it imminent? *How* will she kill herself? *What* is the method? *Who* has she told? *What* might prevent her from dying? We'll pick up the dialogue with Trinity as we assess for the presence of a suicide plan.

Y:	So most of you wishes you were dead? *[Intent]*
T:	Yeah.
Y:	Have you thought about how you would do it? *[Assessing for plan]*
T:	It?
Y:	Kill yourself.
T:	I don't know. *[Never take "no" or "I don't know" as a final answer]*
Y:	Is it you don't know or don't want to tell me?
T:	I really don't know. *[The general question is not working, so we'll use one of Shea's techniques: denial of the specific]*
Y:	Have you ever thought about overdosing on pills? *[Denial of the specific]*
T:	No.
Y:	How about hanging yourself? *[Denial of the specific]*
T:	No.
Y:	Shooting yourself with a gun? *[Denial of the specific]*
T:	Oh my god, no! I don't even own a gun.

Y: I know these questions sound really intense, but it is my job to figure out what's going on. When you're feeling so sad and alone and having thoughts of ending your life, have you ever considered cutting or stabbing yourself? *[Anchoring the question in an affective state]*

T: Ummm . . . yeah, cutting my wrists. In a bathtub. After taking pills.

Y: What pills would you take?

T: Sleeping pills.

Y: How many? 10, 20, 30?

T: As many as I needed.

Y: Do you have these pills at home currently?

T.   Yup. I often have trouble sleeping.

Y: Do you have a bathtub in your house?

T: Yeah. The door locks.

Y: So no one could get in. You've thought this through haven't you?

T: Yeah.

Y: What kind of knife would you use?

T: We have lots of them at the house. One of the sharp ones. *[Remember this when you talk with the parents. They will need to agree to lock up/remove all of the knives, search their daughter's room for pills, knives and razor blades, and consider removing the lock on the bathroom door.]*

Y: When are you planning on ending your life?

T: I don't know.

Y: Tonight? This weekend? Next week? *[Denial of the specific]*

T: I really don't know. Not tonight, not this weekend. I don't really want to, but I like knowing I can.

At this point, you know that Trinity has a specific plan, access to the means, and that her plan involves a fair amount of lethality. You've also identified something that you need to talk with the parents about—removing pills, knives, and razor blades and removing the bathroom lock. The way you would report this in your documentation is, "Trinity reports having a specific plan to die by locking the bathroom door, taking sleeping pills, getting into a bathtub, and cutting her wrists. She reports no intention to activate her suicide plan in the near future."

In addition to finding out about her plans for the future, it is helpful to find out about prior attempts. A prior suicide attempt is the most significant risk factor for a future attempt. Asking about prior attempt(s) can help you identify what precipitated it, what method was used, and what prevented the student from dying (did someone else interrupt it, or did the student abort the attempt?). If the prior attempt was precipitated by the same cluster of risk factors as the student is currently describing, and the plan is the same, then the student is likely to be at much higher risk for suicide than if there were no prior attempt(s). In his Interpersonal Theory of Suicide (Joiner, 2007), Joiner hypothesizes that we are biologically predisposed to survive. As was discussed in chapter 1, in order end your life, you need to acquire the capacity for suicide.

Y: Your plan is very specific and well-thought out. I'm wondering if you've ever done anything to attempt to end your life before? *[Prior attempt]*

T: No. I've thought about it a lot. I've seen movies where people die like that in the tub. I always thought it was because they wanted to make it easier for people to clean up, but now I know it is because the water keeps the blood flowing.

Y: You've really thought through this. . . . like you've been suffering for a long time. How old were you the first time you thought about killing yourself?

T: Nine. But I didn't think about how I would do it until the beginning of this school year.

Y: What has stopped you from following through so far this year?

T: I don't know. I guess, like I said, when I get home, it seems to be better.

Y: Can you think of anything that would make being at home as bad as being at school?

T: If those girls follow me home or mess with me online.

Y: Are you friends with them online?

T: Yeah, but we're not really friends.

Y: On Facebook?

T: Yeah, but mostly Instagram. I don't Snapchat with them. And no, they don't follow me on Twitter.

Y: If they were to mess with you online, could you tell your parents?

T: Not my dad because he's still on deployment. I could tell my mom, but I don't really know what she could do about it. I don't want her coming to the school and making more problems for me.

Y: What else would keep you from following through with your plan?

T: Honestly, I don't think I could do it to my little cousin. She lives with us and I love her so much. So, I don't know.

At this point you've determined that although Trinity has had thoughts of suicide for the past four years, she first planned how she would do it about four months ago. Furthermore, you have established that there is low risk for her to activate her plan because it is located at home where she rarely experiences suicidal ideation. You gathered information about how cyberbullying could increase risk at home, and how her parents are possible—but not certain—resources for her. Finally, and most importantly, Trinity let you know one of her most compelling reasons for living—her little cousin.

Section IV: Strengths and Resources

Protective factors are individual and environmental strengths and resources that reduce the likelihood of suicidal behavior and suicide (Shea, 2002; King et al., 2013). In order for something to be a protective factor, it must reduce risk associated with some characteristic. For example, if your student identifies as multiracial, then taking pride in his or her multiracial identity could protect against some of the risk conferred by his or her multiracial status. Because protective factors are specific to the individual, in section IV of the *Suicide Risk Assessment Form*, we have suggested questions that you can ask to elicit strengths and resources that might protect against suicide risk.

Section V: Risk Factors and Warning Signs

Suicide risk factors are characteristics that precede and increase the likelihood of suicidal behavior or suicide (King et al., 2013). Researchers establish risk factors by identifying which characteristics are significantly more likely to be present in a person who reports suicidal ideation, attempt, or death than in someone who does not (see Chapter 1 for a comprehensive list). We have listed a number of empirically based risk factors in Section V of the *Suicide Risk Assessment Form*. You should assess for as many of those risk factors as possible. Some risk factors will be easy to assess for during the clinical interview, such as dissatisfaction with grades, general dislike of school, and recent disciplinary action such as suspension. Other risk factors, such as psychiatric disorders (e.g., post-traumatic stress disorder, and major depressive disorder), would require more time to establish than is possible during a suicide assessment. Such information might be available in the student's records or from the student himself or herself. If not, you should note which risk factors you were unable to assess for. *Warning signs* are characteristics that indicate imminent risk for suicide. Because risk factors describe risk for suicide across a population, they are invaluable for research, developing prevention and intervention programs, identifying groups of students who might benefit from support, and establishing school policy. But when it comes to assessing imminent risk for an individual, we look for acute, proximal risk factors, also referred to as warning signs (King et al., 2013). Warning signs are statements that you hear a student say or actions that you see a student take (see Chapter 2 for examples) that suggest he or she is at risk for suicide in the very near future (within the next few days). An easy way to remember the difference between risk factors and warning signs is with the analogy of a stroke. Risk factors for a stroke include high blood pressure, smoking, and obesity, and the warning signs for a stroke are numbness or weakness in your face, arm, or leg, especially on one side; trouble seeing; and trouble understanding other people (http:// www.webmd.com/heart/atrial-fibrillation-stroke-11/signs-of-stroke). You would always note risk factors for a condition, but having the risk factor does not mean a stroke *will* happen. It is the warning signs that could possibly save a life.

Section VI: Presentation/Clinical Observations

One of the reason SMHPs are in the best position to conduct comprehensive SRAs is because of their clinical training in the observation of clients. It is important that SMHPs observe and describe the mental status of the student under the domains of emotionality, cognition, and behavior and use this information alongside information provided by the student and those from the student's home and school environments. Information regarding mental status can be obtained either from the student telling you directly (i.e., "I'm exhausted" or "It's all my fault.") or by your observations of the client (client's speech is delayed or student is responding in an agitated fashion to questions) during the assessment interview. When assessing the student's presentation at the time of the assessment, be sure to take cultural considerations into account with regarding to differing behavioral norms and expression of emotions. Issues of language, developmental level, and intellectual functioning should be addressed before making assumptions about cognition.

Assessing the Social Environment

Section VII: School Environment/Peers/School Staff Support

Gathering information about the school environment is one of the most valuable pieces you can add to the youth's assessment, regardless of the student's triggers. In Trinity's case, gathering information about the peer interactions that appear to be triggering the suicide risk will be essential in reducing her suicide risk over the long term. You are in a unique position to give external providers the school-based context for the student's suicide risk. As seen embedded within the SRA, this may include information about school events (e.g., triggers due to testing and assessment or milestone events such as the death of a teacher or student), interpersonal conflict between the student and peers or school staff, or risk factors that might be documented in a student's file such as cognitive impairment, disciplinary infractions, and academic achievement history. If you are not familiar with this information, then it is reasonable to interview school staff members. This information adds a unique component to the SRA.

Section VIII: Home Environment/Parental Support

One of the most robust environmental factors in determining suicide risk is the quality of the student's relationship with his or her parent(s). Research has found that high family conflict, low parental support, or highly critical parents increase risk for suicide (Borowsky, Ireland, & Resnick, 2001). A thorough SRA, therefore, requires assessing the child and the parent(s). SMHPs should evaluate the parents' ability to fulfill *essential functions* (e.g., provision of resources, maintenance of a safe and nonabusive home) and *parenting functions* (e.g., limit setting, healthy communication, nurturing, and positive role modeling) (Rudd et al., 2001). The overall suicide risk will go up or down depending on the parents' ability to fulfill both the essential and parenting functions. For example, if Trinity reports infrequent, not-distressing or low intensity suicidal ideation, a general plan but no intention to follow through and no access to the means, then she would meet criteria for low risk for suicide at the time of the assessment. Is your assessment complete? Can you safely say that your student is able to go back to class and go home without risk for suicide? No. You have not yet assessed her parent(s). Imagine that one of Trinity's triggers for suicidal ideation is constant criticism from her parents regarding academic performance. You would want to assess the parent(s)' ability to maintain a safe and nurturing home—even for 24 hours. If the parent(s) cannot do that, your client's suicide risk would increase from low to moderate. The timeframe for assessment would look something like this:

1. Assess Trinity.
2. Call parent(s) to discuss the assessment.
3. If parents are reluctant to come in, tell them their child has something they really want to talk about.
4. When Trinity's parent comes in (or if unable to come in, then assess over the phone), either you or the student can talk with the parent about the student's suicide risk.
5. Target your questions around access to lethal means, as well as parent's willingness and ability to engage in positive parenting practices and avoid behaviors that might trigger Trinity. (The SRA provides you with a framework for these questions.)
6. Make a final determination based on both the parent and student assessment.

Sections IX and X: Level of Risk and Recommendations

Everything Trinity has disclosed suggests she is at moderate risk for suicide. Again, moderate risk is defined as youth who report frequent suicidal ideation with limited intensity and duration. They may report some specific plans to kill themselves, but report no intent. Moderate risk youth will demonstrate good self-control, some risk factors, and be able to identify reasons for living and other protective factors. Levels of risk are discussed in far more detail in Chapter 7 as are specific actions steps to take and recommendations for support based upon suicide risk level.

Assessment Tools

There is no standardized assessment measure that can replace the clinical interview described above or the rapport and care established by talking to an individual who is hurting. Standardized assessment measures, however, can be a valuable adjunct to the clinical interview. If used across a district they provide consistency in measurement of risk. Assessment measures, unlike people, never miss a question or presume to know what is going on with a student. When you use an assessment measure over and over again, you begin to learn the questions and type of information gathered, which can improve your clinical skills. The SAMHSA Toolkit (2012) lists five brief assessments for adolescents with established psychometric properties. Unfortunately for most SMHPs, nearly all suicide risk assessment measures with well-established psychometric properties that have been evaluated in school settings (e.g., the Suicidal Ideation Questionnaire—Gutierrez & Osman, 2009) are copyrighted and available only by purchase, and most have been developed for adolescents rather than children.

Conclusion

Determining a student's level of suicide risk is difficult, but not impossible. We have created three instruments that you can use in your work with suicidal youth. The first is the *Suicide Risk Screening Form*, which can be used with any student to quickly identify the need for a more thorough assessment of suicide risk. The second, the *Suicide Risk Monitoring Tool*, is intended to be used on a session-by-session basis to evaluate and monitor ongoing suicide risk in students. We have included two versions of the *Suicide Risk Monitoring Tool* to account for students' differing ages, developmental levels and cognitive abilities: one which uses a 3-point rating scale and another that uses a 5-point rating scale. The third is the *Suicide Risk Assessment Form*, which we explored in detail throughout this chapter. You will find Word document versions of these three instruments on the eResource website. They can be duplicated and used freely.

References

Barrio, C.A. (2007). Assessing suicide risk in children: Guidelines for developmentally appropriate interviewing. *Journal of Mental Health Counseling, 29*(1), 50–66.

Berman, A. L. (2009). School-based suicide prevention: Research advances and practice implications. *School Psychology Review, 38*(2), 233–238.

Berman, A. L., Jobes, D. A., & Silverman, M. M. (2006). *Adolescent suicide: Assessment and intervention.* Washington, DC: American Psychological Association.

Berman, A. L., & Silverman, M. M. (2013). Suicide risk assessment and risk formulation part II: Suicide risk formulation and the determination of levels of risk. *Suicide and Life-Threatening Behavior,* n/a–n/a. doi:10.1111/sltb.12067

Bongar, B. M., & Sullivan, G. (2013). *The suicidal patient clinical and legal standards of care* (3rd ed.). Washington, DC: American Psychological Association.

Borowsky, I. W., Ireland, M., & Resnick, M. D. (2001). Adolescent suicide attempts: Risks and protectors. *Pediatrics, 107*(3), 485–493.

Centers for Disease Control and Prevention [CDC]. (2014a). 1991–2013 High School Youth Risk Behavior Survey Data. Available at http://nccd.cdc.gov/youthonline/. Accessed on October 1, 2014.

Centers for Disease Control and Prevention [CDC]. (2014b) *Web-based Injury Statistics Query and Reporting System (WISQARS)* [Online]. National Center for Injury Prevention and Control. (Fatal Injury Reports, 1999–2011, for National, Regional, and States [RESTRICTED]). Retrieved from http://www.cdc.gov/injury/wisqars/index.html. Available at http://www.cdc.gov/injury/wisqars/index.html. Accessed September 25, 2014.

Gutierrez, P. M., & Osman, A. (2009). Getting the best return on your screening investment: An analysis of the suicidal ideation questionnaire and Reynolds adolescent depression scale. *School Psychology Review, 38*(2), 200–217.

Horowitz, L. M., Bridge, J. A., Teach, S. J., Ballard, E., Klima, J., Rosenstein, D. L., . . . Pao, M. (2012). Ask Suicide-Screening Questions (ASQ): A brief instrument for the pediatric emergency department. *Archives of Pediatrics & Adolescent Medicine, 166*(12), 1170–1176. doi:10.1001/archpediatrics.2012.1276

Joiner, T. E. (2007). *Why people die by suicide.* Cambridge, MA: Harvard University Press.

King, C. A., Foster, C. E., & Rogalski, K. M. (2013). *Teen suicide risk: A practitioner guide to screening, assessment, and management.* New York: The Guilford Press.

Lieberman, R., Poland, S., & Cassel, R. (2008). Suicide intervention. In A. Thomas & J. Grimes (Eds.), *Best practices in school psychology,* V. Bethesda, MD: National Association of School Psychologists.

Nock, M. K., Green, J. G., Hwang, I., McLaughlin, K. A., Sampson, N. A., Zaslavsky, A. M., & Kessler, R. C. (2013). Prevalence, correlates, and treatment of lifetime suicidal behavior among adolescents: Results from the National Comorbidity Survey Replication Adolescent Supplement. *JAMA Psychiatry, 70*(3), 300–310. doi:10.1001/2013.jamapsychiatry.55

Posner, K., Brown, G. K., Stanley, B., Brent, D. A., Yershova, K. V., Oquendo, M. A., . . . Mann, J. J. (2011). The Columbia-Suicide Severity Rating Scale: Initial validity and internal consistency findings from three multisite studies with adolescents and adults. *The American Journal of Psychiatry, 168*(12), 1266–1277. doi:10.1176/appi.ajp.2011.10111704

Ribeiro, J. D., Bodell, L. P., Hames, J. L., Hagan, C. R., & Joiner, T. E. (2013). An empirically based approach to the assessment and management of suicidal behavior. *Journal of Psychotherapy Integration, 23*(3), 207–221. doi:10.1037/a0031416

Rudd, M. D., Joiner, T. E., & Rajab, M. H. (2001). *Treating suicidal behavior: An effective, time-limited approach.* New York: The Guilford Press.

Shea, S. C. (2002). *The practical art of suicide assessment: A guide for mental health professionals and substance abuse counselors.* Lexington, KY: Mental Health Presses.

Singer, J. B. (Producer). (2012, September 11). #74 - The Chronological Assessment of Suicide Events (CASE) Approach: Interview and role play with Shawn Christopher Shea, M.D. [Episode 74]. *Social Work Podcast* [Audio podcast]. Retrieved from http://www.socialworkpodcast.com/2012/09/the-chronological-assessment-of-suicide.html

Singer, J. B. (2005). Child and adolescent psychiatric emergencies: Mobile crisis response. In A. R. Roberts (Ed.), *Crisis intervention handbook: assessment, treatment, and research* (3rd ed., pp. 31 –361). /New York: Oxford University Press.

Singer, J. B., & Slovak, K. (2011). School social workers' experiences with youth suicidal behavior: An exploratory study. *Children & Schools, 33,* 215–228. doi:10.1093/cs/33.4.215

Steinhausen, H.-C., & Metzke, C. W. W. (2004). The impact of suicidal ideation in preadolescence, adolescence, and young adulthood on psychosocial functioning and psychopathology in young adulthood. *Acta Psychiatrica Scandinavica, 110*(6), 438–445. doi:10.1111/j.1600–0447.2004.00364.x

7 Intervening With a Potentially Suicidal Student

From Assessment to Intervention

In Chapter 6, we reviewed the components of a suicide risk assessment (SRA). At the end of a thorough assessment, you are able to make a statement about a student being at low, moderate, or high risk for suicide. Over the next few pages, we'll talk about what to do when you have students at these three levels of risk. We will talk about the first intervention: developing a safety plan. We will review how and when to break confidentiality, some ways to think about engaging parents and discussing youth suicide risk with them, and how to document a risk assessment. Although we realize that most school mental health professionals (SMHPs) do not have the luxury to "do therapy" with students, we included a brief review of attachment-based family therapy, a clinical intervention with demonstrated efficacy at reducing suicide risk. We discuss how to manage when a student re-enters school following hospitalization for suicide risk. We end with a review of how to use the *Suicide Risk Monitoring Tool* (available as part of your online eResources).

STANDARD OF CARE

Consultation: Any time you conduct a formal SRA, regardless of the outcome, you should consult with a clinical supervisor or colleague. No one is expected to conduct an SRA alone. Consultation reduces the likelihood that you have missed information or come to an unwarranted conclusion. This protects both you and the student. Although protocols vary by school and by district, you will probably need to inform an on-site administrator about the suicide assessment and final determination.

Parental notification: You should inform the parent(s) any time you conduct a suicide assessment or screening, regardless of the final determination. This includes situations in which the youth reports NO suicide risk. Parents have the right to know when school personnel assess for suicide risk, as long as there is no indication that such information would put the child at risk for abuse or neglect. Parents should always be involved in any suicide assessment because of their insight into prior history of suicide risk, current stressors, and home environment. In addition, contacting parents can establish good will, rapport, and a line of communication that will be invaluable if the time comes when the SMHP needs to let the parents know that their child is at risk for suicide. Finally, we must remember that parents have information we do not. For example, this information may help them decide how and when to deliver potentially triggering news to the student (e.g., "We have decided to get a divorce"). Some schools require parents to sign an *Emergency Notification Form* to indicate that they have been told about the suicide assessment. In one court case (*Eisel v. Board of Education of Montgomery County*), the school district was found liable in the suicide death of a child because the school counselor assessed the child, found no risk, did not notify the parents, and the child subsequently died by suicide (see Chapter 4 for more detail).

Low Risk

Youth who are at low or moderate risk for suicide report passing suicidal ideation, no intent, and no plan. They are considered safe to maintain in the community. That is, they can stay in school, continue with existing mental health treatment, and participate in on-going extra-curricular activities.

What to do: Create a safety plan with the student. Notify parents of your assessment and recommend that they make an appointment with an out-patient mental health professional (if the student is not already connected with one). Connecting students to mental health services is as important for students who are experiencing their first thoughts of suicide as it is for youth with recurrent suicidal ideation. If this is the student's first experience with thoughts of suicide there is an important window of opportunity to address whatever issues are contributing to the suicide risk. If you find that youth with recurrent suicidal ideation are connected with community mental health centers (CMHCs), you can keep tabs on whether those services are adequately addressing the student's suicide risk. If not, help the student and family to find a therapist that knows how to work with suicidal youth. You need to make sure that parents sign release of information (ROI) forms so that you can communicate with CMHCs and so they can communicate with you. For elementary-aged youth experiencing their first suicidal ideation, getting connected with mental health resources is essential. You might have to convince the adults in the child's life that his or her suicidal ideation should be taken seriously. Many adults find it hard to believe that a third grader, for example, could be serious when he or she makes suicidal statements. However, research has found that elementary-aged youth who reported *even passing* suicidal ideation report more serious problems over the long-term than middle school and high school youth who report more frequent and enduring suicidal ideation (Steinhausen & Metzke, 2004). Also, you will have to find a CMHP who works with children *and has experience* with suicide risk. There is a strong likelihood that the CMHP that everyone says is excellent might not have the expertise in youth suicide that another therapist might possess. For information about how to determine if a CMHP meets minimum requirements for working with suicidal youth referrals, please see the *Screening Mental Health Providers Form* in the online eResources.

A final reason why it is so important to connect youth at low risk for suicide with mental health services and other supports is to prevent low risk youth from becoming moderate- or high-risk youth. Recent research has suggested that the average length of time between first suicidal ideation and first suicide attempt in adolescents is less than one year (Nock et al., 2013). However, not all youth who report suicidal ideation will go on to make an attempt: 12% of youth report ever having had serious thoughts of suicide in their lifetime versus 4% who reported making a plan or attempting suicide (Nock et al., 2013). Parental awareness and monitoring and psychotherapy services are two ways of reducing the likelihood that youth with ideation will become youth who attempt suicide.

What not to do: Some schools have a policy of suspending a student from school until a CMHP (e.g., psychiatrist, social worker, psychologist, counselor, psychiatric nurse) determines that the youth is not at risk for suicide. For some students, school is the only place they are able to have supportive and connecting relationships with peers and adults. Unless the student is at high risk or suicide triggers are school based, suspension punishes the student for being honest about suicide risk and places the burden of monitoring on the parent, who in all likelihood is not a trained professional. The relationship between the school and parent should be collaborative. Schools have trained mental health professionals, families don't. Finally, unless there is an agreement in place with an agency or provider to conduct suicide assessments, it creates a burden on the parent and possibly the social service system to get a suicide assessment for a youth who has already been identified as safe to maintain in the community. We recognize that for some youth, home might be the safest place, especially if there is a close connection to a stay-at-home parent. However this is the exception to the rule.

Instead of suspending a student and sending him home, the school should maintain the youth in school and set up a plan for how to keep the student monitored during school hours until either a professional can come in and assess on school grounds or the student can safely be transported by a parent or other authority to a CMHC or hospital for a thorough assessment.

Moderate Risk

Youth at moderate risk for suicide. These youth report frequent suicidal ideation with limited intensity and duration. They will report some specific plans to kill themselves, but report no intent. Moderate risk youth will demonstrate good self-control, some risk factors, and be able to identify reasons for living and other protective factors.

What to do. Youth at moderate risk for suicide present the most challenging management issues for professionals. Consider this: Youth with either low or high risk require minimal management. If you determine that the youth is at low risk, you send him or her back to class (and monitor). If you determine that the youth is high risk, you send him or her to the hospital to be assessed. But what about the youth at moderate risk? Do you send him back to class? Do you send her to the hospital? Do you call the parent and recommend that the student be taken immediately to the local CMHC for an intake? Youth who are at moderate risk for suicide benefit from regular reevaluation of suicide risk to identify increased or decreased risk. You can use the *Suicide Risk Monitoring Tool* to standardize your reevaluation. Before leaving your office, develop a safety plan with the student and the parent if possible (see below for details), and include the number for the local 24-hour crisis center/hotline. If the student is not in outpatient treatment, he or she should be connected immediately with someone who has experience working with suicidal youth. If the student is participating in outpatient therapy, the frequency and intensity of treatment should be increased until the youth's suicide risk is assessed to be low or none. The student should be evaluated by a psychiatrist or psychiatric nurse practitioner for medication. The school staff should maintain close contact with the student and his or her parent(s) and CMHPs.

High Risk

If you have determined that the student has active ideation, a desire to die, a specific plan, access to the means, and few or no reasons for living, you need to get the student assessed for hospitalization. Although there are no data to support the idea that hospitalization is an effective intervention against suicide, most communities do not have the resources or treatments available to maintain high risk youth safely. Therefore, your job is to get the student an assessment with someone who can determine whether he or she meets criteria for hospitalization (typically hospital-based social workers, counselors, psychiatric nurse practitioners, or psychiatrists). The specific steps to take with this student are the following:

1. Supervise the student at all times while in the building (including bathrooms).
2. Contact the parents.
3. Coordinate with the CMHC that provides crisis suicide risk assessments and liaisons with the local hospital (we strongly recommend that you try to coordinate these connections in your school or district ahead of time).
4. Call the hospital directly and alert them of an incoming assessment.
5. Arrange for transportation to the hospital.

    a. The student should only be released to a parent who has agreed to take the student either to the appropriate CMHC or hospital.
    b. If the parent will not agree, the child should be transported only by law enforcement or school personnel if available, can be done safely, and it is within school policy to transport students.

Safety Plans

If you were trained in the 1960s through mid-1990s, you were probably taught to have students sign no-harm or no-suicide contracts (Poland, 1989). These were preprinted contracts with blank spaces for names and phone numbers specific to the student. The suicidal student was asked to sign a document that said something like: "I promise not to do anything to end my life. If I have suicidal thoughts or impulses to act on suicidal thoughts I promise to contact Adult A, Adult B, Adult C, call 911, or go immediately to the emergency room." The student would sign the contract, you would sign the contract, and then everyone would go about their business. We thought that it would protect the provider from liability. This turned out not to be the case. The no-harm contract actually increased liability when it appeared that the provider committed sins of omission (i.e., they did not do what they should have done) because they assumed they were protected by the contract (e.g., *Witsell v. School Board of Hillsborough County*; see Chapter 4). Furthermore, there are no data that support the idea that no-suicide contracts reduce suicide (Rudd, Mandrusiak, & Joiner, 2006) or if a student in the midst of a suicidal crisis would decide not to make an attempt because he or she signed a piece of paper.

"No Suicide Contracts" are

- "widely used, but there is increasing controversy regarding their use;
- neither contractual nor ensure genuine safety;
- emphasize what students won't do rather than what they will do;

- may be viewed by students as coercive, since failure to sign may force hospitalization; and
- may give school mental health professionals a false sense of security" (Miller & Lieberman, 2006, p. slide 24).

In place of a no-suicide contract, the current best practice standard of care is to create a safety plan. There are many variations on what components to include in a safety plan and what to call it (Brent, Poling, & Goldstein, 2011; King, Foster, & Rogalski, 2013; Stanley & Brown, 2012). The basic idea behind a safety plan is that rather than being a legal document, it is a clinical tool that the student can use before and during a suicidal crisis. Students who are in a suicidal crisis often think that their situation will never get better and that the only good solution is suicide. Students can read over their safety plan—a document they helped create—to remind them of coping strategies, peer and adult supports, and professional resources that they can access in the hopes of moving them through the crisis. The last thing you want is for your students to have to be creative during a time when they are certain that all of their ideas are bad—except for one (suicide).

Based on the work of Barbara Stanley and Gregory Brown (Stanley & Brown, 2012), David Brent (Brent et al., 2011), and Cheryl King (King et al., 2013), we recommend the following categories be included in a safety plan. We recommend using the student's own words whenever possible. A formatted version of this *safety plan* that you can use with students can be found as part of the online eResources.

1. Think of the most recent suicidal crisis. Write a one to two sentence description of what triggered the suicidal crisis. What are the thoughts, emotions, or behaviors that let the youth (and those around him or her) know that he or she was in crisis?
2. Internal coping: What can the youth do on his or her own to distract from suicidal thoughts?

    a. If this is the first instance of suicidal thoughts and behaviors (STB) or suicide attempt (SA), document the student's reasons for living and general strategies for successful coping (e.g., listening to music, playing video games, texting with friends).
    b. If the student has a history of STB/SA, find out what the student has done in the past (Socratic questioning) that has helped to reduce suicidal ideation and attempt.

3. External coping:

    a. Identify people the youth likes to hang out with and activities that the youth enjoys doing. These are not people to whom the youth will express suicide risk.
    b. Identify people with whom the youth can talk about suicide risk.

4. Create a plan:
   a. Drawing from #2 above, list the activities the youth would most enjoy doing on his or her own. These items should be activities that the student enjoys doing and can easily access when feeling suicidal.
   b. Drawing from #3 above, list the people (e.g., school staff members, parents, community or religious leaders) and organizational resources (e.g., hospitals, CMHCs, mobile crisis/support teams) that the youth could contact to discuss suicide risk. Include your contact information.
5. Provide the student with the number for the local crisis hotline, National Suicide Prevention Lifeline 1–800–273–TALK (8255), and 911.
6. Get agreement that lethal means will be removed.
7. Sign, provide phone numbers, date, and make sure the student and parent leave with a copy. Talk about where the student will keep the safety plan to access when needed.

Engaging Parents

The simple fact is that parents (we use *parents* as a generic term to describe any legal guardian, regardless of biological relationship to the youth) are ultimately responsible for securing mental health services for their child outside of school. While students of a certain age (typically between 14 and 18 depending on the state) might be able to consent for mental health treatment, parental involvement is necessary any time there is a psychiatric emergency. Parental involvement can range from full participation in assessment and intervention to temporarily authorizing others to make medical decisions about their child. The exceptional parent is the one who is aware of his or her child's needs, is willing to seek and participate in treatment, has the financial and transportation resources to be able to participate, and is ready to act. It is more common to find a parent who is aware, willing, able, or ready, but not all at the same time. In some situations, parents actively block professionals from getting youth the level of care that is deemed necessary, a problem described in more depth below. SMHPs already have to negotiate the personalities and bureaucracy of the school staff and the needs of the child. Engaging parents adds a level of complexity to an already complicated crisis situation. And yet, if one is successful in engaging the parent, it simplifies the SMHPs job and is likely to improve the long-term outcome for the student (Slovak & Singer, 2012).

So, how do you engage parents? As with so many aspects of working with suicidal youth, this is an area where there is more practical wisdom than empirical findings. There has been only one study that has looked at how mental health professionals engage with parents following a suicide assessment (Slovak & Singer, 2012). The study was a qualitative analysis of focus groups of mental health professionals who worked in schools, substance abuse treatment facilities and outpatient mental health clinics. We briefly review the findings and make recommendations specific to SMHPs.

Imagine that you have conducted an SRA with the student and spoken with her teacher. You know that in order to complete the assessment you have to talk with the parents. The purpose of talking with the parents is twofold: You have to share your findings with them (assuming that you have not found evidence that such a disclosure would place the student at greater risk, such as child abuse) and you have to assess their ability to provide a safe, nurturing, and risk-reducing environment for the student (Rudd, Joiner, & Rajab, 2001). If the student is at low or moderate risk for suicide, you would want to know that the parents are willing and able to take the student home, watch for warning signs, and make an appointment and/or follow up with outpatient mental health services. If the student is at high risk for suicide, you need to know that the parent is willing, able, and ready to transport the student to an emergency department to be evaluated for imminent risk and possible hospitalization. Even more important for the long-term success of treatment is the parent(s) attitude: being supportive, nurturing, encouraging, and committed to helping their child. Since some parents are not likely to default to these behaviors and attitudes, one of your jobs is to help them along. Unless you had a relationship with the parent prior to the suicide assessment, there is no way to know how they will react or respond to the news that their child is suicidal. Three common reactions are shock (at a loss for words), denial (acknowledging your concern but saying it is not as bad as you're making it out to be), and frustration/anger (actively defensive or dismissive of the child's suffering and your efforts to do something about it). Here are some tips for how you can understand and respond to them.

Scenario: You tell the parents that their child made suicidal statements and you would like to talk with them about your assessment and next steps.

Shock: Parents in shock need time to process the information. Some parents are aware that their child is having problems, but might be shocked to find out that he or she is suicidal (e.g., "I knew she had problems, but I never thought she would want to kill herself"). For other parents, this is the first time they have heard that their child might be suffering (e.g., "I don't understand. He's a happy kid, lots of friends, has everything he wants."). They are processing information that has implications for their child and for themselves as parents (e.g., "What kind of parent am I that I don't know my child wants to die?"). It seems self-evident that parents will need time to process, but the practical reality is that your tendency will be to rush them for two reasons: You have been dealing with this crisis for most of the day and know your job is not over until the student is safe and you want to get the parent on board with your agenda. While it is understandable that you want to move things along, rushing a parent in shock will reduce the likelihood of attitudinal engagement, even if there is evidence of behavioral engagement.

How to address shock: The good news is that your basic counseling skills are the best way to move a parent out of shock and into action.

1. Label their feelings ("You seem shocked" or "This seems like a total surprise").
2. Validate their confusion ("I know how confusing this can be to a parent like you who is clearly loving and attentive").
3. Reduce self-blame ("I know your child is the most important thing to you, and that's why we're talking about this").

Denial: There is nothing better than a twenty-first-century suicidal crisis to trigger a nineteenth-century Victorian-era defense mechanism. Denial is a way we temporarily cope with information that might be overwhelming, distressing, or challenging to our understanding of the world. Parents in denial do not deny that there is a problem; rather, they deny suicide risk. Statements that parents in denial might make include, "I know she has problems, but it can't really be that bad," "It was just an essay—she didn't really mean it," or "Kids say things to get attention all the time. I'm so sorry you had to spend time on this today." The concern with these parents is that they will be willing to address a lower-level problem (e.g., attention seeking) without addressing their child's suicide risk.

How to address denial: The good news is that these parents acknowledge a problem, just not the one that you want them to acknowledge. Your goal is to move them from denying the suicide risk to acknowledging it.

1. Emphasize the points of agreement: "I totally agree that sometimes kids don't say what they mean."
2. Praise: "She's really lucky to have a parent like you who is willing to acknowledge that something is wrong."
3. Move sideways: "Even if she's trying to get attention, there must be something really going on for her to be crying out for attention to this degree."
4. Tug at the heartstrings: "The other day I saw a parent who never got a chance to say goodbye to her daughter."

Frustration/Anger: Some parents will actively disagree with you about their child's suicide risk. These might be parents whose child has had a long history of suicide risk and the parent is burned out. Barry Wagner and colleagues (Wagner, Silverman, & Martin, 2003) interviewed parents 36 hours after their child was hospitalized for a suicide attempt. They found that while all of the parents showed concern when they were with their child, when the researcher asked them in private how they felt about their child's suicide attempt, the parents whose child had attempted more than once expressed anger about the attempt. These parents were angry and frustrated that all of their prior efforts seemed to have no effect on reducing their child's suicide risk, about the time it was taking out of their life, and that the professional community was not able to provide more help. The parents you work with might express anger and frustration like the parents described by the mental health professionals interviewed by Slovak & Singer (2012): "We've been through this so many times," or "This kid pulled this so many times and they never followed through with it so they must not be serious," or "I quit, I'm done." The biggest risk with these parents is that they will either refuse to get their child help or they will block you from doing your job.

How to address frustration/anger: The good news is that parents who are frustrated or angry have some energy around the situation. Your goal is to shift their energy from blocking you to moving with you or getting out of your way (this is where your Aikido training comes in handy).

1. Play to their strengths: "I see how frustrating this is to you. Am I wrong to think that you'd like nothing more than for this to stop?"
2. Sympathize: "It is exhausting to go through the same cycle over and over and over again. I wish I could tell you it will be different this time. The only thing I can tell you is that you're doing the right thing by taking him for an evaluation."
3. Give them an out: "Look, I know this is a really hard decision. If you want, I'll do it for you. Just give me the word and I'll arrange for her to be transported and evaluated. That way I'll take all the blame if she gets angry."
4. Play hardball: "Bottom line is that she's going to be evaluated for hospitalization with or without your cooperation. I'm a well-respected professional who did a thorough assessment and believe she might do something to end her life in the next 24 hours. I will call the emergency department and tell them to expect an intake in the next 30 minutes. If you can't agree to drive her and consent to the assessment, I'll call law enforcement. They'll be happy to transport her." (Note: hospitalization procedures, accessibility, and availability vary widely; however, all states have protective services and they should be called when parents are uncooperative and not taking the suicidal crisis seriously.)

It is likely that you will encounter a greater variety of parent responses than those described above (e.g., defensive or relieved). With the exception of the parent who actively blocks your efforts to get the student help, your job is to engage the parent on an emotional level as well as behavioral level. In a crisis, SMHPs tend to favor behavioral engagement, "I don't care what their attitude is, as long as they work with me to get this student help." However, research has suggested that parental attitudinal engagement is one of the factors that keeps youth in treatment over the long run (Staudt, 2007). By using the techniques described above to tap into parents' fears, expectations, and concerns, you are priming them for attitudinal engagement. Mental health professionals in the community will love you for that. And ultimately, the student will benefit.

Documenting a Suicide Risk Assessment

There are few times in a mental health professional's career when the old adage "If it wasn't documented, it didn't happen" is truer than in the case of a suicide risk assessment. SRAs should be documented thoroughly and immediately for several reasons:

1. SMHPs will always transfer suicidal youth to someone else's care. Thorough documentation limits the amount of information the student and parent will have to repeat, and make it more likely that the receiving provider is on the same page about the context, triggers, and rationale for post-assessment intervention (whether that was hospitalization or a referral to community mental health).
2. In the event of a lawsuit, your documentation is the only proof that you did what would have been reasonable for someone in your position, responsibility, and level of education. Both an unethical and an ethical lawyer will look at thorough documentation and see that there is no case, assuming that you provided and documented appropriate services.
3. Writing out a suicide assessment is one way to process and organize an enormous amount of information. It is likely that at the end of writing up your SRA you will have a better sense of what you know and what you would like to know than you did before you wrote it up.

What follows is a sample write-up of a suicide risk assessment of Trinity, the 13-year-old from the previous chapter. We suspect that this detailed, formal write-up is not a requirement of your job and that your documentation of suicide risk will probably end with the notes you have written on the *Suicide Risk Assessment Form* or the *Suicide Risk Monitoring Tool*. Even if you do not have to write up this type of detailed documentation as part of your job, it is valuable to know how you can translate the notes you took during an assessment and write them out in a formal assessment.

Trinity is a 13-year-old African-American female who was referred by her teacher for concerns of suicide risk. Trinity submitted a homework assignment with a graphic description of a 13-year-old African-American female cutting her wrists and dying by suicide. When

I spoke with Trinity, she seemed anxious and depressed, was somewhat lethargic, but was able to speak clearly and logically when asked
specific questions. She was oriented to person, place, and time. *[Note:
This summarizes the information in Section VI of the SRA Form.]*

I spoke with Trinity for approximately 45 minutes in my office at
school. At the time of the assessment, Trinity reports having current and
frequent suicidal ideation. Her suicidal thoughts last about 10 minutes
at a time but are not distressing and do not appear to interfere with her
ability to do school work. She reports thinking, "They are probably right,
I should probably kill myself." The "they" she is referring to are a group
of girls she used to consider friends who have now become "worse than
enemies." She reports suicidal ideation primarily when she is at school,
in part because she is able to distract herself when she's at home. She
reports having considered ways to die by suicide: taking sleeping pills
and cutting her wrists while in a bathtub. She stated that the bathroom
door locks, suggesting that she has thought through her plan to consider
the possibility of someone interrupting her attempt. She reports having
access to bathroom, pills, and knives. She reports no prior attempts. Her
reasons for living include her cousin, "I couldn't do that [kill herself] to
her," strong family connection, "they are my rock," and not wanting to
give the girls who victimize her the pleasure of knowing they won. *[Note:
This documents the information from Sections I, II, III, and IV.]*

As noted on the *Suicide Risk Assessment Form*, Trinity reports the following risk factors: recent humiliation in front of peers (being called
a slut in the lunchroom), social isolation (her former group of friends
now victimizes her), and anxiety. School records indicate no history of
anxiety disorder or medication for anxiety. She endorsed no other risk
factors. *[Note: It is very important to document what was assessed but is not
present, rather than not documenting it at all.]* Her anxiety appears to be
due to changes in her social situation. *[Note: This documents the information from Section V].*

After speaking with Trinity, I considered her to be at moderate risk for
suicide at this point because she reported frequent suicidal ideation with
limited intensity and duration. She reported some specific plans to kill
herself, but reported no intent. She reported relatively few risk factors
and very strong reasons for living.

I then spoke with the teacher to get information about Trinity's peers.
Her teacher confirmed that Trinity's former friends are now victimiz-
ing her. We talked about the steps that the teacher is taking to reduce
the amount of harassment Trinity experiences. When I spoke to Trinity's mother, she reported that they had recently lost their home and
were living with a friend. Mother reported that Trinity's father returned
after a being absent for three years. Mother reported that Trinity had
always seemed like a quiet, possibly depressed or anxious youth. Trinity

has prior experience with outpatient mental health services. When Trinity was 10, her mother brought her in to talk about her father leaving. At that time Trinity was not assessed for medication. Trinity's mother stated that she was confident that Trinity could be safe at home and that she would monitor her. We agreed that it would be excessive for Trinity to sleep on the floor in her mother's room. We agreed, however that mother would check on Trinity every two hours. *[Note: This covers information from Sections VII and VIII.]*

Formulation: After I spoke with Trinity's teacher and parent, I determined that Trinity met criteria for *moderate risk for suicide* because she had some risk factors and some very strong protective factors. After consulting with the district head of counseling about the risk assessment, we agreed that Trinity would not be at imminent risk for suicide based on Trinity's reports and mother's ability to provide a safe and nurturing environment. *[Note: This covers information from Section IX.]*

Plan: Trinity's mother made the phone call to set up a psychotherapy appointment for Trinity in one week. Mother states she will attend the session because mother believes strongly in the value of mental health services. We completed a safety plan (a copy is attached to these notes). I will check in with Trinity tomorrow, reassess for suicide risk, review the safety plan, and support her in practicing her coping strategies. Trinity's teacher will continue to monitor the behaviors of Trinity's former friends. *[Note: This covers information from section X.]*

The following are ways to document low, moderate, and high risk for suicide.

Low Risk

It was determined that because client was at a low or mild risk for suicide, hospitalization is not recommended. Client is not imminently dangerous to self and will be safe from serious self-injury or suicide until the next contact with me or primary therapist for the following reasons: problems that contributed to suicide risk are being resolved; suicidal ideation and/ or intent reduced by end of session; credible agreement for safety plan and no self-injury or suicide attempts; suicide being actively addressed by primary therapist/psychiatrist; protective factors outweigh risk factors (provide example from data section).

Moderate Risk

There is some danger of serious self-injury or suicide. However, emergency interventions such as hospitalization are likely to exacerbate rather than resolve long-term risk. The following also apply: (use above list).

High Risk

Emergency intervention (such as hospitalization) is needed to prevent imminent danger of medically serious self-injury or suicide. Therefore,

I called the parent who agreed to transport the student to the ER; called child welfare after the parent refused to transport the student to the ER, and then arranged transport through the sheriff/police/CMHP to the ER; arranged for involuntary commitment (describe process, who, when, how, etc.); called 911 for a welfare check; called 911 for emergency medical services; hospitalized at _____, to be admitted by Dr. _____; on _____ (date and time).

Connecting the Dots During a Suicidal Crisis

As a SMHP, you have unique knowledge of the student's specific educational ecosystem—the culture of the teachers, the peers, the neighborhood in which the school is located, the academic requirements and supports, and the emotional and behavioral supports offered in the school. SMHPs are often aware of, but find it difficult to place, their services in the broader social service context in which their clients live and move outside of the system in which she or he has direct influence. We sympathize. Your daily duties can include a variety of tasks including educational evaluations, individualized education plans, behavior intervention plans, consultation with parents and teachers, personal and group counseling, crisis response, course scheduling, college selection, and possibly administrative tasks. It can be overwhelming to be responsible for the identification, assessment and intervention of a suicidal student and then have to take into consideration all of the other systems of which the student might be a part. But if *you* are overwhelmed by it, imagine how overwhelmed the student and her or his family might be as they try to navigate multiple systems during a suicidal crisis.

The Process of Being Admitted to an Inpatient Psychiatric Unit

After the parent, CMHP, or law enforcement officer has transported the youth to the hospital, the student will have an intake with a social worker, nurse, and/or psychiatrist who will then make a determination about the appropriateness of hospitalization. The purpose of inpatient hospitalization is to maintain the safety of the child. Hospitalization, contrary to popular belief, is not intended to eliminate a student's suicide risk or treat underlying psychosocial issues for several reasons. First, as nearly all youth who are hospitalized for suicide risk report some combination of psychopathology, significant interpersonal problems, substance use problems, or other stressors, it is unreasonable to expect that those problems could be addressed by a brief (two–five day) in-patient stay. Further, youth are removed from a distressing environment for a brief period of time, placed in the hospital, and then returned to the same distressing environment without any explicit efforts to change that environment. So even if youth experience symptom remission in the hospital, it is likely that those symptoms would return upon discharge. Therefore, although youth might be discharged with an appointment to see a CMHP and have a temporary supply of medications, they will return to school needing significant support from school staff and family members in order to have a successful re-entry. School personnel should make sure they are following up with the hospital to get any relevant notes, assessments, or discharge plans.

Benefits of Hospitalization

So, what happens when a student is admitted to a psychiatric hospital for suicide risk? At a minimum, youth

- are evaluated for medication; or if currently prescribed, medication type and dosage are re-evaluated;
- have access to a qualified mental health professional with whom they can talk about the issues that led up to their suicide attempt or serious suicidal ideation, either in an individual or group setting (or both).

Discharge From the Hospital

By the time the student is discharged, there has to be enough of a reduction in suicide risk that the psychiatrist can say that the student is safe in the community. In some areas, youth are discharged to an intensive outpatient program or a partial hospitalization program. According to the Pennsylvania Code,

> Patients in partial hospitalization programs shall receive a minimum of 3 hours of planned treatment programs per hospitalization day. These programs shall emphasize a therapeutic milieu, and include therapeutic, recreational, social and vocational activities, individual, group, or family psychotherapy, psychiatric, psychological and social evaluations, medication evaluations and other activities as determined by the treatment team. (PA Code, § 5210.39, http://www. pacode.com/secure/data/055/chapter5210/chap5210toc.html).

What to Do When a Student Returns From the Hospital

Let's imagine for a moment that Trinity met criteria for high suicide risk, was evaluated at the local psychiatric emergency department, and then admitted in-patient for three to five days. She received very little psychosocial treatment, and there was very little coordination with the school during that time. Trinity was discharged on a Tuesday. The discharge worker coordinated with Trinity's mother to arrange an outpatient psychiatric appointment for 10 days out (the first available appointment). Trinity's mother was also given the phone number to set up an intake at the local CMHC. Both Trinity and her mother were eager for Trinity to return to school. What needs to happen now?

Re-entry Meeting

A re-entry meeting should be held prior to the student's return and might include the school-based case manager as well as the student, parents, SMHP, school nurse, and school administrators to address issues of mental health, attendance, behavior, medication, and academics. The purpose of this meeting should be to create a re-entry plan to address the above stated concerns, any other concerns of the students and family, and to address follow-up services:

- Parents must be involved in this process.
- Teachers should be informed of necessary protocols and to monitor suicide warning signs, while maintaining confidentiality of the family and student.
- Find out if the student has appointments with any outside service providers with whom exchange of information would be important in developing a safety plan.
- Have the parent(s) and student sign a ROI, even if the appointment has not yet happened.
- Anticipate that the student will feel emotions upon return to class ranging from numb to debilitating distress.
- Collaboratively develop a plan for what to do if the student becomes upset in class (i.e., deep breathing, exit the room to take a break).
- Decide what actions will be taken by the student, teacher, SMHP, and parent(s).
- Discuss and practice with the student potential phrases they can use if friends or peers say something potentially triggering such as, "Where were you last week?" or "Hey, I heard you got sent to the loony bin." Rehearsal will help the student feel confident in responding and may include statements such as "I was overly stressed and needed a break to calm my nerves" or simply "I was really sick."

The case manager should maintain frequent contact with the family to be informed of changes in the family situation, outpatient services, medication, etc. The case manager should also serve as a liaison between the student and the teachers to discuss academic concerns, arrange tutoring, modify the student's schedule or course load if needed, and work with teachers to allow adequate time to make up academic work and exams without penalty. The case manager should discuss with the guardians and the student *what* they would like teachers to know. Some families prefer to maintain confidentiality and prefer teachers are simply told the student was "sick" or in the hospital while leaving out details. Other families feel that their child will get more effective support if teachers know the truth. In this case, continue to ensure confidentiality outside of these boundaries. Teachers should be careful not to discuss the child in the lunchroom, the faculty room, or in the hall or elevator. Only the teachers who currently have this student in class need to know the details.

Finally, it is also a good idea at the re-entry meeting to assign a SMHP to meet with the student on a weekly basis (or more often if needed). The goal of these meetings is to "check-in" regarding the student's progress and needs, provide a safe place for the student to share concerns, ensure outside treatment plans are followed with efficacy, and monitor the student's continued risk for suicide.

Monitoring Suicide Risk

We mentioned back in Chapter 1 how frightening the possibility of suicide is. We know that a student does not return from a hospitalization being free of suicidal thoughts. There is no evidence hospitalization is even an effective *treatment* strategy; rather, it is a means by which to keep an individual *safe* in the short-term (Miller, 2011). So, once a youth's suicide risk has decreased enough to be maintained in the community, the hospital will discharge him or her. The responsibility for monitoring his or her suicide risk is now on you and any outpatient providers the student is connected to.

Let's make this a little more concrete. Imagine Trinity has just returned to school after her five-day hospitalization. You have conducted your re-entry meeting and everyone is on board with the plan for her to make up her academic work and how to handle feelings of distress or overwhelm. So, Trinity returns to class. Now what? Will Trinity be able to focus in class? Is she still depressed? After her hospitalization, has her suicide risk decreased at all? What if it has increased (which sometimes happens if students are angry or embarrassed about the hospitalization)? How will we even know? Her outpatient psychiatrist appointment is not for another 10 days and an appointment has not yet been made for community mental health treatment. Is it the school's ethical responsibility to monitor Trinity's risk until treatment outside of school has begun? How do we do this given all the other demands on our time? We created the *Suicide Risk Monitoring Tool* to help answer these questions and to monitor ongoing suicide risk.

Suicide risk can increase and decrease rapidly in youth. Therefore, one of the clinical challenges faced by SMHPs working with suicidal youth is monitoring and responding appropriately to these fluctuations in levels of risk. An effective approach to measure these fluctuations seems to be missing from suicide protocols and mental health professionals have often asked for a best practice technique to monitor ongoing suicide risk. Conducting a comprehensive suicide risk assessment week after week is not realistic: It is laborious and would not allow clinicians time to talk to Trinity about *anything* else that may be going on. In a world of data-based decision making, the new *Suicide Risk Monitoring Tool* provides a clinical framework for SMHPs to monitor variations in a student's unique profile from week to week and focus treatment based upon his or her weekly reports. This tool was designed specifically to link assessment findings directly to intervention decisions.

We have created two versions of the *Suicide Risk Monitoring Tool*: one for elementary to middle school students and one for middle through high school students. The forms are exactly the same, except one uses a 3-point scale and the other uses a 5-point scale. This is based on the fact that older children prefer more choices when responding and feel pigeonholed when not presented with enough choices, whereas younger children cannot readily decipher between them. For middle school age, we suggest that you consider the student's grade (middle schools often range from fifth through eighth grades) and developmental level when choosing which form to use. When using the form with high school students, we suggest a collaborative approach. During the first session, you complete the tool with the student, carefully explaining each section and ensuring understanding. For subsequent sessions, as developmental level dictates, students would be able to complete the form independently followed by you collaboratively discussing any fluctuations with them. For elementary school students, the practitioner completes the form each time with the child, presenting each question in a developmentally appropriate manner. As this is not a standardized tool, alter the language as needed so that the child understands what you are asking. It is suggested that the form be completed at the *beginning* of each session in order that increased STB can be addressed immediately in the session.

To provide a brief illustration of the tool's utility, imagine, for example, that you meet with Trinity individually after the re-entry meeting and complete the high school version of the monitoring tool with her. Trinity reports moderate levels of hopelessness (rating = 3), high levels of depression (rating = 5), mild levels of disconnection (rating = 2), and moderate feelings of being a burden to others (rating = 3). These first ratings provide us with a baseline of her affective state upon return from the hospital. Because this scale has not been validated and normed, there is no magic number (i.e., clinical cutoff) above or below which you need to do something. The decision to do something (e.g., call the parents, recommend being evaluated at a hospital, etc.) is based on relative changes to Trinity's own ratings. For example, when you meet with her the next day, she completes the monitoring tool and has the same scores. For the next four weeks her scores decrease slightly, indicating slight progress. When you meet with Trinity two months later, her ratings are as follows: hopelessness = 5, depression = 5, disconnection = 4, and burdensomeness = 4. While she previously reported thinking about suicide daily, she now thinks of it hourly and instead of the thoughts lasting only a few seconds, they last for many minutes at a time. What does this tell us? Well, it certainly indicates that Trinity's distress levels are increasing, that her suicide risk has increased, and that something needs to be done; her parents and outpatient therapists/doctors made aware of her increased risk, a medication management review, increased treatment strategies, increased supervision and removal of means, along with continued safety planning. If Trinity further reports having a plan, we would then refer her for another assessment for hospitalization.

The second page of the form is for clinicians to determine the current level of risk and quickly identify the follow-up strategies initiated by easily checking the appropriate boxes. As Trinity always has some level of suicidality, we cannot send her to the hospital weekly. The monitoring tool allows us to compare current functioning to her baseline levels after her first hospitalization and make decisions as we see a broader picture of Trinity week to week. Finally, the tool allows us to identify Trinity's protective factors—the things she enjoys doing and the supports she feels she has in her life, including family, friends, peers and other adults. This not only provides a measure to assess her strengths and resources but

Standard of care: I use the *Suicide Risk Monitoring Tool* after *any* suicide risk assessment, even if the child was not hospitalized. Think about a child who was found to be at low to moderate risk during your initial assessment. The child was not hospitalized but continues to see you weekly. Then imagine that the student had a major life event happen; his father died of a heart attack, his mother lost her job, or he failed anatomy and now cannot walk with his class at graduation. Any of these traumatic life events could impact this student who already had many risk factors for suicide. The *Suicide Risk Monitoring Tool* will allow you to assess if his life challenges have increased this risk. Finally, as with most data-based monitoring tools, if I find that a student presents with no or extremely low suicide risk for multiple weeks in a row, I begin to decrease the frequency of monitoring from weekly to biweekly, then to monthly and bimonthly. This may continue until either graduation or until there continues to be no risk for many months in a row. This also will be exemplified in the case study presented in Chapter 11.

has clinical utility identifying on an ongoing basis what areas need to be continually fostered and built upon.

The *Suicide Risk Monitoring Tool* is, in essence, an abbreviated form of the comprehensive *Youth Suicide Risk Assessment Form*. We have added common warning signs that a student may be suicidal (Substance Abuse and Mental Health Services Administration, 2012) to measure ongoing risk; feelings of sadness and hopelessness as well as Joiner's two signs of a desire to die—perceived burdensomeness and low belongingness. As you will know your individual students' risks and warning signs best by this point, we have left a blank space for you to identify their individual triggers in order to also monitor those over time. The final case study for this text (Chapter 11) walks you through a comprehensive case where we screen, assess, and monitor the suicidality of a high school student utilizing each of the forms discussed in Chapters 6 and 7. This case study analysis provides you with an enhanced example of the forms' real-life utility.

Psychotherapy Interventions

SMHPs rarely have the luxury of conducting ongoing psychotherapy with students, let alone families. For those who do, there are very few interventions developed to address suicide risk in youth and there is even less empirical support for those interventions (Corcoran, Dattalo, Crowley, Brown, & Grindle, 2011). The most commonly researched psychotherapies take a cognitive behavioral approach and work primarily with the individual student such as David Brent's cognitive behavioral therapy (CBT) (Brent et al., 2011) and Marsha Linehan's dialectical behavior therapy (DBT) (A.L. Miller, Rathus, & Linehan, 2007). CBT and DBT are structured interventions that focus on skill building (e.g., addressing "all-or-nothing" thinking, reframing thoughts, or recognizing and synthesizing ideas that seem to be opposites). Although it is beyond the scope of this text to summarize all of the treatments for suicidal youth (for a complete list please see the National Registry of Evidence-Based Programs and Practices (NREPP; http://www.nrepp.samhsa.gov/), we provide a brief summary of a relatively new treatment, attachment-based family therapy (ABFT; Diamond et al., 2010), because it fills an important gap in our understanding of how to work effectively with families of suicidal youth. ABFT has a psychodynamic and family systems basis, is the only family-based intervention with empirical support for the reduction of suicidal ideation in youth, and targets affective, rather than behavior change to reduce suicide risk.

Attachment-Based Family Therapy (ABFT)

ABFT is a trust-based, emotion-focused psychotherapy model that aims to repair interpersonal ruptures and rebuild an emotionally protective, secure-based, parent-child relationship. ABFT restores youth's hope that they can have a life worth living, and re-establishes the family as a source of strength and support during suicidal and other crises. Although ABFT is a family-based model, the therapist meets individually with the student and parent(s) to address issues central to reducing suicide risk. The ABFT treatment manual describes the five treatment tasks in great detail (Diamond, Diamond, & Levy, 2013). We have identified three concepts that SMHPs can easily integrate into their work with suicidal youth and families.

The first ABFT concept is to *get the parent(s) and youth to see the youth's suicidal thoughts and behaviors as a family problem.* When you meet with the parent and youth, have the youth describe some of the things that have contributed to his or her suicidal thoughts. Make sure the parent does not challenge the youth's experience. Find out if the youth has been able to talk with the parent about his or her problems. It is likely that the youth has not. Turn to the parent and ask if the parent would like their child to be able to talk to him or her about those problems. It is likely that the parent will say yes. Then ask the youth what has gotten in the way of going to the parent. Regardless of what the youth says, you can respond by saying something along the lines of "Your parent is one of the most important partners you can have in life. There are lots of things that are okay to not talk with parents about, but thoughts of suicide is one of the things that you should absolutely be able to talk with your parent about. I know it is hard to go to your parent [for the reason stated by the student], but he or she clearly wants to be there for you. Would you be willing to work with me over the next couple of days to make it easier for you two to talk with each other about suicide?" Once the family is on board with the idea that the youth's suicide risk is a family problem, it is easier for them to consider the family as a solution.

The second ABFT concept is *talking with the youth about what makes it hard for him or her to talk with adults (particularly his parents)* about depression, anxiety, bullying, suicide risk, etc. You would set up your session with the student by saying, "I know things have been hard for you lately. I was really impressed with how honest you were with your mom/dad, especially since you said that talking to him or her is really hard. I've talked with enough students to know that everyone has a different reason for what makes it hard to talk with parents, especially about something like suicide. I was wondering what are some of the things that get in the way of you talking with him or her about it?" If the student says, "I just don't want to talk with her about it," or "I would never tell him/her about something like this," you want to get more detail about what the student has done in the past. Some questions include, "What would happen if you did talk with him or her? Have you tried in the past? What happened?" If the student says, "I'd love to" or "I have tried" then follow up with questions like "How has your parent responded?" and "How would you like him or her to respond differently?"

The third ABFT concept is *teaching the parent to listen and validate their child's concerns before problem solving.* You would meet with the parent alone and let them know that you realize how scary/confusing/frustrating/hopeless it is to parent a child who is actively suicidal. If the child is in elementary school, explain that the child is not likely to respond well to direct questions about how they are feeling and instead teach the parent about engaging in activities like drawing, playing with clay, or even playing video games together while having a conversation. For parents of middle school- and high school-aged youth, provide the following context for the parents about how to listen so their child will talk:

1. Adolescents in a suicidal crisis often have thoughts and feelings that are confusing, scary, and/or embarrassing. Because they are so overwhelmed, they can't be creative about how to feel better.
2. Adolescents assume that since they don't feel entitled to their feelings, that no one else will feel the are either.
3. One of the best ways to show an adolescent that you value their feelings is to listen and validate their experience.
4. Once adolescents feel "heard," then it is easier for them to problem-solve on their own.

After parents understand these basic ideas, teach them reflective listening skills and how to make statements that validate and affirm the youth's feelings (even if the parent disagrees with the logic behind those feelings). It is a great idea to role play with the parent. Start out by taking the role of the youth. Share the issues and listen to (and watch) how the parent responds. After the role play use the same skills you just taught the parent—listen and validate! You can expect that the parent will need some time to learn these skills, after all it took most of us "helping professionals" years to become experts in accurate listening, reflection, and genuine and honest validation. Once you review these basic skills with the parents, you can switch roles. You be the parent and the parent practices disclosing as the youth. This serves two purposes. First, it gives you the opportunity to model for the parent the types of responses you are expecting. Second it provides you with insight into how well the parent understands the youth's issues, as well as gives the parent an opportunity to feel what it might be like for their child to approach them with this information.

The three concepts presented here provide the foundation for the attachment task in ABFT. Briefly, the attachment task is a conversation that the youth has with his or her parent(s) about why it has been so hard to go to them when things are difficult. The goal is for the youth to have a new experience of the parent as safe, nurturing, loving, protective, etc. and change his or her view of the parent(s) as someone that cannot be a resource to someone who can be a resource. The parent has an experience of being the parent he or she has wanted to be—loving, supportive, and there for the youth. Once the parent and youth have this new experience of each other, the remaining sessions are focused on helping the family engage in normative problem solving, which was previously impossible given the attachment ruptures. For an authoritative review of the model with illustrative case examples and specific techniques, we refer you to the ABFT treatment manual (Diamond et al., 2013).

References

Brent, D. A., Poling, K. D., & Goldstein, T. R. (2011). *Treating depressed and suicidal adolescents: A clinician's guide.* New York: The Guilford Press.

Corcoran, J., Dattalo, P., Crowley, M., Brown, E., & Grindle, L. (2011). A systematic review of psychosocial interventions for suicidal adolescents. *Children and Youth Services Review, 33*(11), 2112–2118. doi:10.1016/j.childyouth.2011.06.017

Diamond, G. S., Diamond, G. M., & Levy, S. A. (2013). *Attachment-based family therapy for depressed adolescents.* Washington, DC: American Psychological Association.

Diamond, G. S., Wintersteen, M. B., Brown, G. K., Diamond, G. M., Gallop, R., Shelef, K., & Levy, S. (2010). Attachment-based family therapy for adolescents with suicidal ideation: A randomized controlled trial. *Journal of the American Academy of Child and Adolescent Psychiatry, 49*(2), 122–131.

King, C. A., Foster, C. E., & Rogalski, K. M. (2013). *Teen suicide risk: A practitioner guide to screening, assessment, and management.* New York: The Guilford Press.

Miller, A. L., Rathus, J. H., & Linehan, M. (2007). *Dialectical behavior therapy with suicidal adolescents.* New York: The Guilford Press.

Miller, D. N. (2011). *Child and adolescent suicidal behavior: School-based prevention, assessment, and intervention.* New York: The Guilford Press.

Miller, D. N., & Lieberman, R. (2006). School crisis prevention & intervention: Suicide. [PowerPoint slides]. Retrieved from National Association of School Psychologists http://www.nasponline.org/prepare/Suicide presentation nasp 2006 final version.ppt

Nock, M. K., Green, J. G., Hwang, I., McLaughlin, K. A., Sampson, N. A., Zaslavsky, A. M., & Kessler, R. C. (2013). Prevalence, correlates, and treatment of lifetime suicidal behavior among adolescents: Results from the National Comorbidity Survey Replication Adolescent Supplement. *JAMA Psychiatry, 70*(3), 300–310. doi:10.1001/2013.jamapsychiatry.55

Poland, S. (1989). *Suicide intervention in the schools.* New York: The Guilford Press.

Rudd, M. D., Joiner, T. E., & Rajab, M. H. (2001). *Treating suicidal behavior: An effective, time-limited approach.* New York: The Guilford Press.

Rudd, M. D., Mandrusiak, M., & Joiner, T. E. (2006). The case against no-suicide contracts: The commitment to treatment statement as a practice alternative. *Journal of Clinical Psychology, 62*(2), 243–251. doi:10.1002/jclp.20227

Slovak, K., & Singer, J. B. (2012). Engaging parents of suicidal youth in a rural environment: Engaging parents of suicidal youth. *Child & Family Social Work, 17*(2), 212–221. doi:10.1111/j.1365-2206.2012.00826.x

Stanley, B., & Brown, G. K. (2012). Safety planning intervention: A brief intervention to mitigate suicide risk. *Cognitive and Behavioral Practice, 19*(2), 256–264. doi:10.1016/j.cbpra.2011.01.001

Staudt, M. (2007). Treatment engagement with caregivers of at-risk children: Gaps in research and conceptualization. *Journal of Child and Family Studies, 16*(2), 183–196. doi:10.1007/s10826-006-9077-2

Steinhausen, H.-C., & Metzke, C.W.W. (2004). The impact of suicidal ideation in preadolescence, adolescence, and young adulthood on psychosocial functioning and psychopathology in young adulthood. *Acta Psychiatrica Scandinavica, 110*(6), 438–445. doi:10.1111/j.1600-0447.2004.00364.x

Substance Abuse and Mental Health Services Administration. (2012). *Preventing suicide: A toolkit for high schools*. HHS Publication No. SMA-12–4669. Rockville, MD: Center for Mental Health Services, Substance Abuse and Mental Health Services Administration. Retrieved from http://store.samhsa.gov/product/Preventing-Suicide-A-Toolkit-for-High-Schools/SMA12–4669

Wagner, B.M., Silverman, M.A.C., & Martin, C.E. (2003). Family factors in youth suicidal behaviors. *Atemmerican Behavioral Scientist, 46*(9), 1171–1191. doi:10.1177/0002764202250661

8   The Aftermath

Immediate Suicide Postvention
Step-by-Step

Case Study: There Is a Loaded Gun

Jacob, a 17-year-old soccer player, is an introverted student who's smart and works hard. He grew up on the same block as his friend, Michel, and they did everything together until recently, when Michel's father got a job transfer and the family moved out of state. The sudden loss of his best friend threw Jacob, who had a history of depression, into a state of despondency; he couldn't focus, he couldn't sleep well, and his motivation toward school waned. He was caught cheating on an algebra test and suspended from the soccer team, disappointing and embarrassing his family. He withdrew even more. He didn't want to see a therapist about his depression because he hated talking and just wanted to be normal.

On a Friday afternoon, Jacob met his girlfriend for pizza. His attitude was bleak; they began to argue. In frustration, she yelled that she could no longer stand him. He needed to get help for his depression, and she was tired of him taking it out on her. They both left the pizza shop in a huff.

Jacob was clearly upset when he got home and shared his distress with his parents. They listened as he continued on about feeling like he didn't have any friends and would never fit in. His parents comforted him until it was time for them to leave to meet friends for dinner. Jacob's father had never thought twice about having guns in the home because he had grown up in a rural area where guns were commonplace. As soon as his parents were out the door, Jacob called 911 and told the police he had a loaded gun and "would be dead before they got there." He did not want his parents to find him. He wrote them a note that simply said, "I love you. I'm sorry. It's not your fault," and then shot himself.

Jacob's death devastated a community and changed the lives of his friends and family forever. The school mental health professional (SMHP) leads the team that will guide the greater school community through the crisis, managing the suicidal risks of other students, the distress of the teachers, and the anxiety of the school district lawyers and administrators. The crisis team had laid the groundwork for a smooth response; the true work of postvention starts now and continues in the days, weeks, and months to follow.

What happened next? The school crisis team (counselors, social workers, and support staff), administrators, a teacher representative, and a community liaison convened immediately and quickly determined they would need additional assistance. The principal, who had gotten my contact information as an outside crisis consultant from attending one of my workshops, asked me to organize the postvention activities. By 10:00 AM Saturday, I was joining the crisis team to carefully plan the next steps. After many hours, we were ready to face the week.

Thirty minutes before school opened on Monday, teachers and staff arrived for the first information meeting, having been notified of the suicide over the weekend by the principal via the school's phone chain. The teachers were shocked and sad but ready to support their students as they were handed an announcement to read to their homeroom class during a classroom meeting. A letter to the school community was posted on the school district website and sent home with students sharing about the loss of Jacob, explaining signs of grief, and announcing that additional counselors would be available. At the morning meeting, a gym teacher who was well liked, volunteered to follow Jacob's roster throughout that first day, actually sitting in Jacob's seat. The gym teacher was joined by a school counselor who addressed each class to see if Jacob's peers had questions or concerns, to help dispel rumors, and to remind students where to go for counselor assistance. Safe rooms were established in the library, counseling center and faculty room. Students were allowed to come to safe rooms at will, sign in, and see counselors either individually or in small groups. The safe rooms were flooded, and additional counselors were pulled in to help, myself included.

I found myself facilitating a safe room group of 11 students who were the closest friends of Jacob. While this is a larger group than typical, they all wanted to grieve together, so I allowed it. We signed agreements of confidentiality, discussed group rules, and began to talk. As I asked the students to say their names and tell a bit about themselves, it came to my attention that both Jacob's girlfriend and ex-girlfriend were sitting in my room. I immediately went to remove one, but they insisted they were friends and preferred to be in the same group. Again, I allowed it, but monitored this situation closely. After introducing themselves and beginning to discuss Jacob, it became clear that some of Jacob's friends were feeling guilt as they thought they should have seen the signs that Jacob was becoming more depressed as he had begun to withdraw. Others expressed sadness at the loss and anger that Jacob had not come to them to talk. It did not escape me that Jacob felt as if he had no friends, yet here were 11 students right in front of me who cared greatly. His girlfriend clearly loved him. I spent a good deal of time with Jacob's friends, normalizing their emotions and discussing healthy coping strategies (no drinking!). Each student considered who they could call if they began to feel distressed, including each other, family members as well as one beloved music teacher. I consulted with the principal who agreed that, due to the closeness of their relationships to Jacob, I would meet with this group again the next day to check in.

On Tuesday, our safe room group met again. We again normalized feelings, discussed how each coped the night prior, and agreed to make cards for Jacob's family. As these were Jacob's close friends, his parents knew them well and would likely appreciate this gesture. A friend who was also Jacob's neighbor volunteered to deliver the cards and offer to do errands for the family. Before they were delivered, I read all the cards to ensure appropriateness (I have before seen cards say, "I'll miss getting high with you" or other such words that would only be upsetting to the family). We created support plans for the following days, and many students again mentioned their music teacher. One student continued to express feelings of guilt, and Jacob's girlfriend became extremely tearful as the reality of the loss set in. A few students expressed concern about going to the funeral because they had never attended one. It was to be a Catholic mass, and I asked students who had previously experienced one to share what to expect—it is more impactful that they hear this from peers than from me.

As for follow-up, both the student who felt guilt and Jacob's girlfriend were provided continued care in individualized safe rooms and were referred for individualized therapy. Not forgetting that staff need support too, I asked a crisis team member to check in with the music teacher who had been mentioned several times. She was provided a substitute teacher so she could talk individually with a counselor. After the funeral, I met the students one more time briefly to ensure they were doing okay. Most felt that the funeral service provided closure, and they were happy they participated in it. The students expressed a desire to do something in Jacob's name, so they put up posters throughout the school asking each person to do one *random act of kindness*, a wonderful tribute to Jacob's memory. Resources on normal expectations of grief and when a student may need additional help were sent to all parents and teachers so they knew what to look for, and Jacob's family was referred to a local Survivors of Suicide group. There are many more intricacies that occurred throughout the days following Jacob's suicide death, but this provides a general understanding of what occurred and which steps your school may wish to consider in an event such as this.

Preparing for Postvention

As you read the postvention activities that took place after Jacob's death, did they sound comprehensive? Would your school have done things differently? Would you have changed anything? Is your crisis team prepared? The worst time to figure out how to respond to a student suicide is right after the suicide. Schools are best equipped to respond when they have adequate and appropriate resources, a well-trained staff, an intimate knowledge of the student body, and policies and procedures established ahead of time. Your school will then be in a better place to help students return to pre-crisis levels of academic and emotional functioning as quickly as possible. Failure to respond effectively could result in drastic psychological consequences, increased disciplinary referrals, and increased attendance problems—all of which impact the learning environment.

In this chapter and the next, we take you through an entire year following a suicide death. We talk about what to do on a procedural level and what to think about therapeutically. This chapter focuses on immediate interventions (within the first 24 hours) following a suicide while Chapter 9 takes you through longer-term support and care. The best practice suggestions and strategies provided here are drawn from the small body of empirical literature, the authors' decades of experience doing postvention work, and the expert consensus guidelines *After a Suicide: A Toolkit for Schools* (AFSP & SPRC, 2011) and *The PREPaRE Curriculum Workshop 1* (Reeves et al., 2011) *& Workshop 2* (Brock, 2011). The handouts, media guides, and sample letters described in the chapters are all available for download in the online eResources; as with all of the eResources in this book, we hope that you will modify the documents to meet the needs of your school staff, student body, and district policy.

Advanced Preparation: Before a Crisis

Logistical arrangements that enable a smooth response to a suicide loss should be made in the beginning of the school year to make sure no steps that can impact mobilization are missed. In the case of Jacob, the crisis team ran smoothly in part because they had already developed a teacher telephone tree, had my emergency contact information at home, and were prepared for many of the advanced preparation steps.

Develop a Staff Phone Tree

Suicide deaths may occur on weekends or during the evening. Having ready access to a staff phone tree will allow an administrator to contact faculty members, give the details of the event, and report where and when staff should gather for a briefing. While automated text or email systems are now readily available, these should be used judiciously with such highly sensitive information. An in-person phone call will also be a means through which to assess staff members who may themselves be greatly impacted or traumatized by the event.

Prepare a List of Home/Cell Numbers of Outside Support Personnel

If school counseling staff members need assistance due to the elevated impact of a suicide, they will want to have met personnel ahead of time and ensure personnel have police, FBI, and/or child abuse clearances required by the state or district. Construct relationships with local community menth health centers (CMHCs), crisis centers, and private counselors before a crisis occurs and develop a *memorandum of understanding (MOU)* that they are willing to help in the event of a crisis (a sample MOU and provider screening questions are provided in the eResources). Make sure to keep home or cell phone numbers on hand for emergencies. One organization that can provide crisis response, postvention consultation, and training is the National Emergency Assistance Team (NEAT) of the National Association of School Psychologists. The NEAT Team is available to all school personnel for either in-person support or phone/email consultation (http://www.nasponline.org/resources/crisis_safety/neat.aspx). Further, many states also have resources available through the Office of Education and the Suicide Prevention Resource Center (SPRC) maintains contact information for selected individuals working in suicide prevention in each state who can assist in identifying local experts (http://www.sprc.org/states).

Assess Cultural Diversity and Provide Sensitivity Training

As schools are already aware of the various cultural groups within their community (Ortiz & Voutsinas, 2012), potential barriers to think about before a crisis occurs include language (Are handouts and letters sent home translated?), socioeconomic status (Does everyone in the school community have computer or smartphone access to receive emergency alerts?), beliefs in mental health services (Does every culture see counseling as a positive approach?), and varied views on grief, death, and suicide (Is suicide considered a sin?). Ortiz and Voutsinas (2012) suggest that all members of the crisis team receive cross-cultural and sensitivity training to ensure best practice response.

Plan Space for Meetings and Safe Rooms

In the event of a suicide, there should be spaces designated for the following purposes: counseling students, unannounced parent pickup, and journalists who show up at the school. The media space is particularly important to designate ahead of time so the media does not have access to grieving students and staff. Safe rooms are detailed later in the chapter.

Prepare Go-Kits

Go-kits are often backpacks, bins, or rolling cases that are portable and easily accessible and include emergency supplies that may be needed quickly in safe rooms. The kits include tissues, water, nonperishable snacks, sign-in sheets, and passes for students to return to class. Many students benefit from drawing, writing, or creating cards for the family of the deceased, so kits should also include writing paper, art or construction paper, poster board, scissors, glue pens, markers, crayons, pens, pencils, and rulers. Paper bags may be helpful in case a distressed child hyperventilates.

Develop Policies for Memorials and Funeral Attendance

Develop uniform policies for both memorializing students and attending funerals, where all are treated the same, regardless of the manner of death. More specific policy information can be found in Chapter 9, but they are mentioned now to prompt you to create procedures before a suicide occurs, so you can stand firm on the policy when emotions are running high.

Using Social Media Networks

Research has found that if schools establish a presence on social network sites before a crisis occurs, they are better able to reach parents and community members in the event of an emergency (Flitsch, Magnesi, & Brock, 2012). Users are likely not to follow a site solely devoted to crisis information and may not have familiarity and practice using a network that is activated only infrequently. Schools should assess the culture of their school community to determine which social media tools to use. They should consider creating a general school Twitter account or Facebook page, which can become a platform for communication in the event of a crisis. Establish social media policies and protocols at the onset and teach students to think critically about the effects of any messages and images they post online (Flitsch et al., 2012).

Designate a Media Spokesperson

School districts should be prepared for contact from local news stations in the event of a suicide, particularly if the deceased student was a popular athlete or otherwise well known in the community. Determine ahead of time who will take such calls as it is best if this media contact has knowledge of suicide and resources for help. For a high profile suicide, the communications specialist or superintendent will likely handle media requests, although in most cases, it is the principal who will speak with the media.

Establish a Relationship With Your Local Media

Developing a positive relationship with the media ahead of time by sharing positive stories about the school and student achievements will help build a personal relationship of trust and accountability to ensure a suicide death is reported *safely*, as discussed later in this chapter.

Intervening Immediately Following a Suicide

The steps presented throughout this chapter and in the next address goals of returning to the normal academic routine quickly for those who are ready, facilitating natural coping responses, providing resources for those impacted, identifying the ongoing needs of the school community, and preventing contagion (Hart, 2012).

Issues Concerning Contagion

Hart's goal of preventing contagion is important as exposure to a completed suicide increases the risk that an individual will attempt suicide, particularly for adolescents (Hart, 2012). Youth at particular risk for contagion have prior existing risk factors (e.g., psychopathology or previous losses) and typically knew the decedent but were not best friends with him or her (Brent et al., 1989). Why is this? It seems that while the best friends are acutely aware of the pain and suffering caused by the suicide death, acquaintances are somewhat removed from the intense pain and turmoil and are not the ones at the decedent's home, seeing how torn apart his or her family is. A new study by Abrutyn & Mueller (2014) provides important information regarding contagion among adolescents:

1. Suicide attempts made by friends and family do indeed trigger the development of suicidal thoughts and sometimes attempts in adolescents.
2. The effects last at least a year and up to six years, and possibly longer for girls.
3. When exposed to a suicide attempt, girls are more susceptible to developing both suicidal thoughts and attempting, whereas boys may develop thoughts (but not attempt).
4. Peers continue to have a greater influence than family for both boys and girls, though girls may also be susceptible to contagion when a family member attempts suicide, though boys are not.

Overall, this study suggests that danger of contagion as exposure to the suicidal thoughts and behaviors (STB) of others "may teach individuals new ways to deal with emotional distress, namely by becoming suicidal" (Abrutyn & Mueller, 2014). If a suicide cluster has begun to evolve, Cox and colleagues (2012) identify six main postvention strategies for schools to use to contain it:

1. Developing a community response plan
2. Offering educational/psychological debriefings

3. Providing both individual and group counseling to affected peers
4. Screening high-risk individuals
5. Reporting the suicide cluster responsibly in the media
6. Promoting long-term health recovery within the community to prevent further suicides

As graphic images or details, sensationalizing the act, and romanticizing the deceased can lead to contagion, AFSP has worked with journalists and community organizations to create recommendations for safely reporting on suicide (found within the eResources), which has been updated to include suggestions for online media, blogs, and social networking sites. AFSP's website also has sample news reports that use what AFSP experts find to be safe media reporting strategies (http://www.afsp.org/news-events/for-the-media/reporting-on-suicide).

If a Suicide Occurs on Campus

If suicide occurs on campus, several steps must be taken immediately; call 911, notify the school nurse, institute lockdown procedures, isolate the area, do not allow staff or students exposure to the body, and treat it as a crime scene (touch nothing) until police arrive. Anyone who viewed the body should be provided immediate support, including the nurse, whomever found the body, administrators, and facilities staff. To mitigate trauma, contact an outside agency to clean up the site as school maintenance/custodians may have known this student or seen him frequently roaming the halls.

The First 24 Hours: A Step-by-Step Approach

Now that you have implemented the necessary steps to be *prepared* for a potential suicide, we will take you through the steps if you do have the unfortunate task of dealing with the loss of a student, teacher, administrator, or other staff member to suicide. Many of these will look familiar as they were implemented after the death of Jacob. We expand upon them here and provide a greater rationale of why each is important.

Notify Key Personnel

In the age of the internet and social media, students now often hear about a tragedy well before we do. Encourage teachers, staff, parents, and students to share information heard with the school principal who will inform the crisis team and superintendent's office. It is up to these key personnel to determine if it is a rumor, so discourage any further discussion of the death until it is verified, reminding students that rumors are often inaccurate and can be deeply hurtful. Protecting a family who has suffered a tragedy is important, and releasing inaccurate information can add to the trauma that the family is already experiencing.

Mobilize the Crisis Team Immediately: Plan Steps and Assign Responsibilities

As described in Chapter 3, all schools must have crisis teams and should include suicide postvention activities in their crisis plans. Upon hearing of a death, the principal should activate the crisis team, meeting face to face if possible, to plan for the following days. This includes arranging a faculty meeting as soon as possible to share facts and prepare teachers and staff to deal with students' issues, questions, concerns, and reactions. At this time:

- Determine if siblings attend school there or elsewhere and notify those administrators.
- Arrange to have someone meet with every class the student attended for at least the first day (this was done by a beloved gym teacher in the case of Jacob).
- Remove the student's name from school computer lists so no phone calls or notices are automatically sent home and teachers do not see the name on attendance sheets.
- Elicit student input to help make decisions regarding upcoming extracurricular events—while getting back to a normal routine is the goal, some events may be inappropriate.

Verify the Facts

Vignette: "Suzy is out of school because her Mami died," a student told the attendance office. When you read that out loud to yourself, who do you assume passed away? That sounds like 'mommy' to many of us. This was a mistake made where condolences were offered to Suzy's father for the passing of his wife. But, actually, it was her grandmother who died. In this Latino community, Mami can refer to many familial women. Oops!

The lesson learned in the above scenario is to first confirm that a death occurred, *who* is deceased, *when* the death occurred, as well as *where, why,* and *how* it happened, if relevant. Designate a staff member to contact the family as soon as possible to verify this information, offer the family condolences, and query how the school can assist them (i.e., perhaps parent-teacher association members can organize a meal calendar?). When calling, we should seek permission to communicate openly about the cause of death (more to follow), ask about funeral arrangements, be equipped to provide the family with grief resources, and be prepared to discuss the return of their child's personal belongings from their desk or locker. If the family does not initiate these discussions, they can be brought up on a future call when the family is ready. The staff member who made the initial call should be a comforting liaison with the family throughout.

If the parents are unreachable, an administrator should verify the cause of death with the local police, coroner, or medical examiner's office. Ask law enforcement if there is an ongoing investigation before speaking with students who may need to be interviewed by authorities. Once information has been verified and if the family allows disclosure, share the *facts* with the school community to dispel further rumors and ease questioning. Youth often feel that adults keep secrets from them, so share this information quickly. There are times when a cause of death is unknown. In this case, schools can state that the cause has not yet been determined and they will share information once discovered.

Respect Family Privacy

We must respect the privacy of the family if they do not want information about the cause of death disclosed. If the family is hesitant to disclose the cause, a staff member with a good relationship with the family should contact the family and discuss this further, preferably visiting the family in person. The family may change their perspective once it is gently explained that students are already talking about the cause of death amongst themselves and having adults in the school community talk to students about suicide and its causes can help keep students safe.

If the family continues to refuse to permit disclosure, school staff can state something like, "*The family has requested that information about the cause of death not be shared at this time. As you would want your privacy respected, let's be sure to respect theirs and not allow rumors to flow.*" The After a Suicide Toolkit created by SPRC & AFSP (2011) suggests using this as an educational moment, telling students that we realize there is speculation the death was suicide and taking the opportunity to educate on warning signs and how to get help for themselves or peers who may be showing signs of depression or suicide.

Notify Teachers and Staff

How and when school crisis teams hear about a suicide death will influence the next steps. If over the weekend or in the evening, crisis teams have sufficient time to communicate with staff by phone tree and convene prior to the school day to prepare a response and action plan. If, however, facts are discovered during the school day, crisis teams must work far more efficiently and proceed quickly. In this case, a crisis team member should be assigned to notify each classroom teacher in person. This not only makes it more personal, but also allows the team member to assess teachers' responses and need for additional support when they share this distressing news with their class.

Conduct a Staff Meeting

Hold a staff meeting before school, if possible, to share information about the suicide death, allow teachers to express their own reactions and concerns, plan for the day, and introduce any additional counselors or crisis responders. AFSP & SPRC's downloadable After a Suicide Toolkit (2011) includes sample agendas for this meeting. The administration should recognize that teachers may be grieving, allow them breaks from their classrooms, and make counselors available to them as well. If the suicide is discovered during the day, follow notification procedures mentioned above and have a staff meeting at day's end. Provide staff with a death announcement to read to their students and provide fact sheets with anticipated reactions from students and key phrases for how to respond. Also provide office staff with a copy of the fact sheet, as concerned parents will often flood the front office with phone calls. Having a prepared statement will reduce rumors, ease parental concerns, and free office staff from the anxiety of now knowing what to say. Remind all staff of the important role they play in identifying changes in behavior among the students they know and see every day, and ensure they know how to refer these students for counseling support. Confirm that all staff members know who has been identified as the media spokesperson and that *only* this individual is to communicate with the media.

Responding to the Death of a Staff Member

Realizing that the teachers in schools are actually at greater risk for suicide than our students, we must plan for this as well. Additional considerations include arranging substitutes for staff members who wish to participate in funeral arrangements, providing assistance to students who are grieving the loss of their teacher and dealing with a mid-year transition to a new teacher, and providing referrals, such as the Employee Assistance Program (EAP), to staff members who are in need of additional support.

The Three Tiers of Crisis Postvention

It is helpful to look at postvention within the framework of the three-tier model (Figure 8.1) described in Chapters 3 and 5 to effectively provide

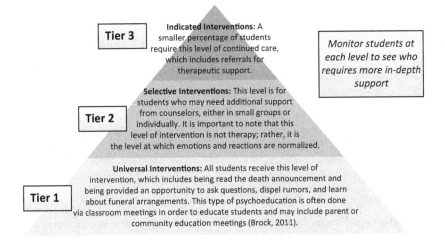

Figure 8.1 Levels of School-Based Postvention After a Suicide Loss

students appropriate levels of service. Specific strategies for Tiers 1 and 2 are presented in this chapter, while Tier 3 interventions, including grief groups and longer-term care, are discussed in Chapter 9.

Tier 1: Universal Interventions

Consider Cultural Differences

When implementing universal strategies, we must take into consideration the diversity of our school building and community as we strive to understand familial dynamics in each culture (how family is defined and who we reach out to if a student needs more support), what languages are spoken in our school, what community resources are available and appropriate for varied cultures, how we will translate death notifications to varied languages, and how to achieve equity in our responses. Establishing equity or fairness means that members of *all* cultural groups feel that they were provided the same quality of care and attention (Ortiz & Voutsinas, 2012).

Ensure Physical Health and Safety

The first priority in crisis events is to ensure the physical safety of students and staff (Brock et al., 2009, p. 111). As most suicide deaths occur off school grounds, issues of physical safety are not typically of concern. However, there are cases where a gun may be brought into school; in a 2006 incident in Springfield, PA, a teenager brought a rifle to school, fired shots within the building, and then shot himself (Associated Press, 2006). We should never tell students they are safe if we are not completely sure it is true. In the Springfield example, police could confirm there was no longer a threat as the student was deceased. Maslow's hierarchy of needs suggests that individuals' physiological (survival) and safety needs must be met before any other needs become relevant (Koltko-Rivera, 2006), such as emotional needs.

Determine Level of Response

Once safety is ensured, crisis teams determine the level of response required and begin responding to the emotional needs of staff and students.

Expert tip: It is important when planning crisis response that we do not over- or under-respond, but make a careful determination about the level of response required.

We obviously need enough staff to provide counseling to those in need, but overstaffing may send a message that the event is worse than originally thought. This may suggest to students that their naturally occurring supports are not sufficient and that significant help is needed, further increasing feelings of unease and anxiety and associated risk for trauma (Brock et al., 2009, p. 5). NASP's PREPaRE model (Brock et al., 2009, pp. 5–6) describes levels of response:

- *Minimal response*: The crisis is small enough that people can respond within their typical job duties. For example, if one student's uncle (who is not known in the school) takes his life, this student and perhaps his friends would need support from a counselor.
- *Building-level response*: The crisis is small enough that the school can respond without additional assistance, but people may need to leave their normal job duties to respond. An example might be the suicide death of the eighth-grade teacher, who is new to the school. Only the eighth graders would have had this teacher in class, so it would not impact the lower grades. Most teachers would not have had time to get to know the new teacher very well. School counseling staff will likely be sufficient to meet the needs of this crisis event.
- *District-Level Response*: This level of response requires assistance of more school district members as many students and staff are affected. An example might be the suicide death of a well-known high school football player who has three siblings of varied ages in the school district. Support is needed for the siblings' schools in addition to the high school.

- *Regional Response*: This type of response requires the assistance of the community. An example here is a train suicide. A suicide by train will not only devastate the family, but will involve community members, CMHCs, nearby schools, police, fire, Amtrak, etc.

Coordinate External Resources if Needed

If outside supports are needed, refer to the MOUs created earlier, and contact known personnel to assist. School counseling staff should remain mindful of their own limitations and consider bringing in trained trauma responders from other school districts or local mental health centers to help as needed. In particularly complicated situations (and provided that sufficient funding is available), schools may even consider bringing in local or national experts in suicide postvention for consultation and assistance. Such steps should generally be taken in consultation with the community liaisons, and all outside experts must of course be carefully vetted and references checked.

Triage Throughout the Day

Psychological triage is the process through which the level of intervention each student might need is identified (Brock, 2011). While initial determinations regarding levels of support were made, collaborate with teachers and staff throughout the days that follow to assess if more/less support is needed and have backup counseling personnel ready on call to be contacted if needed.

Prioritize Students Needing Immediate Support

Although staff can never quite tell which students will suffer emotionally in response to a traumatic event, it is important to identify, monitor, and follow-up with students who may be at risk. Friends, family, neighbors, office staff, bus drivers, and teammates of the deceased can help you identify other students who may have been heavily impacted but are unlikely to come to the safe room. In Chapter 3, we discussed the following framework for identifying which individuals are most likely to present with traumatic symptomology. Students who present with one or more of these are at particularly increased risk.

- First is *geographical proximity* to the crisis exposure, which refers to how close students were to the actual event. This will include students who witnessed the suicide or found the body. In Jacob's case, he contacted the police so his parents would *not* find him.
- Second, *psychosocial proximity* relates to how well a student knew the deceased. This may include close friends, neighbors, and family

members, the last person to talk to the deceased, and students on teams or in clubs with the deceased. It may also include students who were estranged, had a fight with the deceased, or who express guilt that they should have seen the signs that their friend was suicidal. Jacob's girlfriend, as well as a friend who felt this guilt, received follow-up.

- Next, we address *populations at risk*, which relate to the risk factors (internal or external vulnerabilities) a student presents with at the time of the crisis that influence how they cope with difficult situations. *Internal vulnerabilities* may include poor coping or problem-solving strategies, a history of mental illness or suicidal ideation, or a history of trauma or loss. *External vulnerabilities* relate to students' lacking social supports.

- Finally, *threat perceptions* refers to students perceiving the event to be extremely negative and highly threatening, such as students who felt their own lives may have been at risk. An example is the Springfield case where a student brought a gun to school.

Notify Students About the Death: Class Meetings

Notifying students of the death personally, holding classroom meetings, and offering safe room support are important because students some-times feel the deceased was erased by school and not to be spoken of and remembered. Any siblings, family, or very close friends of the deceased should be notified of the death individually; how a child hears about a suicide death can have a profound impact on the resultant response of the child (Hart, 2012). Stay calm and collected as adult reactions greatly impact children's understanding of how threatening a crisis event truly is (Brock, 2012).

For the remainder of the student body, their classroom teacher should read a death notification statement. Students should be provided with this formal announcement from school staff as soon as possible as they are most likely becoming aware of the incident via online social media sites faster than staff can formally distribute the news. Be sure to translate the statement into the languages spoken by families in your school. It is *not* a good idea to announce the death over the loud speaker or in an assembly, as this can cause hysteria, may be confusing, and feels imper-sonal. Students feel most familiarity with their own teachers, who can therefore provide the most comfort, particularly for younger children. As in the case of Jacob, classes expected to be greatly impacted (or those where the teacher is uncomfortable) should be assigned a support per-son (e.g., school counselor) to assist them in disseminating the informa-tion. Also arrange coverage for any staff members who feel they cannot be involved at all and need a break from their classroom.

This classroom meeting is not a time to share stories or get deep into emotions. It is not counseling or therapy. The authors of this text view the classroom meeting as actually a combination of what the PREPaRE model identifies as a classroom meeting and a psychoeducation group (Brock, 2011). Whereas, in the PREPaRE model, classroom meetings do not include education on how to manage crisis reactions, these authors feel that all students should be provided this information in the classroom meeting. We see it as an opportunity to educate all students about managing crisis reactions regardless of how impacted they are by this particular event.

STEPS FOR CLASSROOM MEETINGS:

1. Introductions (of any additional staff in the classroom)
2. Provide crisis facts
3. Dispel rumors and answer questions
4. Normalize reactions and prepare students for what to expect
5. Educate students on effective coping strategies
6. Triage, refer students in need of more support, and teach self-referral strategies

Adapted from the PREPaRE model (Brock, 2011).

After we introduce ourselves and notify the students of the death (provide crisis facts), allow children to ask questions and clarify misperceptions or rumors. Offer verified facts only, be considerate of the family's wishes for disclosure, and provide only details that are asked for as anything more may be traumatizing for those not ready to hear it. For younger children, explanations should be simple and facts may need to be repeated until they comprehend it. Help children understand what reactions are normal (this information can be found in the eResources) and when to refer themselves or peers for additional support. Provide information on procedures for safe rooms so that teachers and students know how to access counselors if needed. Help students establish means of healthy coping and offer information on funeral arrangements if available as well as ways to help the family through donations, etc.

Talking points for teachers/staff after a suicide:

- Give the facts only—if you don't know, tell students you don't know but will inform them if you learn further information.
- Students may blame others and seek revenge. Discuss this and briefly explain the role of mental illness in suicide.
- Students may say they don't understand why their friend took their own life—Perhaps tell them that if they do not understand, it could

be because they've never experienced *that* level of sadness or depression and that is a *good* thing.

- *Never* discuss graphic details about the method of suicide death as this can create traumatic images. If asked, it is okay to give basic and developmentally appropriate facts about the method.
- Students may feel guilt that they should have known their friend was suicidal, particularly if they were close to the deceased student. These students should be reassured that we can never predict someone else's behavior and they should be referred to a counselor.
- Encourage help-seeking behaviors if students are feeling down.
- Help students learn to monitor their friends and refer each other to counselors if needed.
- Encourage healthy coping strategies including drinking enough water as well as eating and sleeping well. Discourage self-medicating behaviors such as using drugs or alcohol.
- Help students feel they are actively helping by sending the family of the deceased condolence cards, making dinners, or offering to do errands as was seen in the case of Jacob at the beginning of this chapter.

What not to say:

Some of us get flustered in the midst of tragedy and have trouble finding the right words. As you follow the protocol for classroom meetings, here are a few things to avoid saying:

Your friend is in a better place—(No! A better place would be here with me!)

They are with God now—(How do you know if I even believe in God?)

I understand how you feel—(How? Did *your* best friend take their life at 15?)

Keep your chin up—(Why? My dad died . . . is it not okay for me to cry?)

Remember, it's God's will—(Then, that is one mean God, I want no part of Him any longer.)

You had many wonderful years together, you are fortunate—(My mom just died and you are telling me I am fortunate? You must be insane. You don't understand at all!)

Be strong for your mother—(Strong? I want to crawl under a rock. Who will be strong for me?)

Notify Parents and the School Community

It is important that a letter be sent home providing information on the death as well as how caregivers can talk to their child about it (see sample letter in the eResources). In the age of technology, letters are often emailed to parents as well as posted on the school or district website. Paper copies are still recommended, however, as we cannot assume all families have the technology or ability to access materials electronically. Translate it to any languages of families in the district. This letter should include:

- The nature of the incident
- What the children have been told
- Funeral arrangements, if known
- Emotional responses parents may see in their children
- Atypical reactions that suggest students may require more support
- Suggestions on how to help their child
- Information on a parent meeting held, if possible, to provide opportunities to ask questions, share concerns, and debrief
- Resources

Coordinate Parent/Community Meetings

Traumatic events can impact everyone in the school community and a community/parent debriefing is suggested. Separate the children from the adults as parents may not speak freely if they feel they have to be strong in front of the children. Parent meetings are similar to class meetings for students as they are a time to share facts, dispel rumors, discuss normal grief, and provide suggestions for positive coping strategies as well as indicate where to get further help if needed. Stress to parents the importance of accompanying their children to a funeral service and provide information on arrangements if known. Pass out index cards so people who wish to remain anonymous with their questions can do so and have floaters to collect the cards and assist someone who needs Kleenex, etc. The facilitator will likely be the school principal, crisis team leader, or school psychologist.

Remember That Staff Hurt Too

Staff members are impacted by suicides as well. Pay special care to a deceased student's current and past teachers, coaches, club facilitators, or any other staff who may have had a special relationship with the deceased student. Staff may also have their own personal experiences triggered by the suicide death. Allow staff to say no to certain duties without judgment if responsibilities become too much for them to handle at this time.

Debrief at the End of the First Day

It is advisable to have an all-staff debriefing meeting at the end of the first day. This meeting provides an opportunity to take the following steps:

- Offer verbal appreciation of the staff.
- Review the day's challenges and successes, share experiences, and ask questions.

Vignette: It was Monday morning at 9AM when a school learned about the death of a teacher aide, Amelia. Her special education coworkers had to go through their day as normally as possible for the sake of their highly disabled students, and a staff meeting was scheduled immediately after school. At this teacher debriefing, some staff spoke and shared stories about Amelia, while many remained silent. The head teacher in that classroom, Eric, was the one who had known Amelia best. While Eric shared a few thoughts at the meeting, he indicated no need to talk further. The next day, a SMHP started routine conversation with Eric about the weather, his students, etc. Little by little, Eric began to share stories (memories) about Amelia. He shared a story about his drive home the previous night with great emotion. He told of how he would often drive Amelia home after school, and he spoke of one road where he would always hit a large pothole no matter how hard he tried to miss it. Eric sighed, stating that he always felt badly as he jostled Amelia, who was not so young. He went on to tell that upon his dreary drive home last night, he (finally!) missed this sacred pothole and could not help but think of Amelia, grieving his loss greatly. Eric then smiled as he remembered his friend with fondness. Eric's grief and experiences were normalized. While he did not need counseling, per se, Eric was hurting and wanted to share stories about his friend as a helpful part of his grieving process. Listen carefully and attend to those affected in a way that they, as individuals, need.

- Disseminate updated information regarding the death or funeral arrangements.
- Discuss the schedule and determine additional support needs for the following day.
- Check in with staff to assess who might be hurting and refer accordingly.
- Remind staff of the importance of self-care.
- Remind staff to document crisis response efforts for future planning and evaluation.

Debrief Caregivers

Once all teachers and staff have been debriefed, it is time to go home! But, wait a minute. *Who ran the teacher debriefing meeting? The school psychologist? School counselor or social worker? The school principal in conjunction with the others mentioned?* These individuals need debriefing as well. *Yes, that means you.* As much as we want to head to our homes and families, we need to do our loved ones a favor and take the time to debrief ourselves before leaving for the day. There is more on this in Chapter 10, but it is an important step to mention here as well.

Proactively Use and Monitor Social Media

Social media is ever changing, but sites such as Facebook, Instagram, Snapchat, Google+, YouTube, and Twitter are rapidly becoming the primary means of communication for people of all ages, especially youth. Following a suicide death, students may immediately turn to social media to transmit news about the death (true or untrue), call for impromptu memorials or candlelight vigils, create online memorials, post messages about the deceased, and sometimes blame others as the cause of the suicide. In the emotionally charged atmosphere that can follow a suicide death, schools may be inclined to try to control or stifle such communications by students—a task that is *virtually* impossible.

Schools can, however, strategically use social media to dispel rumors, communicate facts about the death or funeral arrangements, and provide information on grief or mental illness, using the forum to educate the community. Ask students to identify which social networking sites are being used and disseminate information about warning signs of suicide and safe messages that emphasize suicide prevention to minimize the risk of suicide contagion. As students will inevitably post messages after a suicide, school staff can provide students with specific language that is appropriate to distribute (Flitsch et al., 2012). Information on resources where students can get help in school or in the community can be posted on sites. Students who need further support may be identified by monitoring their social communication, posts, comments, and blogs as they may post distressing comments such as "*I have no reason to go on anymore . . .*"

A deceased person's social profile page may become a memorial itself as friends and family post memorial messages and discuss the suicide, which increases risk of contagion. Schools can take steps to support students, including language as suggested by the PREPaRE curriculum (Reeves et al., 2011, handout 19), "The best way to honor (person's name) is to seek help if you or someone you know is struggling. If you are feeling lost, desperate, or alone, please call the National Suicide Prevention Lifeline at 1–800–273-TALK (8255). This call is free and confidential and crisis workers are available 24/7 to assist you. To learn more about the Lifeline, visit http://www.suicidepreventionlifeline.org."

Work With the Press Using Established Media Guidelines

Media are often not educated in suicide reporting, and harmful portrayals, sensationalizing, and romanticizing can occur as a result, possibly influencing suicide contagion. Journalists have an almost impossible task when it comes to reporting on a suicide death. Their job is to pull together a comprehensive, accurate, and compelling story complete with expert interviews and appropriate human interest content in a matter of hours. However, it is often difficult to establish all of the facts, particularly when the only person who can provide this information is the one who is deceased. The worst case scenario is that the journalist will report on the sensational features of the story without making it about suicide prevention. Establishing a good relationship with journalists will ensure that they know about and respect the media reporting guidelines made available by the AFSP, available within your eResources.

Assist the media by developing a fact sheet that includes concise, informative, and unbiased messages using layperson's terms. Remember that the media seek dramatic stories; state facts only, keep it brief, don't sensationalize, and take the opportunity to educate the public on mental illness and available resources. Finally, guide the media to stories of hope and recovery, information on how to overcome suicidal thinking, and strategies to increase coping skills. Include steps that the school will be taking to support staff and students and ensure information provided protects the privacy of the deceased's family and does not jeopardize any legal investigations.

Tell students, staff, and parents they have a right to refuse to talk when approached by the media, and ask them to refer all media inquiries to the designated media spokesperson. Quickly identify a briefing area that does not allow easy access to the school building or children as the media may arrive unexpectedly. Security may need to assist with the flow of traffic and with media and crowd control.

Tier 2: Selective Interventions

As we triage throughout the first day and the days that follow, schools will recognize which students require additional support. We begin to implement Tier 2 interventions as soon as these students are identified.

Consider Cultural Differences

In Tier 2, it is important to ensure we have diverse counselors available to provide culturally competent counseling strategies in safe rooms. As was suggested, make these mental health contacts and MOUs ahead of time. Be sure to respect different perceptions of suicide postvention activities (Ortiz and Voutsinas, 2012) as some families, for example, may believe this is the responsibility of the family and not the school. Build trust with families and involve community leaders of varied spiritual, religious, and ethnic backgrounds when possible.

Safe Rooms

Safe rooms are locations where grieving students can go for a safe place to express their fears, grief, and sadness as well as positive memories of their loved one. Encourage upset students to stay at school and use safe rooms to get help, rather than signing out where they are unsupervised. Some students will come individually and others will come in small groups of friends, teammates, etc. The PREPaRE curriculum refers to safe rooms as classroom-based crisis intervention (Brock, 2011). We find this term confusing as safe rooms are typically not held with an entire class or in a classroom. To clarify, we did mention a classroom meeting earlier, which we define as a Tier 1 universal intervention where students are told of the death and coping strategies are provided to the entire class in the classroom. Safe rooms are Tier 2 interventions for selective individuals who need further support. We suggest schools identify ahead of time what rooms might be used such as group counseling rooms, conference rooms, libraries, a staff lounge, or empty classrooms. The room should have comfortable chairs, be at a comfortable temperature and be light filled. Most importantly, the room should *feel* comfortable. Go-kits should be in the rooms, and water and snacks should be provided. Keep in mind your Parent Teacher Associations as they often want to assist in a crisis and asking them to supply refreshments is a great way to involve them in the healing process.

Students who are impacted deeply may need altered academic expectations to either attend safe rooms or quietly heal. While routines are comforting as they offer predictability and familiarity, administrators should give teachers clear directions to temporarily set aside curriculum and postpone tests. Be patient as some students take longer to get to pre-crisis levels of functioning than others and take the cue from students as to when they are ready to return to curriculum. Even then, a student grieving intensely may have trouble concentrating, may be late in turning in assignments, or may need to make up exams they could not perform well on.

Managing Students: Safe Rooms

It is important to know *where* students are *when, who* saw them, *if* students' *parents* were contacted, and if *follow-up* is needed. Have a sign-in sheet to ensure accountability (a sample is available in the online eResources). This will help keep tabs on who was seen, who needs follow-up, and who has not been seen by the end of the day but should be.

Group Facilitators

A good rule of thumb is to have two adults assigned to each safe room. At least one adult will be a counselor trained in suicide postvention (school counselor, social worker or school psychologist). The second adult may be another counselor or the classroom teacher, which is often beneficial as the teacher knows the students best. If a student becomes upset and needs to leave the room, one facilitator can escort the student while the other stays with the group. This also allows for two sets of eyes; while one facilitator is talking, the other is watching the group for signs of who may be particularly upset. It is important that facilitators present with a demeanor of calmness as students take cues from how the adults helping them react (Ruzek et al., 2007). If the counselor facilitating the safe room is not on staff of the school, he or she should learn as much as possible about the climate and culture of the school as well as procedures and resources before beginning. Know who to report to, where to refer students who require more support, and who will be doing follow-up once you are gone.

Regardless of qualification, we use the term *group facilitator* here because the facilitator is there to do just that—facilitate—as it is not counseling per se. However, it is important that one facilitator be a SMHP as some students will require more directive strategies. Safe room groups work best when they are child-centered and student-led. For example, we may learn that students actually want to discuss fears or remorse whereas we had planned on discussing the sadness of grief. Safe rooms are less about students receiving counseling and more about ridding stigma and normalizing their reactions amongst peers. Arrange a lunch break or have food brought in for the counseling staff as they are often so busy talking to students that they do not have a chance to eat. Also ensure that facilitators are provided adequate bathroom breaks.

Including the Classroom Teacher

Many young children accidentally refer to their preschool or elementary school teacher as "mom" at some point in the year as teachers are caregivers that are familiar and comforting to these young children. The calm presence of the classroom teacher in the safe room may help the child gauge the crisis event to not be overwhelmingly stressful, thereby reducing threat perceptions and resultant psychological trauma (Brock, 2012; Brock et al., 2009). It is okay for a student to see their teacher tear up as this may even provide modeling that it is okay to cry. However, it is counterproductive if a teacher loses complete emotional control in front of his or her students (Brock et al., 2009). If teachers have been traumatized themselves, it is important to know when they should break and let other caregivers assist their class.

Safe Room Participants

As was mentioned, safe room participants may include individual students or small groups. Homogenous groupings in safe rooms are important as these group members will likely have had similar experiences, feelings, and thoughts. It is through these shared experiences that students' reactions are normalized. Homogenous groupings should be of similar age and developmental level, have a similar relationship with the deceased, and should not have witnessed the death. Having a similar relationship is important because a suicide will likely impact a sibling, neighbor, or close friend differently than a classmate who was not as close with the deceased. Those who have witnessed the suicide should not be in a group with others as they may inadvertently traumatize others with unpleasant details of what they witnessed. Further, students who are significantly distressed may cry uncontrollably, hyperventilate, or shake and may require more individualized care. Do not to let the group get too large—usually about 8–10 students (space permitting). Other students that come in should be directed to a new group, so it may be necessary to have several group rooms available. Parents should not be allowed into safe rooms, as they will sometimes ask.

Some students come to safe rooms because this suicide triggered other personal losses they have experienced, whether or not by suicide. They may be re-experiencing their own trauma and these individuals should be seen individually as there is no homogenous group for them. Students who have been suicidal in the past should also be checked in with individually.

Safe Room Guidelines

Appropriate discipline must be maintained in the safe room in order for students to feel safe. Clear rules should be established and having students decide upon the rules helps to ensure ownership and accountability. A general rule is that while safe room participants are encouraged to share their thoughts and feelings, it is not mandatory (other than sharing their name and grade level). Many students report anecdotally that while they did not talk much, safe rooms were extremely beneficial as their feelings were normalized, they learned to describe their grief as others "put into words what they were thinking," and they no longer felt alone in their grief.

Students should be encouraged to return to class after spending an hour or so in the safe room. Let them know that they can return later if they continue having a tough time. Teachers should not make decisions about who to allow to a safe room. Rather, any student is allowed to go, with the SMHPs monitoring who is ready to return to class and who may need further intervention. At the same time, some students will try to take advantage of time away from class and SMHPs should be savvy and aware of this, sending them back when appropriate. While safe rooms provide an outlet for those who need it, they also allow teachers to get back to teaching for those students who are ready to return to their typical school routine.

Goals and Activities

The goals of safe rooms are to provide emotional comfort and support, allow students to share stories, manage and normalize stress reactions, establish healthy coping strategies, and ensure students know where to go for help; remembering that our ultimate goal is get students back to their education. Other goals include re-establishing connection with social supports (family, friends), identifying who may need further care, promoting a psychological sense of safety, and protecting students from unnecessary exposure to additional trauma and trauma reminders (Ruzek et al., 2007). Activities may include crafting artwork or writing creatively to express their feelings. It is not a time to interpret their work, but rather to emphasize commonalities in their feelings.

Obtain Parental Permission

It is always prudent to seek parental permission prior to meeting with students individually or in small groups. However, in a crisis situation, it may be necessary to provide immediate interventions to distressed students prior to obtaining this consent (Jacob & Feinberg, 2002). It is critical in this case to contact the parent or guardian as soon as possible after meeting with the student (Brock et al.,2009). Not only do schools have an ethical responsibility to inform parents, but a parent or guardian would want to know that their child was seen and if their child needs further support. This also allows doors of collaboration to open between the school and families. For group interventions, it may be possible to use a passive consent form, but policies on permission required and forms used should be determined by each school district's legal counsel.

Limits to Confidentiality

Jacob and Feinberg (2002) remind us of the importance of discussing limits of confidentiality with students. Clinicians must break confidentiality if it is discovered that the student is thinking of hurting him or herself or another person, if the student is being harmed by another (i.e., abuse), if the student requests that information be shared, or if there is some other legal obligation to do so. Peer confidentiality in safe rooms is of utmost importance and rules of confidentiality should be made clear. While we have students sign confidentiality agreements in safe rooms as we did in the case of Jacob at the beginning of this chapter, peers are not bound to the same legal and ethical guidelines as clinicians and there is therefore no absolute guarantee of confidentiality. On the other end of the spectrum, some adolescents are so weary of breaking confidentiality that they do not discuss anything from the safe room, not even with their parents. We find it is best to explain to students that they may readily disclose safe room discussions as they pertain to their *own* feelings and thoughts shared, but that they may not share anything about another member of the group. We want to ensure that we are not promoting a lack of communication with families, but rather a safe environment to share.

Follow-Up and Referrals

Students in safe rooms should be continually monitored for STB themselves (see suicide warning signs in Chapter 1). This is particularly important as students who lose a friend to suicide are more likely to think of suicide as an option themselves. Students who are so overcome with grief that they cannot function at school may need to have a parent come pick them up and referrals to outside agencies should be made for families as needed.

Conclusion

Suicide is complex. Suicide postvention as we have described it *is also suicide prevention*—how we respond after a suicide death can help build resiliency of students and encourage further use of naturally occurring supports and coping strategies. We hope that a suicide never occurs in your district, but we cannot stress enough the importance of being prepared in case it does. The guidelines outlined in this chapter help to ensure needed students are checked on, that adequate counseling staff is available, that we do not over- or underwhelm students or staff, and that we do not inadvertently traumatize students. By planning ahead for an event, your school can minimize psychological risk, thereby minimizing academic impact for your student body. While this chapter focused on the details of steps to take during the first 24 hours after hearing about a suicide, the next chapter takes you through the days, weeks, and months that follow. Finally, as with all crisis plans, a school's suicide response protocol should be reviewed and updated after a crisis event. Be sure that new staff members receive a copy of the revised protocol and are trained appropriately. The lives of our children are in our hands.

References

Abrutyn, S., & Mueller, A. S. (2014). Are suicidal behaviors contagious in adolescence? Using longitudinal data to examine suicide suggestion. *American Sociological Review, 1–17.* doi:10.1177/0003122413519445

American Foundation for Suicide Prevention & Suicide Prevention Resource Center [AFSP & SPRC]. (2011). *After a suicide: A toolkit for schools.* Newton, MA: Education Development Center, Inc.

Associated Press. (2006, December 12). Teen commits suicide in hallway of Pennsylvania school. *Fox News.* Retrieved from http://www.foxnews.com/story/2006/12/12/teen-commits-suicide-in-hallway-pennsylvania-school

Brent, D.A., Kerr, M.M., Goldstein, C., Bozigar, J., Wartella, M., & Allan, M.J. (1989). An outbreak of suicide and suicidal behavior in a high school. *Journal of the American Academy of Child & Adolescent Psychiatry, 28*(6), 918–924. doi:10.1097/00004583–198911000–00017

Brock, S. E. (2011). *PREPaRE Workshop 2: Crisis intervention and recovery: The roles of school-based mental health professionals* (2nd ed.). Bethesda, MD: National Association of School Psychologists.

Brock, S. E. (2012). Preparing for school crisis intervention. In S. E. Brock & S. R. Jimerson (Eds.), *Best practices in school crisis prevention and intervention* (2nd ed., pp. 265–283). Bethesda, MD: National Association of School Psychologists.

Brock, S. E., Nickerson, A. B., Reeves, M. A., Jimerson, S. R., Lieberman, R. A., & Feinberg, T. A. (2009). *School crisis prevention and intervention: The PREPaRE model.* Bethesda, MD: National Association of School Psychologists.

Cox, G. R., Robinson, J, Williamson, M., Lockley, A., Cheung, Y.T.D., & Pirkis, J. (2012). Suicide clusters in young people: Evidence for the effectiveness of postvention strategies. *Crisis, 33*(4), 208–214. doi:10.1027/-227-5910/a000144

Flitsch, E., Magnesi, J., & Brock, S. E. (2012). Social media and crisis prevention and intervention. In S. E. Brock & S. R. Jimerson (Eds.), *Best practices in school crisis prevention and intervention* (2nd ed.). Bethesda, MD: National Association of School Psychologists.

Hart, S. R. (2012). Student suicide: Suicide postvention. In S. E. Brock & S. R. Jimerson (Eds.), *Best practices in school crisis prevention and intervention* (2nd ed.). Bethesda, MD: National Association of School Psychologists.

Jacob, S., & Feinberg, T. (2002). Legal and ethical issues in crisis prevention and response in schools. In S. E. Brock, P. J. Lazarus, & S. R. Jimerson (Eds.). *Best practices in school crisis prevention and intervention.* Bethesda, MD: National Association of School Psychologists.

Koltko-Rivera, M. E. (2006). Rediscovering the later version of Maslow's hierarchy of needs: Self-transcendence and opportunities for theory, research, and unification. *Review of General Psychology, 10*(4), 302–317.

Ortiz, S. O., & Voutsinas, M. (2012). Cultural considerations in crisis intervention. In S. E. Brock & S. R. Jimerson (Eds.), *Best practices in school crisis prevention and intervention* (2nd ed.). Bethesda, MD: National Association of School Psychologists.

Reeves, M. A., Nickerson, A. B., Conolly-Wilson, C. N., Susan, M. K., Lazzaro, B. R., Jimerson, S. R., & Pesce, R. C. (2011). *PREPaRE Workshop 1: Crisis prevention & preparedness: Comprehensive school safety planning* (2nd edition). Bethesda, MD: National Association of School Psychologists.

Ruzek, J. I., Brymer, M. J., Jacobs, A. K., Layne, C. M., Vernberg, E. M., & Watson, P. J. (2007). Psychological first aid. *Journal of Mental Health Counseling.* Retrieved from www.homeland1.com/print.asp?act=print&vid=424682

9 The Bereaved Student, School, and Community

Case Study: Enduring the Pain

Imagine it is the worst winter you remember—it's bitter cold, dark, and dreary, and your school has called more snow days this year than in the last decade or more. Less than a month ago, a male high school student was riding his bike without a helmet, was hit by a car, and died from blunt force injuries to his head and neck. If you were a staff member in this school, in the last month you would have spent one to two weeks of intense crisis intervention and another week or two of things getting back to normal.

Imagine now getting a phone call about a suicide pact involving three female teens. You quickly receive another call that two of these girls have just died after being struck by a high-speed southbound Amtrak Acela train. Can you even begin to imagine a third suicide within a month as another student was found after hanging himself inside a nearby mill? Now, go on to imagine a fourth suicide occurring within about another month. While this 18-year-old does not attend your high school, and there appears to be no direct connection to the girls, he lives in the same county and also killed himself by train. Is your school crisis team prepared to handle this? Could your school district ever be prepared for such horrific multiple tragedies? What would you do first? Who would you turn to for additional support? There are many questions that would need to be answered.

This scenario actually happened and made national headlines in 2010. Three best friends waited together on the train platform after making a suicide pact. The girls each had their own plights; normal teenage relationship issues, parents divorcing, and issues with the law. One's own father had taken his life six years prior. One had been the girlfriend of the young man who died on his bike. As the train approached, two of the girls headed onto the track and hugged each other in those last seconds. As reported by Schaefer, Panaritis, and Farrell (2010), the third girl changed her mind after her brother called her cell phone and told her "Don't do it!" and she screamed for the other two to stop. She witnessed the scene, and her friends were dead upon impact.

It was snowing as emergency responders, classmates, family, and friends began showing up at the train station. The families were in shock and could not wrap their heads around such a tragedy. An impromptu candlelight vigil was held at the station the following night, with the distressing noise of the train coming by every so often. A spontaneous memorial was fashioned out of letters, pictures, and Valentine's Day teddy bears. The media were everywhere, perhaps giving this tragedy too much attention and glorifying the deaths of these two young ladies who appeared on the front pages of the papers nearly every day. It was a media frenzy, and the girls' parents could not get a break from it. Even national television personalities were calling relentlessly. Only a few media outlets used this as an opportunity to educate the public on suicide warning signs and where to get help; most seemed to be chasing viewer ratings. Experts in suicide became fearful of contagion, as there were reports of youngsters relating to these girls, even if they had never met them. There were memorial walls on Facebook and gossip was flying.

There were many rumors associated with this story, including that there were drugs and alcohol involved, that the girl who had dated the boy that died on the bike was pregnant with their child, and that there were multiple others involved in the pact expected to complete suicide within the next few days. None of these rumors were founded and were squashed by school administration.

Schaefer et al. (2010) report that they could not reach the school superintendent who focused her efforts on helping her school and community heal and begin to move forward. The high school consulted with experts in the field to ensure best practices were followed and engaged a community level response, pulling additional counselors from the district's middle and elementary schools and from local mental health agencies in the county. They collaborated with community spiritual leaders, and a nearby church housed an interfaith caucus of ministers available to talk to students. They also organized a two-hour parent information meeting to guide families in helping their grief-stricken children.

The school continued a comprehensive response and the superintendent posted updates on the district's blog, provided information on the grief and stress students and staff may experience, and gave resources on where to go for help. School administrators followed social media closely for concerning comments, rumors, and bullying as many wanted to blame others for the deaths. The school held a wellness night, focusing on positive ways to improve mental health, instituted a bullying prevention program for their underclassmen, and began providing character education to incoming freshman. The school put posters around the school the following September as students returned from summer break letting them know where to go for help if needed; they put information on their website around the holidays about how to get through difficult holiday times; and they ensured their staff was trained on suicide warning signs by providing a three part series on suicide prevention. The school also implemented focus groups, asking students what else they could do to create a positive school climate and reach out to those in need. Multiple fundraisers were organized by local families to raise funds for the families including cut-a-thons, silent auctions, and dinner benefits.

On the one-year anniversary, the school carefully planned activities for the week of the anniversary, shying away from candlelight memorials in fear of glamorizing the suicides. The school began a memory quilt where students could purchase hearts for the quilt made by the home economics department. They also piloted a student chapter of the Yellow Ribbon program, with many students stopping by an information table to learn more and sign up to be involved. Many students also wrote down memories to put in a memory box. Finally, the year the girls were supposed to graduate, two years after their deaths, the student body continued efforts to educate their community and prevent future suicides. The senior class held a fundraiser similar to the television show *The Dating Game*. Their own classmates were the contestants and there was an entry fee for attendees. The school reportedly had a great time organizing, conducting, and watching this game and all proceeds raised were donated to the county's local suicide prevention task force. These events seemed to be successful in helping students remember their beloved classmates and heal in positive ways.

A single suicide death will have an effect on a community. The community was devastated by three suicides following the accidental death of a well-liked recent graduate. It would have been unreasonable to expect the school to manage the community's shared trauma. While the school was managing its own postvention activities, the regional Suicide Prevention Task Force stepped in to mobilize community supports. A task force will look different in every locale, but the goal is typically the same as all members strive to minimize the loss of life due to suicide. The stakeholders on a task force will vary by region as a task force can be organized by the school, the county or township, or by the state. The members of this regional suicide prevention task force included representatives from behavioral health agencies, the county educational intermediate unit and other school personnel, community religious leaders, as well as county government, police and probation officers, local hospitals and crisis centers, the medical society, the medical examiner's office, and survivors of suicide. With all of these expert professionals coming to the table, additional counseling supports were offered to the school, a press release was created after the tragic events, outreach to the media on effective reporting of suicide was organized, and a call to action statement was developed. This task force was one approach to mobilizing the community in a way that the school alone could not have done. As with so many systems discussed in this book, having the task force in place prior to a suicide death was essential in ensuring that supports were already in place to rally when the deaths occurred. Responding to a succession of deaths including a suicide pact is a nearly impossible task for the school to take on alone.

The Days Following: After the First 24 Hours

This chapter provides a framework for assisting survivors of suicide, those left behind after a suicide loss. While the previous chapter focused upon the first 24 hours after hearing about a suicide death, this chapter takes you through the remainder of the first year, discussing the grief process and traumatic response, how to cope, and strategies to help your students and school community begin the process of moving forward. School response often focuses on the immediate aftermath of a suicide, rarely including longer-term grief support. Steps for long-term planning will be laid out, including indicated interventions (Tier 3) such as grief counseling, therapeutic support, and planning for the anniversary of a suicide death within the context of culturally appropriate intervention. There is a tendency to want to return to normal as soon as possible, but for many students, staff, and community members, life will never be the same. In addition to triage efforts, school staff members need to address other issues, such as funeral attendance by staff and students, planning memorials, and what to do with the empty desk left behind by the deceased student. What follows are recommendations based on expert consensus, not empirical research. Your school/district culture and policy will influence how you respond. Unless an explicit policy is already in place, we encourage you to discuss these recommendations at your next staff meeting.

Culturally Appropriate Care

This is not the time to figure out which providers in the community have the expertise to work with grieving, traumatized, and possibly suicidal students—that work needs to be done well in advance. In addition to evaluating a provider's training and experience, referrals should be evaluated for their ability to provide culturally relevant intervention (Ortiz & Voutsinas, 2012). For example, you may refer a student who, because of her religious beliefs, conceives suicide as a sin but is struggling with her own thoughts of suicide following her friend's death. Culturally relevant services could address her religious beliefs *and* provide the appropriate clinical services to address her suicide risk. Evaluating providers' views on grief, suicide, death, and mourning is one way to get a sense of which providers would be the best fit with which student and within your community as a whole.

Self-Disclosure

It is important to discuss the appropriateness and effectiveness of clinician self-disclosure. Let's imagine a school psychologist in her 40s who lost her mother 20 years prior. The psychologist has grieved fully and strong emotions are no longer triggered when hearing about maternal loss. There may be elements of her experience where she can relate to a teen girl grieving her mother's loss. This school mental health professional (SMHP) may wonder if she should share this information with the teen as perhaps it would help normalize the girl's feelings if she knew she wasn't alone in them. These are important questions to ask. Regardless of whether she shares it or not, the caregiver may have a better understanding of the teen because of her own experiences. Reflecting on the pros and cons before deciding to disclose is integral. The general rule of thumb is that a SMHP err on the side of non-disclosure unless the clinician is certain that the self-disclosure of his or her own grief will lead to client growth (Tsai, Plummer, Kanter, Newring, & Kohlenberg, 2010). In the context of a strong therapeutic relationship, these researchers found that for some clients who avoid their own pain, therapist self-disclosure can create deeper discussions, increase trust, model communication, and normalize emotional intensity, particularly as clients may notice a change in the therapist's behavior. However, clinicians must be prudent and not discuss personal losses with clients/students if there is *any* potential whatsoever to re-traumatize the individual with the disclosure (Tsai et al., 2010). Self-disclosure should always be a thoughtful process, and never a knee-jerk reaction. If that is the case, hold off on disclosing until you can carefully weigh the potential risks and benefits to the student or client.

To Attend or Not Attend the Funeral?

In most cases, children and adolescents should be allowed to attend funerals if they wish to go. Children who are not allowed to attend may feel they didn't get closure or a chance to say goodbye, particularly if they were close friends, in the same class or homeroom, or in the same activities or sports teams with the deceased. On the other hand, children who are forced to attend a funeral may feel resentful and should not be criticized if they do not want to go. It is best to allow students to make an informed decision by explaining what a funeral service is, why they are held, and what they can expect to happen, especially if they have never before attended a funeral, wake, or memorial service.

Children and teens expect us to be clear, direct, and honest in our explanations. After a suicide, the world as these children knew it has completely changed, and additional surprises and unfamiliar situations can complicate the grieving process. Students may not realize an open casket is a possibility and may not be prepared to see their friend or loved one's body. Help prepare students on what to wear, appropriate behavior, and what to say to the mother or other relatives of the deceased. Funerals and memorial services vary greatly based upon culture; students who have attended services in their own culture may not anticipate a difference in ritual. It is best to find out as much as possible ourselves so we can explain what to expect to those who may attend. For example, some cultures see a memorial mass as a celebration of the person's life, rather than as a time to mourn. This can be a shock to those not expecting grievers to be sharing stories of their loved one, laughing, or perhaps partaking in food and drink.

Schools may encourage families to have services after school hours, though this is often not possible. As mentioned in Chapter 8, each school should have a policy for student attendance at funerals, and it is recommended that school buses not be used to transport students to and from services (American Foundation for Suicide Prevention & Suicide Prevention Resource Center [AFSP & SPRC], 2011). Many schools require parents to sign out their child from school and transport them themselves. This is the best option as it allows parents to be a primary support for their child during this challenging time and provides them opportunities to observe their child's behavior and emotional response at the funeral and assess the potential need for follow-up. This is particularly true for young children who may find aspects of the funeral confusing and upsetting and need a parent nearby for comfort. The regular school schedule should remain intact to maintain normality for those not impacted by the death.

Districts should also have policy on funeral attendance by staff. If it were a teacher or other staff member who died, many school staff may wish to attend. In this case, multiple substitute teachers may need to be assigned. Not allowing teachers and staff to attend funerals can inhibit their grief process and can lead to bitterness or anger toward the school or administration. It is suggested that SMHPs and a senior administrator attend the funeral to provide further support (AFSP & SPRC, 2011).

Memorials

School communities often wish to memorialize a student who has died. While a memorial might seem like an appropriate and respectful way to

Expert tip: Risk for contagion deaths can be increased if the suicide has been glamorized making the student larger in death than they were in life (Brock, 2011).

honor a deceased student, memorials must be approached with caution as schools must consider how to appropriately remember the student without increasing the risk for suicide contagion.

In the past, schools responded to this concern by not recognizing the loss at all if it was a suicide death. However, to not recognize a loss may make students resentful as they are still suffering the loss, regardless of the manner of death. In the Suicide Toolkit developed by AFSP and SPRC (2011), it is recommended that schools have a consistent policy to treat all deaths in the same way. For example, if your school has a yearbook page for a student who died in a car accident, do the same for a student who died by suicide. We caution against permanent memorials in any cause of death. Why should incoming freshman, who likely never met the deceased, be faced with a permanent memorial as an unnecessary reminder of loss? Further, permanent memorials such as trees or gardens are at risk of dying, which might trigger students.

AFSP and SPRC recommend living memorials such as a donation to charity or research foundation or the purchase of a suicide prevention program as these types of memorials help students find meaning in their loss. In the case of the suicide pact, the senior class raised money while having fun with it as they staged a game show. Other effective activities include handing out information on mental illness, having wellness instruction, and educating the school community on how to get help if needed. If the deceased student participated in sports, clubs, or other school activities, teams have been known to wear colored armbands in memory of their teammate, and school shows have been dedicated in their honor. These tributes can provide opportunities for students to appropriately acknowledge and express their loss.

Schools may wish to make poster board and markers available so that students can gather and write messages. It is advisable to set up the posters in an area that can be avoided by those who don't wish to participate (i.e., not the cafeteria or front lobby). Also advisable is to have each student fill out individual cards/papers to be posted onto a banner rather than writing directly on a banner itself as students sometimes write comments that are upsetting, such as references to drugs and alcohol or negative comments about the deceased. Instead, create a "Wish Upon a Star" banner where star shapes are cut out, written/drawn on, and posted on a banner of a night sky. Staff can monitor individual stars and inappropriate ones not hung (while explaining this to the student who wrote it and offering them a chance to redo it). It is suggested that memorials be removed after the funeral or approximately five days, after which they may be offered to the family as a remembrance (AFSP & SPRC, 2011).

When spontaneous memorials occur off campus, it is more difficult for schools to facilitate their removal. Schools can encourage a responsible approach by explaining the potential for trauma if items remain (AFSP & SPRC, 2011). In one case, an expansive memorial was placed on a busy road outside a building adjacent to the school, forcing students, staff, and the thousands of employees who work in this building to pass the memorial daily. It remains there over three years later and seems to serve as a constant negative reminder of this trauma.

Candlelight vigils are common expressions of loss and remembrance, though these can at times become large, dramatic, and chaotic, resulting in increased trauma. Some students also feel pressured to attend when it seems everyone else is going. These vigils are not optimal, particularly when unsupervised. It may be necessary to enlist the assistance of local police or security to monitor these for safety and to have SMHPs on site for guidance and support (AFSP & SPRC, 2011).

The Empty Desk

A loss by suicide is traumatic. Coming into school the next day to see the deceased's belongings gone can be even more traumatic as students may feel that school staff are trying to erase any memory of their peer . . . their friend. Yet, seeing the chair where their classmate should be noticeably empty day after day can be overwhelming. The best option is to wait until after the funeral (or about five days) (AFSP & SPRC, 2011) and then have students participate in discussions about when and how to remove their peer's belongings. Classmates may find it healing to gather the belongings themselves, particularly good friends or teammates of the deceased who may then deliver the items to the parents. The class may decide to write cards for the family to accompany the belongings or to read a statement in their friend's honor (AFSP & SPRC, 2011). Most importantly, the desk, the locker, or the student's parking space for teens, should not become a shrine as this will be a constant reminder of the loss.

In elementary classrooms, where there might be an exact number of desks for each student, remove the desk and chair from the room completely as it could serve as a frequent reminder. As high school classrooms may not be able to rid of the desk since it is used in other class periods, it will be important to reconfigure the entire class to create a new environment.

Weeks 2–4

During the second to fourth week, you will see some students and staff return to pre-crisis levels of functioning. They will respond to the ups and downs of school, home, jobs, and interpersonal relationships much as they did before the death. If students and teachers had conflict, they will return to having the same type and intensity of conflict as before the death. If they laughed and joked often before the death, they will start to laugh and joke again. They will generally be functioning at the same level as before the crisis—for better or worse. Others will experience a new normal that is not better or worse, just different. Their peer group might look different because of bonds made or broken as a result of the death. They might find that they have a newfound interest in English class because Hamlet suddenly speaks to them in a way that chemistry does not, or vice versa. Survivors living a new normal might do things differently but be functioning at the same level. A third group will neither return to normal nor create a new normal. These survivors will function poorly in school, home, and/or at work. They are likely experiencing intense grief and, depending on how close they were to the person who died, they might be traumatized. The following is a review of common grief reactions, what may constitute a more complicated grief or trauma, and indicators that someone may need additional supports.

Kübler-Ross' Stages of Grief

In her 1969 book *On Death and Dying*, Kübler-Ross described a five-stage model of how people make sense of their own impending death. Kübler-Ross later expanded the model to describe anyone who is suffering loss, including the death of a loved one. While individuals spend differing lengths of time in each stage, they universally move between stages before achieving an acceptance of the death. Kübler-Ross suggested that the five stages do not necessarily occur in order and are not meant to be a complete list of all possible emotions after a loss. Rather, her theory was intended to help grievers understand where they are in their grief process to attempt to resolve each phase to work toward acceptance. Her stage model has been widely adopted with both clients and providers finding comfort in the stages. Research on grief and loss, particularly the work of Bonanno (2009), has not found support for the model. Because the model makes intuitive sense, however, we briefly review the five stages (popularly known by the acronym DABDA) and then present an empirically supported model of grieving.

Denial: Denial is a defense mechanism that can be a conscious or unconscious refusal to accept facts or the reality of the situation. For example, a child may talk about his deceased friend as if he were still alive: "*Joey is the first one I tell everything to. There's no way he wouldn't be around to hear if I passed my driver's license test!*"

Anger: In this second stage, the child recognizes that denial cannot continue. As anger can manifest itself in different ways, individuals may become angry with themselves or others. As an example, a child whose father died by suicide may think, "*Dad, how dare you leave me? I am so mad that you did this to me! It's not fair!*"

Bargaining: The third stage involves a wish to bring a deceased loved one back. Usually, the negotiation for an extended life is made with a higher power in exchange for a reformed lifestyle. A child who has lost his mother to suicide may bargain, "*I would do anything for my mother to be at my graduation ceremony. I can be a better daughter and not get in trouble.*"

Depression: During the fourth stage, the grieving person begins to understand the reality of death and may spend time crying and grieving. It's natural to feel sadness, regret, fear, and uncertainty when going through this stage. For a child whose best friend died by suicide, she may think, "*I am so sad. I miss her so much. Why bother caring anymore? Why go on alone?*"

Acceptance: In this last stage, individuals begin to come to terms with their loss. This stage varies according to the person's situation. A child may still miss his or her father who died by suicide, but may begin to realize that "*Mom and I are going to be okay. We will never forget daddy, but we have the support of his family and we will be okay.*"

Contemporary Model of Grief and Loss

Refuting Kübler-Ross, Bonanno (2009) has identified three main grief patterns: The first, *prolonged grief*, is an extreme and enduring grief that never seems to get better and leaves survivors yearning for their lost loved one for years on end, if not forever. The second pattern is *recovery*, as grievers' experience intense suffering, but for a shorter period of time, usually not more than a year. While these survivors slowly return to normal and are generally healthy, they continue to hurt and grieve through the years. The third pattern, *resilience*, was interestingly found to be the most common. These individuals struggle with acute grief for a few days or weeks, but then manage the pain and continue to meet the demands of their life. "They even laugh and experience moments of joy. They accept the loss, readjust their sense of what is, and move on," (Bonanno, 2009). Bonanno (2009) further reports that he and colleagues have seen these same patterns both cross-culturally and after other traumatic events, such as divorce, job loss and even survivors of the 9/11 terror attacks. It seems that resilience is more common than realized. In 2007, the *Journal of the American Medical Association* published the Yale Bereavement Study (YBS). Also counter to stage theory, this study found acceptance to be the norm in the case of natural deaths, even in the initial months post-loss (Maciejewski, Zhang, Block, & Prigerson, 2007).

Expectations of Grief

The typical grieving process differs by individual and is characterized by a unique constellation of physical, cognitive, psychological, and spiritual symptoms, though in most cases, "bereaved individuals are able to integrate the loss and continue to function" (Strada, 2009).

Expert tip: It is important to remind survivors that everyone grieves differently and there is no right or wrong way to grieve after a suicide loss.

Grieving students, faculty, and staff must give themselves permission to grieve in whatever ways and in whatever timelines work best for them. Bereaved adolescents often suffer a multitude of emotions, including confusion, anger, fear, and despair (Balk, 1996). As students sometimes feel as if they are "going crazy," the best thing teachers and school staff can do is let students know that what they are experiencing are *normal* reactions to a challenging situation.

COMMON GRIEF RESPONSES

Emotional reactions: *fear, guilt, anger, anxiety, sadness, denial*

Behavioral reactions: *crying, shock, withdrawal or isolation, numbing, apathy*

Physical reactions: *headaches, stomachaches, tense, trouble eating/ sleeping*

Cognitive reactions: *difficulty concentrating, flashbacks, trouble making decisions*

Spiritual reactions: *questioning if there is a God, wondering how this could happen*

As grief responses vary based upon age, it is particularly important that teachers and school personnel are sensitive to these reactions and prepared to help students deal with them (A handout with further developmental reactions to grief and a booklet for teens describing how they may feel after a suicide loss are both included in the eResources). As peer relationships play a critical role in early adolescence, 11- to 15-year-olds suffering loss may withdraw as they now feel different from peers, increasing the potential for long-term negative effects (Davies, 1991). Those in late adolescence, however, seek connections to give meaning to life after the death of a loved one (Balk, 1996), though they still report feeling different than peers as their sudden maturity and seriousness about life interferes with developmentally appropriate activities of childhood (Davies, 1991). For these students, "their friends' interests, behaviors, and antics were perceived as trivial and judged as intolerable" (Davies, 1991).

How long will the grief last? Give it time. According to Humphrey and Zimpfer (1996; cited in Regehr & Sussman, 2004), the process of normal grieving is expected to last somewhere between one and two years; depending on the circumstances surrounding the death and the nature of the relationship with the deceased. The amount of time it takes to adjust to the loss of someone loved dearly is different for everyone. The lives of survivors are forever changed by this tragedy but, for most, the intense pain eventually becomes tolerable. Survivors can then begin to focus more on the positive memories of their dear loved one rather than just their death (or how they died).

The Complexity of Suicide Grief

Some students will have a harder time with the suicide death than others. There are many factors which contribute to the difficulty experienced, including if a survivor witnessed the suicide or found the body, if the suicide scene was treated as a murder scene, or if the suicide was widely publicized and memorialized. There are many cases where it is not conclusively known if the death was a suicide or was an accident (i.e., drug overdose) or perhaps murder (i.e., there was a case where a father went missing, and his truck was found on the highway)—not knowing can complicate trauma and grief. While children are resilient, it is much more difficult to process a loss when the details surrounding it are not known.

Expert tip: Sudden deaths such as suicide often take much longer to process due to the overwhelming shock and disbelief the survivor is facing along with a difficulty comprehending *why* this happened.

Teens who respond with healthy coping strategies, such as developing new interests, volunteering, turning to religion, or confiding in friends and family, will typically find their grief symptoms to slowly subside. Those with unhealthy strategies, such as withdrawing or turning to alcohol, have the potential to complicate their grief further. Strada (2009) has identified a list of factors that may impede upon the normal grieving process. We have expanded upon this list by providing definitions and applying them to youth and suicide loss to better understand their potential impact in context. We find these factors particularly important when triaging students and identifying those that may need additional or more intense supports.

Factors Related to the Nature and Circumstances of the Loss

Degree of suddenness: As a suicide is often unexpected and sudden, children frequently report that they "*had no time to say goodbye*" to their loved one, inhibiting their sense of getting closure. The suddenness is at times linked to the shock and difficulty understanding *why* their loved one took their life. It is difficult to wrap their head around it all as opposed to a death by cancer, for example, which is more commonly understood and there is time to say goodbye.

Length of illness prior to the death: If a battle with cancer was long, it may result in an eased grieving process as there was time to say goodbye. The student may even be relieved that a loved one's physical suffering has ended upon death. A similar experience may be had with suicide loss. Imagine an adolescent whose mother, diagnosed with bipolar disorder, has attempted suicide multiple times over the years. This adolescent may similarly report a level of relief or respite that her mother is free from the enduring emotional pain.

Perception of preventability: Suicide is preventable. Death that is preventable is more difficult for children (and adults) to understand and accept. Even more so, deaths that are human-caused create even more complexity in understanding "*Why would my father choose to do this to himself?*" Children can more easily integrate and understand a heart attack that could not have been prevented and are not human caused.

Psychosocial context of the death: As a person's behavior is a dynamic interaction between him or her and the social context in which he or she lives, those bereaving a suicide death will be impacted by the relationships and beliefs of the deceased. This may include cultural and religious beliefs and practices as well as their involvement in the community. For example, a student may struggle to understand the suicide of her father who was a beloved police officer, "*Why would such an important man kill himself when so many people depend on him?*"

Factors Related to the Relationship With the Deceased

Psychological character: This is related to a deceased person's personality traits and temperament. A child who lost his mother who he described as the most loving, warmest, and kindest person he ever met may struggle more with his grief than another child who felt her mother was terse, aggressive, and callous.

Strength: The strength of the relationship will also impact a child's grieving. An adolescent who views her grandmother as her best friend and the only one who understands her may struggle with the grief of her grandmother's suicide more than a teen who did not see his grandmother all that often.

Security of the attachment: The security of the relationship may have an opposite effect on a grieving child or adolescent. For example, if a teen never doubted her father's love for her, she may miss their father greatly, but she can move forward feeling love in her father's memory. Another child, however, may have had a dismissive father who he never trusted. This child may have always hoped they would be close some day, but he will never have the opportunity now that his father has died.

Amount of unfinished business between the deceased and the bereaved: As teens and adolescents are at a developmental stage of seeking independence and identity, they often have a tumultuous relationship with one or both parents. If a parent dies during this time, it can be challenging for the teen to resolve this relational conflict and may challenge the grieving process.

Level of ambivalence in the relationship: As an example, a teen may have conflicting feelings about her relationship with a peer who died by suicide. Let's say that she did not like this peer who teased her relentlessly. Yet, she grew up with this peer who lived on the same block and attended the same schools. This teen may feel ambivalence as she is saddened by the death, but also remembers all the times this girl taunted her.

Roles of the deceased in the bereaved's life and social system: "*My mother is the one who drove my girlfriends and I to all the dances, took us dress shopping, and talked to us the next day about which boys we danced with.*" For this teen who lost her mother, grief may be complicated. Not only will she face the grief of loss, but will feel the impact of all the ways her mother was there for her. This teen may wonder who will help her pick out the best dress now, who will drive her and her girlfriends to dances, and who will she tell when that perfect boy finally asks her to dance.

Factors Related to Characteristics of the Bereaved

Previous experience with grief and loss: Losing someone close to you is a risk factor for suicide, particularly if that person also died by suicide. If a child or adolescent has had other previous losses, these compound and can complicate grief further. These losses are not always death but can be the loss of his childhood home, loss of a pet, or losing a friend group. In some cases, however, a previous loss can have the opposite effect in building resiliency. For example, a child who previously lost their grandfather to old age, grieved it appropriately, and moved on with the support of family may have gained strength, realizing that she will be okay again.

Presence of concurrent losses or other stressors: When a parent dies, a child's life may be turned upside down. For example, think of a teen whose father was the primary breadwinner, while mom was a stay-at-home mom. Upon dad dying, significant stressors include how to make mortgage payments, pay the electric and gas bills, and pay for school activities. The child may no longer be able to participate in sports, may have to move, and may have to change schools.

Mental health prior to the loss: A child who was already suffering from mental illness or already had suicidal thoughts and behaviors are at even greater risk and often have a more difficult time evolving through the grief journey after a suicide loss.

Developmental stage of life: The developmental stage of a student may impact how well they can understand the suicide death and how they cognitively interpret the loss within their current schema. A child who is less cognitively flexible may have more difficulty integrating the loss than someone who can perhaps understand the deceased's emotional suffering.

Social, cultural, ethnic, religious, and spiritual beliefs: Just as the deceased's view on death and suicide may impact grief, the survivor's view also impacts the grief process. As one example, if a survivor views suicide as a religious sin, he may have more difficulty with a suicide loss. As another example, in a culture that sees death and funerals as a time to celebrate life, individuals may integrate the loss more effectively, easing their grief process.

Complicated Grief and Trauma

Suicide is often referred to as a *complicated grief* because of the complexities mentioned above as well as the social, emotional, and cultural issues that come with it including stigma, shame, and embarrassment. Similar to Bonanno (2009), Prigerson et al. (2009) describe prolonged grief disorder as a significant form of psychological distress associated with substantial disability that includes a strong yearning for the deceased, difficulty accepting the loss, avoidance of loss reminders, inability to trust others, anger, difficulty moving on, numbness, shock, and feeling that life is meaningless. Suicide survivors' relationship to the deceased may predispose them to complicated bereavement reactions with offspring being the most adversely affected (Mitchell, Kim, Prigerson, & Mortimer-Stephens, 2005). Survivors with complicated grief feel lonelier than the naturally bereaved, are more than two times more likely to attempt suicide (DeGroot, DeKeijser, & Neeleman, 2006), and are five to ten times more likely to experience suicidal ideation (Prigerson et al., 1999; Mitchell, Kim, Prigerson, & Mortimer, 2005). These studies thereby stress the importance of conducting screenings and offering referrals to those left behind after a suicide, particularly as complicated grief is higher in suicide bereavement than other forms of death (Mitchell, Kim, Prigerson, & Mortimer, 2005).

Is there a difference of trauma and grief? Yes, while both trauma and grief "have intrusive thoughts or memories, traumatic memories focus on specific negative or horrifying aspects of the event, while grief memories focus on the lost person and can be either positive or negative in nature". Trauma can be defined as any event that is outside of the usual realm of human experience and is markedly distressing (evokes reactions of intense fear, helplessness, and horror) (Raphael, 1997, as cited in Regehr & Sussman, 2004). Traumatic events such as suicide are often sudden with no warning and render the victims powerless, increasing the likelihood of severe distress. Children who suffer trauma may also have an overwhelming sense of hopelessness, difficulty sleeping, and feelings of isolation as they may feel that nobody understands. Traumatic response can include cognitive deficits such as confusion, disorientation, impaired short-term memory, and an inability to concentrate, which may greatly impact upon academic performance (Horowitz et al., 1997). Some of the most common symptoms of trauma are flashbacks and nightmares as victims re-experience the traumatic event. Some children even experience survivor guilt, wondering why they survived when their beloved peer did not.

When untreated, trauma can result in post-traumatic stress disorder (PTSD) for children, stressing the importance of getting adequate help for survivors as soon as possible. PTSD symptoms are those that have been experienced for a month or more and include intrusion (the traumatic event is persistently re-experienced), avoidance (persistent effortful avoidance of distressing trauma-related stimuli), negative alterations in cognitions and mood that began or worsened after the traumatic event, and trauma-related alterations in arousal and reactivity that began or worsened after the traumatic event (American Psychiatric Association, 2013). The amygdala and hippocampus are the two particular areas involved in the processing of emotionally charged memories, and trauma may actually result in "permanent neuronal changes that have a negative effect on learning, habituation, and stimulus discrimination," (Van der Kolk, 2001). Many people therefore try to avoid trauma reminders, stemming from a desire to not re-experience the distress and horror (Brewin, 2001).

Van der Kolk, Roth, Pelcovitz, Sunday, and Spinazzola (2005) found that trauma that is prolonged, occurs at an early age, and is of an interpersonal nature can have profound effects on children above and beyond those of PTSD, particularly in the first decade of life. These effects can be longstanding and can include affect dysregulation, aggression, dissociative symptoms, and character pathology.

Tier 3: Indicated Interventions in the Following Months

Suicide-Specific Grief Counseling Groups

There were only two studies found that evaluated group interventions for survivors of suicide. The first study conducted by Daigle and Labelle (2012) evaluated the group therapy program for children bereaved by suicide (PCBS), a program for 6- to 12-year-olds. Children were evaluated prior to entering the program and were excluded if PTSD symptoms were present. The program comprised twelve 2-hour sessions for groups of six to nine children. The first ten sessions were held weekly with the last two sessions being biweekly to facilitate separation from the group. Parents were required to attend the last half hour of every session as parental involvement is vital for this age group. While the manual states specific goals, objectives, and principles of intervention, it does not provide practitioners with specific strategies. The study did find improvements in anxiety and depression for these child survivors.

The second study by Groos and Shakepeare-Finch (2013) found participation in suicide bereavement groups to be beneficial in helping survivors adjust to the loss and normalize the bereavement experience as participants realize that suicide loss actually does happen to others as well. This group experience, talking extensively about the loss in a supportive environment, and sharing with others who suffered a similar loss held strong benefits (Groos & Shakepeare-Finch, 2013). Further, exploring why the suicide may have occurred and addressing distressing emotions of guilt, fear, blame, hurt, and anger helped participants make sense of, and find meaning in, the loss. The high level of disclosure in the group led to important social relationships that helped address challenges and did not include pressure to move through the grief process at a faster pace (Groos & Shakepeare-Finch, 2013). The group process also helped participants develop greater compassion for the self and others and allowed participants to learn from others with different suicide experiences, generating hope that the pain will ease and adjustment will improve (Groos & Shakepeare-Finch, 2013). Finally, the model suggests that the "gaining of insight, development of new narratives surrounding the suicide, and schema change are the desirable outcomes from involvement with the suicide bereavement group" (Groos & Shakepeare-Finch, 2013).

If your school or district has SMHPs available to conduct suicide specific grief groups, the research above demonstrates they would be beneficial. We know that teens, in particular, benefit from camaraderie with other teens, that group members can develop insight through others' experiences, and that group work helps reduce social isolation as well as normalize reactions, feelings, and concerns. Gray (1988) found that 76% more teens reported they "felt peers understood them after their loss" compared to nonbereaved teens. There are many activities that can be used in grief groups. SMHPs often come prepared with multiple activities as all students respond differently based upon their developmental level, interests, etc. While there is no research basis for choosing one activity over another, many options are presented within the eResources.

Individualized Therapeutic Treatments

As some students will need more support than the school system can provide, individualized treatments may be necessary and referrals to outside agencies made. It is helpful if schools have resources readily available in their community for therapists that focus on grief or trauma to help parents who may also be grieving quickly access these supports.

While there are many individualized treatment approaches available for students who are surviving the suicide of a loved one, a few studies are mentioned that show efficacy. For treatment of PTSD, one study by DeAngelis (2008) found the following treatments to be effective: prolonged-exposure therapy, cognitive-processing therapy, stress-inoculation training, other forms of cognitive therapy, cognitive restructuring, eye movement desensitization and reprocessing (EMDR), and medication.

Another study found a course of cognitive behavioral therapy (CBT) of up to 16 sessions given one to four months after trauma to be more effective than both supportive counseling and self-help booklets in preventing chronic PTSD symptoms (Ehlers & Clark, 2003). Fewer sessions of CBT (four to six sessions) offered within the first month also led to significant improvement (Ehlers & Clark, 2003), revealing that while immediate CBT interventions are effective, it is never too late as interventions provided later also have positive outcomes. CBT may be beneficial in how it helps participants work through traumatic memories and more effectively interpret their PTSD symptoms (Ehlers & Clark, 2003).

Music therapy has also proven successful for grieving children, particularly given the enormous part music plays in contemporary youth culture (Dalton & Krout, 2006; Hilliard, 2001). Dalton and Krout (2006) developed a grief model based upon a thematic analysis of songs written by bereaved adolescents. The grief themes that emerged were understanding, feeling, remembering, integrating, and growing. These researchers found that the music therapy positively impacted group members as a creative and supportive way to help teens progress through their grief.

A final study examined the effect of cognitive-behavior Internet-based writing therapy on the posttraumatic stress of traumatized individuals (Knaevelsrud, Liedl, & Maercker, 2010). Effectiveness may be attributed to successful cognitive processing of the traumatic event as cognitive restructuring was a focus of this approach, which included identifying any positives that could be learned from the experience through narrative writing (described below).

Writing a Narrative for Healing

Journaling or writing about a traumatic event can be therapeutic, particularly for those who are unable to attend therapy or do not feel they will benefit from traditional therapeutic approaches. Pennebaker, Kiecolt-Glaser, and Glaser (1988) discuss the importance of confronting a traumatic experience where the inhibition or active holding back of thoughts, emotions, or behaviors is associated with stress that can become manifested as physical illness. Their study found that writing about traumatic events had positive effects on autonomic levels, on health center use, and on subjective distress. Those who showed the greatest health improvements were those who were forced to write about topics that they had actively held back from telling others. These researchers purport that "actively confronting a trauma allows for the understanding and assimilation of that trauma" (Pennebaker et al. 1988). Further, while the confrontation may be done either via writing or by talking with another, writing allows an individual to disclose at their own rates and devise their own solutions while also providing an alternative cost-effective approach for those who do not engage in therapy.

A Year In: Anniversaries of the Death

Anniversary dates are times we remember those we have lost and are often triggers for those who had a close relationship to the deceased. Some students have this date tattooed in their brain. It is important that school crisis teams anticipate anniversaries and plan events to console and comfort those who are struggling, not glorifying or sensationalizing the suicide as the risk of contagion continues. Examples of positive anniversary memorials may include handing out suicide prevention materials, organizing a fundraising event to donate money to a suicide prevention organization, or participating in a walk/run for suicide awareness.

Other important dates may include:

- Birthdays
- Opening day or important days for sports the student participated in
- A school show or other activity in which the student was active
- Graduation
- Proms, senior week, and other important class events
- The two-year anniversary. Students often report that the deceased is honored at the one-year anniversary, but is forgotten by the second year. Students describe that by then everyone *assumes* they are doing fine and do not even check in. They begin to feel that the memory of their loved one is fading away and no one even cares anymore.

Help Students Find the Gifts in the Loss

Teens who can find meaning in the loss and redefine it in a positive light may find that their loss has prepared them to face life's challenges (*"If I can get through this, I can get through anything"*) and has fostered a new appreciation for life and gratitude for simple joys. Positives from journeying through this loss can also include emotional growth, trying to reach their fullest potential (sometimes in honor of their lost loved one), wanting stronger connections to others, learning compassion and forgiveness, and wanting to help others and make the world a better place (volunteering). Adolescents may likewise learn to think about what is really important in life, to try new things and live to its fullest, that everybody has their struggles at one time or another, and to never judge another person who is responding nastily in class or is moping through the hall—perhaps they are facing their own personal tragedy in silence.

Cultural Considerations: A Final Note

Many school professionals are unaware of their lack of proficiency in serving culturally diverse populations, but crisis team members should be aware of their own cultural views and biases (Ortiz & Voutsinas, 2012). Cultural diversity can include differences related to gender, language, race, ethnicity, religion, socioeconomics, sexual orientation, and disability. Issues of diversity have been discussed throughout the preceding two chapters, but perhaps most importantly, schools should understand the cultural differences present within their schools and build relationships with families, cultural leaders, and community resources. In summary, issues to think about include responding after a suicide in varied languages, accessing resources such as translators and cultural brokers, having handouts printed in native languages of families, and understanding common expressions and reactions toward death, bereavement, and suicide in advance (Reeves et al., 2012).

Conclusion: Evaluating Postvention Activities

Crisis teams must evaluate response to a suicide loss within the school system and integrate lessons learned into their crisis plan. Questions to ask include: *What did we do well? What was missing? What could we do better next time? Where were the holes in our plan?* Crisis teams should meet to debrief this information within a few days after the crisis event. If the team waits too long (i.e., the following year if updating the plan is typically an annual activity), details of what worked and what didn't will likely be forgotten. Take this as an opportunity to learn and improve for next time . . . although we hope there isn't a next time.

References

American Foundation for Suicide Prevention & Suicide Prevention Resource Center [AFSP & SPRC]. (2011). *After a suicide: A toolkit for schools.* Newton, MA: Education Development Center, Inc.

American Psychiatric Association. (2013). *Diagnostic and statistical manual of mental disorders* (5th ed.). Arlington, VA: Author.

Balk, D. E. (1996). Models for understanding adolescent coping with bereavement. *Death Studies, 20,* 367–387.

Bonanno, G. A. (2009, October). Why we're wrong about grief. *Thriving in the Face of Trauma* [Blog]. *Psychology Today.* Retrieved from http://www.psychologytoday.com/blog/thriving-in-the-face-trauma/200910/grief-does-not-come-in-stages-and-its-not-the-same-everyone

Brewin, C. R. (2001). A cognitive neuroscience account of posttraumatic stress disorder and its treatment. *Behavior Research and Therapy, 39,* 373–393.

Brock, S. E. (2011). *PREP_aRE Workshop 2: Crisis intervention and recovery: The roles of school-based mental health professionals* (2nd edition). Bethesda, MD: National Association of School Psychologists.

Daigle, M. S., & Labelle, R. J. (2012). Pilot evaluation of a group therapy program for children bereaved by suicide. *Crisis, 33*(6), 350–357.

Dalton, T. A., & Krout, R. E (2006). The grief song-writing process with bereaved adolescents: An integrated grief model and music therapy protocol. *Music Therapy Perspectives, 24*(2), 94–107.

Davies, B. (1991). Long-term outcomes of adolescent sibling bereavement. *Journal of Adolescent Research, 6*(1), 83–96.

DeAngelis, T. (2008). PTSD Treatments grow in evidence, effectiveness. *APA Monitor, 39*(1).

DeGroot, M. H., DeKeijser, J., & Neeleman, J. (2006). Grief shortly after suicide and natural death: A comparative study among spouses and first-degree relatives. *Suicide and Life-Threatening Behavior, 36*(4), 418–431.

Ehlers, A., & Clark, D. M. (2003). Early psychological interventions for adults survivors of trauma: A review. *Biological Psychiatry, 53,* 817–826.

Gray, R. E. (1988, January). The role of school counselors with bereaved teenagers: With and without peer support groups. *The School Counselor,* 185–193.

Groos, A. D., & Shakespeare-Finch, J. (2013). Positive experiences for participants in suicide bereavement groups: A grounded theory model. *Death Studies, 37,* 1–24.

Hilliard, R. E. (2001). The effects of music therapy-based bereavement groups on mood and behavior of grieving children: A pilot study. *Journal of Music Therapy, 38*(4), 291–306.

Horowitz, M. J., Siegel, B., Holen, A., Bonnano, G. A., Milbrath, C., & Stinson, C. H. (1997). Diagnostic disorder for complicated grief disorder. *American Journal of Psychiatry, 154,* 904–910.

Knaevelsrud, C., Liedl, A., & Maercker, A. (2010). Posttraumatic growth, optimism and openness as outcomes of a cognitive-behavioural intervention for posttraumatic stress reactions. *Journal of Health Psychology, 15*(7), 1030–1038.

Kübler-Ross, E. (1969). *On death and dying.* New York, NY: Scribner.

Maciejewski, P. K., Zhang, B., Block, S. D., & Prigerson, H. G. (2007). An empirical examination of the stage theory of grief. *Journal of the American Medical Association (JAMA), 297*(7), 716–723.

Mitchell, J. T., Kim, Y., Prigerson, H. G., & Mortimer, M. K. (2005). Complicated grief and suicidal ideation in adult survivors of suicide. *Suicide and Life-Threatening Behavior, 35*(5), 498–506.

Mitchell, J. T., Kim, Y., Prigerson, H. G., & Mortimer-Stephens, M. K. (2005). Complicated grief in survivors of suicide. *Crisis, 25,* 12–18.

National Association of School Psychologists (NASP). (2011). *PREP_aRE Workshop 2: Crisis intervention & recovery: The Roles of School-based mental health professionals.* Bethesda, MD: Author.

Ortiz, S. O., & Voutsinas, M. (2012). Cultural considerations in crisis intervention. In S. E. Brock & S. R. Jimerson (Eds.), *Best practices in school crisis prevention and intervention* (2nd ed.). Bethesda, MD: National Association of School Psychologists.

Pennebaker, J.W., Kiecolt-Glaser, J.K., & Glaser, R. (1988). Disclosure of trauma and immune function: Health implications for psychotherapy. *Journal of Consulting and Clinical Psychology, 56*(2), 239–245.

Prigerson, H.G., Bridge, J., Maciejewski, P.K., Beery, L.C., Rosenheck, R.A., Jacobs, S.C., . . . Brent, D.A. (1999). Influence of traumatic grief on suicidal ideation among young adults. *American Journal of Psychiatry, 156*(12), 1995–1996.

Prigerson, H.G., Horowitz, M.J., Jacobs, S.C., Parkes, C.M., Aslan, M., Goodkin, K., . . . Maciejewski, P.K. (2009). Prolonged grief disorder: Psychometric validation of criteria proposed for DSM-V and ICD-11. *PLoS Medicine, 6*(8), e1000121. doi:10.1371/journal.pmed.1000121

Reeves, M.A.L., Conolly-Wilson, C.N., Pesce, R.C., Lazzaro, B.R., Nickerson, A.B., Jimerson, S.R.,. . . . Brock, S.E. (2012). Providing the comprehensive school crisis response. In S.E. Brock & S.R. Jimerson (Eds.), *Best practices in school crisis prevention and intervention* (2nd ed.). Bethesda, MD: National Association of School Psychologists.

Regehr, C., & Sussman, T. (2004). Intersections between grief and trauma: Toward an empirically based model for treating traumatic grief. *Brief Treatment and Crisis Intervention, 4*(3), 289–310.

Schaefer, M.A., Panaritis, M. & Farrell, J. (2010, May 16). *Special report: Anatomy of a teen tragedy.* The Philadelphia Inquirer, Philadelphia, PA.

Strada, E.A. (2009). Grief, demoralization, and depression: Diagnostic challenges and treatment modalities. *Primary Psychiatry, 16*(5), 49–55.

Tsai, M., Plummer, M.D., Kanter, J.W., Newring, R.W., & Kohlenberg, R.J. (2010). *Therapist grief and functional analytic psychotherapy: Strategic self-disclosure of personal loss. Journal of Contemporary Psychotherapy, 40,* 1–10. doi:10.1007/s10879-009-9116-6

Van der Kolk, B.A. (2001). The psychobiology and psychopharmacology of PTSD. *Human Psychopharmacology: Clinical and Experimental, 16,* 49–64.

Van der Kolk, B.A., Roth, S., Pelcovitz, D., Sunday, S., & Spinazzola, J. (2005). Disorders of extreme stress: The empirical foundation of a complex adaptation to trauma. *Journal of Traumatic Stress, 18*(5), 389–399.

10 Caring for the Caregiver

Burnout, Compassion Fatigue, and Vicarious Traumatization

If you have read the previous nine chapters, you might be feeling overwhelmed by everything school personnel should do to protect the health and well-being of students, families, and staff before, during, and after a suicidal crisis. On one hand, this is healthy realism: Working with suicidal clients has been consistently ranked as among the most stressful of all professional experiences. Ninety percent of school psychologists who reported doing crisis work described negative physical, emotional, and professional consequences (Bolnik & Brock, 2005). On the other hand, there are many downsides of choosing a profession where you take care of others but not yourself: burnout; compassion fatigue; and vicarious, or secondary, traumatization. We start with definitions, provide a case study of compassion fatigue, and end with recommendations for managing stress and burnout at a personal, professional, and organizational level.

While burnout can occur in any profession, those tasked with the care and well-being of others are more likely to experience compassion fatigue and vicarious traumatization.

Case Study: Who Will Die Today?

This case study describes a four-student suicide pact, how a school responded, and the intense emotional reaction of the clinician after the suicide crisis was over. The clinician in the case is Jonathan B. Singer, one of the co-authors of this text. Although he was working as an outpatient therapist, it is deemed a valuable case study to include because the suicidal crisis was located within a school setting. The scene you're about to read takes place at a middle school on a hot day in Austin, Texas. The day started out like so many others. The school mental health professional (SMHP) called the outpatient crisis unit and asked for a crisis worker to come to the school and assess an eighth-grade student for suicide risk. When Jonathan arrived, he learned there were no rooms available for the assessment. The interview takes place in the school's library when no classes are being held there. They have been talking for the past 20 minutes.

Jonathan:	How long have you had thoughts of killing yourself?
Eighth-grade girl:	On and off for years.
Jonathan:	Recently?
Eighth-grade girl:	A lot. Mostly when my parents are being a**holes.
Jonathan:	By 'a lot' do you mean five times an hour, five times a day, five times a week?
Eighth-grade girl:	A couple of times a day.
Jonathan:	Have you told anyone?
Eighth-grade girl:	Sure. My friends know.
Jonathan:	What do they say?
Eighth-grade girl:	They understand. They think about it too.
Jonathan:	Your friends think about killing themselves?
Eighth-grade girl:	Yeah. We all do. We talk about it. If one of us does it, we'll all do it.
Jonathan:	Wow. So y'all have a suicide pact?
Eighth-grade girl:	Yeah.
Jonathan:	Do they know you're thinking of killing yourself now?
Eighth-grade girl:	Yup.
Jonathan:	Did they try to talk you out of it?
Eighth-grade girl:	Yeah. Sort of. But they understand.
Jonathan:	Understand?
Eighth-grade girl:	We're not afraid to die. Everyone dies some day.
Jonathan:	Do they want you to die?
Eighth-grade girl:	No.
Jonathan:	I'm glad to hear that. How many are there?
Eighth-grade girl:	Three.
Jonathan:	There are three of you with a suicide pact, or three plus you?
Eighth-grade girl:	Four of us total.
Jonathan:	Does anyone else know about your suicide pact?"
Eighth-grade girl:	I don't think so.
Jonathan:	Will you tell me who they are?
Eighth-grade girl:	Why?
Jonathan:	Your friends seem really important to you. If one of them takes his or her life, you'll be more likely to kill yourself. I want to keep you safe, and that means knowing who your friends are and if and when they are planning to die by suicide. I genuinely want you guys to be happy and safe.
Eighth-grade girl:	Whatever. If I kill myself, you'll find out.

In the late 1990s, I worked as a mobile crisis worker in an outpatient mental health agency. I was part of a six-person team of graduate-level clinicians who provided crisis assessment and short-term stabilization therapy to suicidal youth ages 4 through 18 and their families (see Singer,

2005 for a detailed case study). We were a tight team; we worked our shifts in pairs and we supported each other. In all my time, there was only one experience that paralyzed me: three weeks of working with four middle school students with a high-risk suicide pact.

After completing the suicide assessment, I told the SMHP about the suicide pact. She knew the student's group of friends. She thought she knew who might be in the pact. She called them into her office one-by-one until she identified the three other students. She called their parents. For the next three weeks, nearly every day I was embroiled in a multi-family, multi-system crisis. Every day I woke up wondering if a child was going to die. Our plan was constant communication between professionals, daily suicide monitoring coordinating with family members, and separating the students. The SMHP switched lunch periods for two of the students. The parents agreed to keep the students from talking with each other over the phone (this was before cell phones). At the end of the third week, one of the students was transferred to another school. After this intensive intervention, my client reported five days of no suicidal ideation or wishes to die. The suicidal crisis was over, and the suicide pact had been broken (before the internet era this was an effective form of limiting communication between students).

Friday night. The crisis was over. The pact had been broken—for now. I came home at 5:00 PM. I felt tired and simultaneously numb and emotional. I curled up on my couch (something I never did). Five hours later I hadn't moved. The phone rang. My friend—a therapist—called to check in. She offered to come over with another friend and bring a movie. They brought *A Little Princess* and said, "This is a great movie. It will cheer you up." I wasn't in the mood to be cheered up, but I didn't have the energy to say no. In the movie, a little girl is orphaned and goes from being a student at a boarding school to being a servant girl. She is teased mercilessly. The movie felt so cruel, so inhumane. Twenty minutes into the movie I lost it. I stood up, screamed at my friends, "I f**king hate this movie. How could you bring this into my home? What a horrible story. F**k you." I stormed to my bedroom. I curled up on my bed wondering what I had just done. This wasn't me. I didn't yell at my friends. I didn't get upset at movies. I couldn't understand. I cried. My friend knocked on the door. I told her to go away. I heard muffled voices in the living room. About 20 minutes later, I heard the front door shut. I was alone. I don't remember falling asleep. When I woke up the next morning in my clothes on top of my bed, I was still in a daze. The whole weekend dragged on. I felt like I was walking through a tar pit. Everything felt heavy. I was emotionally raw. I didn't trust myself. I couldn't handle anything that seemed cruel. Monday came. I woke up feeling like the heaviness was starting to lift, feeling more like me. I wanted to eat breakfast. I did not dread the thought of going to work. I looked forward to talking with my colleagues.

I went to work. I told my co-workers about my experience. They got it. They understood. "You did great work with those students. Instead of four dead kids and a traumatized community, we have four living kids and a community that doesn't know any differently." They made me feel like I wasn't losing my mind. My supervisor told me I should hold off on taking any new cases for a week. Then the phone rang. I felt my heart start to race. It was a mom who had just gone into her 15-year-old daughter's room to wake her up for school and found her standing on a chair holding a rope. I took a deep breath and told the mom that she needed to take her daughter to the emergency room for a suicide assessment. I talked her through everything that might happen, what she should expect, and what we could do for her after her daughter was either medically cleared or admitted to the hospital. There was something about knowing what to say and do that made me feel better in that moment than I had in weeks. Although it took weeks for all of the feelings of fear and anxiety to subside, it took years for me to realize that I had experienced either burnout, compassion fatigue, or vicarious trauma.

Case Analysis: Burnout, Compassion Fatigue, and Vicarious Traumatization

Would you classify Jonathan's reaction as burnout, compassion fatigue, or vicarious traumatization? There is debate in the field about the differences between the three. Let's expand on the brief definitions listed above in Table 10.1, and see what fits.

Table 10.1 Definitions of Burnout, Compassion Fatigue, and Vicarious Traumatization

Burnout	Compassion Fatigue	Vicarious/Secondary Traumatization
Definition: the emotional exhaustion, depersonalization, and reduced accomplishment experienced by the general work you do (can be in any field)	Definition: the natural consequences of knowing about and wanting to help another person suffering from a trauma as a result of high levels of caregiver empathy for the individual's pain	Definition: the psychological distress and permanent disruption in a caregiver's cognitive schema due to their work with traumatized individuals
Signs: fatigue, frustration or anger, negativity, withdrawal, weakened work performance, negative reactions to others	Signs: sadness or grief, nightmares, somatic aches, guilt, increased arousal, detachment and isolation, changes in belief systems	Signs: anxiety, sadness, confusion, apathy, somatic aches, decreased capacity for relationships, loss of control and trust, intrusive imagery

Adapted from Sabo (2011). Overview of burnout, compassion fatigue and vicarious traumatization. *Online Journal of Issues in Nursing.*

Burnout

Jonathan certainly displayed signs of burnout: fatigue, frustration or anger, negativity, withdrawal, and negative reactions to others. And yet, he did not appear to exhibit "weakened work performance" (he was able to return to work after a two-day weekend and feel good about his ability to help others), which suggests he did not experience burnout. Why would this be? Research suggests there are three constructs related to burnout: emotional exhaustion (I feel emotionally drained from my work), depersonalization (I've become more callous toward people since I took this job), and reduced personal accomplishment (I do not feel like I'm helping people through my work) (Motta, 2012). Further, organizational demands such as increased caseloads, decreased control and autonomy, lack of acknowledgement or reward, and limited resources such as training opportunities, social supports, or leadership result in significant environmental stress (Sabo, 2011). There also appears to be a complex relationship between personality characteristics, environmental stressors, gender, and burnout. When school psychologists experience significant job related stressors, those with a pessimistic, negative, or neurotic worldview tend to feel more emotional exhaustion, whereas those with an extroverted, positive, or optimistic worldview are more likely to experience reduced personal accomplishment (i.e., they are more likely to feel they are not helping people through their work) (Mills & Huebner, 1998). Men tend to experience more depersonalization (i.e., they are more callous toward people), and women tend to feel more emotionally exhausted (Purvanova & Muros, 2010). The result of burnout is often an inability to perform job duties well. For helping professionals, this can look like an inability to engage and empathize with clients (Skovholt & Trotter-Mathison, 2011).

Compassion Fatigue

Compassion fatigue has been described as a form of burnout and, like other kinds of fatigue, may exhaust us physically and emotionally (Figley, 2002; Sabo, 2011). Jonathan exhibited about half of the signs of compassion fatigue: sadness or grief, guilt, increased arousal, and detachment and isolation. He did not experience nightmares, somatic complaints, or changes in belief systems. And yet his distress appeared to come directly from being emotionally exhausted from trying to meet the needs of four suicidal youth. Empathy is a key component to compassion fatigue; in our efforts to view the world from the perspective of the suffering, we in turn suffer (Figley, 2002).

Vicarious Traumatization

Jonathan exhibited almost all the signs of vicarious traumatization: anxiety, sadness, confusion, apathy, decreased capacity for relationships, loss of control and trust. However, it is not clear that trauma content was transferred from a client to Jonathan, and his disruptions to life and work were not lasting. While any educator could suffer from burnout, being "exposed to emotionally shocking images of horror and suffering" (McCann & Pearlman, 1990) can result in vicarious trauma, defined as the "post-traumatic stress reactions experienced by those who are indirectly exposed to traumatic events" (Palm, Polusny, & Follette, 2004). Figley (2002) refers to the term STSD or secondary traumatic stress disorder to describe the PTSD-like symptoms experienced by an individual witnessing another person's terror, whereas PTSD symptoms are directly connected to the sufferer themselves.

Secondary trauma symptoms may include crisis responders experiencing their own painful images and emotions after hearing about trauma, and they may even incorporate these events into their own memory systems, resulting in intrusive thoughts or images (McCann & Pearlman, 1990). Hallmarks of vicarious traumatization also include changes in frame of reference or cognitive schema (beliefs about other people and the world), identity, sense of safety, ability to trust, self-esteem, intimacy, and sense of control (Bloom, 2003; McCann & Pearlman, 1990). Crisis responders must be aware of these damaging effects and incorporate strategies to ameliorate them, otherwise risking feelings of numbness and emotional distance that will not allow them to the maintain the empathy needed to be effective in their job (McCann & Pearlman, 1990).

Risk factors for vicarious traumatization include a previous history of trauma, extending beyond the limits of customary service delivery by overworking, ignoring healthy boundaries, and taking on too many trauma survivors (Bloom, 2003). Caregivers are also more vulnerable if they have a history of mental illness or substance abuse or if they lack social and family resources (National Association of School Psychologists [NASP], 2003). Personal vulnerabilities may also impact trauma as caregivers empathize with a traumatized individual presenting graphic or disturbing information (Cunningham, 2004). Finally, research consistently shows that clinicians with less experience are more prone to vicarious trauma symptomatology, as less experienced trauma therapists report greater disruptions in self-trust, self-intimacy, self-esteem, and overall distress (Bloom, 2003).

Symptoms

The symptoms of burnout, compassion fatigue, and vicarious trauma might look quite similar and often overlap. The most important point we want to drive home in this text is for you as caregivers to consistently monitor your own symptomatology. Know what is out of the norm for you and pay attention to it. Concerning symptoms are presented in Table 10.2. If any of these are present in your daily life, perhaps you will

Table 10.2 Symptoms of Concern

Psychosomatic Symptoms	Chronic Fatigue or Sleep Disturbances
Significant irritability or agitation	Changes in appetite
Withdrawal from others	Severe sadness or depression
A compulsion to be involved in every crisis situation and upset/jealous when not	An inability to stop thinking about the crisis or the crisis victims
Excessive worry about the crisis victims	Alcohol or substance use/abuse
Personally identifying with the victims	Suicidal thoughts
Loss of objectivity	Inability to make decisions
Irritability, anger, or rage	Agitation, restlessness, or impulsivity
Maintaining an unnecessary degree of follow-up contact with crisis victims	Inability to return to normal job roles

Adapted from National Association of School Psychologists (2003). Helping children cope with crisis: Care for caregivers, Bethesda, MD.

find that it is time to consider seeking therapeutic services or discussing organizational options with supervisors.

Responses such as fear, shock, terror, anger, rage, and grief are common in the aftermath of a tragedy such as suicide for those directly affected and those responding (Raphael, 2007). Clinicians with higher rates of traumatized clients also report increased isolation from friends and family, increased worry (checking if doors are locked, listening for noises, decreasing their children's activities away from home), increased symptoms of intrusion (visualizations of traumatic incidents) and avoidance (of traumatic stimuli), as well as increased symptoms of stress, anxiety, and sleep disturbance (Chrestman, 1995).

A study assessing the effects of crisis work on school psychologists was conducted by Bolnik and Brock (2005), with results finding that 86% of psychologists had been involved in school crisis response. Of these, over 90% of respondents reported negative reactions, with physical reactions in general, and fatigue/exhaustion specifically, being identified as the most frequent. Other physical reactions reported included sleep difficulty, headache, and rapid heartbeat. Emotional reactions reported included increased sensitivity, anxiety, and helplessness. Behavioral reactions included irritability, moodiness, and withdrawal, while cognitive reactions included difficulty concentrating and preoccupation with the trauma. Interestingly, work performance reactions were reported to be low, with the authors suggesting that this could be due to the fact that a school psychologists' traditional job duties include legal deadlines that must be met, and they cannot allow themselves time away from these duties. What this tells us is that school psychologists must carry on in their typical job roles regardless of what tragedy unfolds. Psychologists, administrators, teachers, and other crisis responders who care so deeply about these children must find ways to monitor and nurture their own well-being despite the daily demands of their profession.

> **Expert tip:** Crisis responders are exceptionally conscientious and steadfast in their care for others, often at the expense of their own physical and emotional wellness.

Managing Stress and Preventing Burnout

There are three domains to consider when managing stress and preventing burnout: personal, professional, and organizational. Although the personal domain is perhaps the most well-known and widely discussed (there are 64,000 books listed under self-help on Amazon.com), research is presented, which suggests that changes in the organizational domain have the greatest impact on burnout prevention and addressing symptoms of secondary trauma.

Personal Self-Care Strategies

Perhaps the most well-known and widely endorsed approach to managing stress and burnout prevention comes in the form of self-care. Most SMHPs recognize the list of self-care strategies in Table 10.3 (a more expansive list of suggestions can be found in your eResources).

Most of you would recommend these suggestions to others, but SMHPs often don't follow their own advice. Furthermore, it is not clear that doing these activities actually leads to a reduction in traumatic stress (Motta, 2012). The most popular strategies among those who engage in self-care are following a normal routine, helping fellow crisis interveners by sharing feelings, realizing those around you are under stress, exercising, getting plenty of rest, and spending time with other crisis interveners (Bolnick & Brock, 2005). If we think back to the case study, Jonathan engaged in these self-help strategies, albeit unintentionally.

Professional Strategies

> **Expert tip:** While I may be the *first* person in my organization called in the aftermath of a crisis or suicide loss, I am certainly not the *only* one who can handle it.

Self-care includes balancing the demands of your personal and professional lives, as well as finding a balance *within* your professional life.

Table 10.3 Sample Strategies for Positive Self-Care

How Often Do You Engage in Each of These Strategies?	None of the Time	Some of the Time	All of the Time
Spend time with loved ones (including animals!)			
Avoiding high-risk behaviors, such as drinking alcohol, to cope			
Saying no			
Setting clear boundaries between work and home			
Eating and sleeping well			
Engaging in physical activity/exercise			
Practicing calming activities (e.g., yoga, meditation, reading)			
Asking family members or friends for emotional support			
Debriefing with experienced colleagues			
Using the tragedy to clarify your own sense of meaning in life			
Taking breaks throughout your day			
Recognizing that you are not alone			
Limiting online media exposure to traumatic events			
Going to therapy			
Acknowledging yourself			

Adapted from National Association of School Psychologists (NASP) (2003). *Helping children cope with crisis: Care for caregivers*, Bethesda, MD.

Working fewer hours, having control over your schedule and caseload, developing a caseload of clients with varying types and degrees of problems, working with populations other than those with trauma, not scheduling two trauma victims in a row, and scheduling breaks during the day are effective professional care strategies (Motta, 2012; Palm, Polusny, & Follette, 2004). One author of this text revels in days where the greatest personal crisis encountered is a teen debating who to ask to prom. Another strategy for reducing professional stress is setting professional boundaries. This can look like saying no to a colleague asking for a favor or declining involvement in a crisis response when you are already distressed.

Vignette: Think back to the high profile suicide cluster discussed in Chapter 9. This event was so sensationalized in the media that everyone was talking about it. There was no escape for one of the authors as even neighbors were discussing the tragedy, asking questions, and sharing their own stories. Burnout and compassion fatigue became a serious concern. While setting boundaries is one of the best ways to prevent burnout, you can imagine how difficult this was when one neighbor personally knew the victims. There would be no way to recharge in the evening prior to returning to the victims' school the next day if boundaries were not carefully set. And, so the truth was told and the importance of mental respite as a crisis responder was explained. And you know what? They all understood. If the author had avoided it or beaten around the bush, so to speak, neighbors may have felt insulted or felt that they just weren't cared about, which certainly was not the case! By learning when to say no and being honest about it, we are better able to take care of ourselves, and subsequently, those around us.

One technique you can use to set up a boundary between work and home is to visualize putting all of your worries, concerns, and challenges into a jar; closing the lid; and putting it on a shelf in your office prior to heading home. The jar will be there in the morning but is left in stillness for the night. This visualization has helped staff relax as they head home, realizing that they can begin in the morning where they had left off and that the time away from the stress of trauma is crucial.

Organizational Strategies

For administrators and supervisors reading this, organizational strategies that can help decrease risk of vicarious traumatization for employees include ensuring *manageable and balanced caseloads* for your staff, fostering a supportive environment, and providing *adequate consultation* opportunities for difficult cases (Palm et al., 2004) to process what steps to take next and to help new staff process the emotionality of such work. Having a mentor available, preferably on-site, can help novice clinicians not feel so alone in the feelings of doubt, isolation, and fear that frequently occur. Administrators and supervisors can further decrease stress by acknowledging crisis responders' efforts in the crisis response as well as normalizing secondary stress reactions. *Debriefing* after an event helps crisis responders feel less isolated, as many report that their families, while supportive, do not quite understand what they are experiencing in the trenches (Palm et al., 2004). The debriefing process includes caregivers constantly self-reflecting on their capacity for crisis response. Perhaps we are not the best person to respond to a crisis at a given time due to our own life circumstance, including relational conflicts or financial struggles, our own grief and loss, or perhaps issues of health, whether our own or of a loved one. Organizations should remain open to caregiver disclosure of their current capacity as caregivers may fear discipline from a supervisor or retribution from peers if this is an expected part of their job duties. Supervisors must allow respite as needed. The debriefing process also includes identifying which school personnel are most in need of mental health services. Developing a school culture that encourages personnel to seek mental health services is likely to reduce secondary traumatization.

Other strategies to reduce distress include increased income, utilization of *additional training* (not necessarily in trauma), and lower percentages of time spent in clinical activities relative to other activities (Chrestman, 1995). Administrators who allow time for professional development activities find that these opportunities not only improve knowledge and skill but increase professional support and referral networks.

Training and Preparation

Providing crisis experience and education to interns, practicum students, and student teachers while under supervision will help build skills, calm nerves, and build confidence (Raphael, 2007). University-based trainers can share their own real-life cases to provide those entering the field with further knowledge and experience to take with them to their own crisis events. Beginners often say that once in a real crisis situation of their own, they recalled a certain story told to them as a trainee to help them remember action steps to follow, possible pitfalls, and normalized emotional responses. Training more individuals to respond to a suicidal crisis in schools will help distribute the response among a greater volume of personnel rather than having it fall consistently on only a few responders who then have an increased likelihood for secondary trauma (Eidelson, D'Alessio, & Eidelson, 2003).

Training by negative case example is also an excellent way to train school personnel to identify signs of burnout, compassion fatigue, and vicarious trauma. For example, the case presented earlier was a positive case example of helpful organizational responses to Jonathan's distressing experience. However, the scenario could easily have turned negative if Jonathan had gone back to work, been given a full caseload of suicidal youth, and encountered colleagues who were unsympathetic and invalidating about his weekend experience. Trainings would then facilitate discussion about what happened and why.

Preventing Burnout by Looking Ahead

Professionals who stay current with advances in the field are less likely to experience burnout. We end this chapter reviewing three promising uses of technology that might address the challenge of identifying and intervening with suicidal youth, especially students who have dropped out of school or who are enrolled in cyberschool. First, use technology for universal prevention: As an example, MoodGym (Powell et al., 2013), is a computerized CBT (cognitive behavioral therapy) program that has been shown to improve emotional well-being at a population level.

Second, use technology for indicated prevention: For example, the Re-frame IT program, currently being evaluated in a randomized control trial, provides interactive CBT for youth who have been identified as at risk for suicide. Youth watch a series of videos, create and upload their own video diaries, engage in weekly activities, use a message board, and interact with a therapist if necessary (http://oyh.org.au/our-research/research-areas/suicide-prevention).

Third, use social networks to monitor and respond to youth suicide risk. As mentioned earlier in the text, Facebook and Siri have programmed options for users to identify and report posts or statements that indicate suicide risk. Anthropologist danah boyd found that the school personnel who were most accessible to students were the ones who engaged with students online (boyd, 2014). Although there are privacy and ethical concerns about school personnel "friending" students, boyd recommends the following:

1.   Create a professional profile.
2.   Give the login ID and password to your administrator.
3.   Let students know about the profile and who has access to it.
4.   Connect with students online only after they have initiated contact (i.e., on Facebook they send a "friend request").

Conclusion

Can you answer yes to any of the following questions?

Do you find that you have no time or energy for yourself?
Do you have work-related nightmares?
Do you have a more negative view of the world than before?
Do you call in sick often?
Has your motivation level dropped at work or are you less productive?
Do you find that you can't stop thinking about certain clients or cases?

If you can say yes to any of the above, you are at significant risk for burnout, compassion fatigue, or vicarious trauma. Perhaps you are already experiencing one or all of these—all educators, SMHPs and staff working in the aftermath of a suicide event are at risk. It is essential that we prevent burnout or fatigue *before* it happens, that we practice self-care, and that we look out for colleagues who may need help and support. A caregiver's genuineness, empathy, warmth, responsiveness, and comforting presence are central to helping survivors (Raphael, 2007). In order to maintain these effective qualities, we must think about what brings us joy and peace and what calms us at the end of the day and practice it.

References

Bloom, S. L. (2003). Caring for the caregiver: Avoiding and treating vicarious traumatization. In A. Giardino, E. Datner, & J. Asher (Eds.), *Sexual assault, victimization across the lifespan* (pp. 459–470). Maryland Heights, MO: GW Medical Publishing.

Bolnik, L., & Brock, S. E. (2005). The self-reported effects of crisis intervention work on school psychologist. *The California School Psychologist, 10,* 117–124.

boyd, d. (2014). *It's complicated: The social lives of networked teens.* New Haven, CT: Yale University Press.

Chrestman, K. (1995). Secondary exposure to trauma and self-reported distress among therapists. In B. H. Stamm (Ed.), Se*condary traumatic stress: Self-care issues for clinicians, researchers and educators* (pp. 29–36). Luterville, MD: Sidran Press.

Cunningham, M. (2004). Teaching social workers about trauma: Reducing the risks of vicarious traumatization in the classroom. *Journal of Social Work Education, 40*(2), 305–317.

Eidelson, R. J., D'Alessio, G. R., & Eidelson, J. I. (2003). The impact of September 11 on psychologists. *Professional Psychology: Research and Practice, 34*(2), 144–150.

Figley, C. R. (2002). Compassion fatigue: Psychotherapists' chronic lack of self-care. *JCLP/In Session: Psychotherapy in Practice, 58*(11), 1433–1441. doi:10.1002/jclp.10090

McCann, I. L., & Pearlman, L. A. (1990). Vicarious traumatization: A framework for understanding the psychological effects of working with victims. *Journal of Traumatic Stress, 3*(1), 131–149.

Mills, L. B., & Huebner, E. S. (1998). A prospective study of personality characteristics, occupational stressors, and burnout among school psychology practitioners. *Journal of School Psychology, 36*(1), 103–120. doi:10.1016/S0022-4405(97)00053-8

Motta, R. W. (2012). Secondary trauma in children and school personnel. *Journal of Applied School Psychology, 28*(3), 256–269. doi:10.1080/15377903.2012.695767

National Association of School Psychologists (NASP). (2003). *Helping children cope with crisis: Care for caregivers.* Retrieved from http://www.nasponline.org/resources/crisis_safety/CaregiverTips.pdf

Palm, K. M., Polusny, M. A., & Follette, V. M. (2004). Vicarious traumatization: Potential hazards and interventions for disaster and trauma workers. *Prehospital and Disaster Medicine, 19*(1), 73–78.

Powell, J., Hamborg, T., Stallard, N., Burls, A., McSorley, J., Bennett, K., . . . Christensen, H. (2013). Effectiveness of a web-based cognitive-behavioral tool to improve mental well-being in the general population: Randomized controlled trial. *Journal of Medical Internet Research, 15*(1), e2. doi:10.2196/jmir.2240

Purvanova, R. K., & Muros, J. P. (2010). Gender differences in burnout: A meta-analysis. *Journal of Vocational Behavior, 77*(2), 168–185. doi:10.1016/j.jvb.2010.04.006

Raphael, B. (2007). The human touch and mass catastrophe. *Psychiatry, 70*(4), 329–336.

Sabo, B. (2011). Reflecting on the concept of compassion fatigue. *The Online Journal of Issues in Nursing, 16*(1). doi:10.3912/OJIN.Vol16No01Man01

Singer, J. B. (2005). Child and adolescent psychiatric emergencies: Mobile crisis response. In A. R. Roberts (Ed.), *Crisis intervention handbook: Assessment, treatment, and research* (3rd ed., pp. 319–361). Oxford / New York: Oxford University Press.

Skovholt, T. M., & Trotter-Mathison, M. (2011). *The resilient practitioner: Burnout prevention and self-care strategies for counselors, therapists, teachers, and health professionals.* New York: Routledge.

11 Comprehensive Case Study

While many school mental health professionals (SMHPs) do not engage in the type of suicide risk monitoring and counseling sessions presented in this case study, this presents a best practice care example of how to work within a systems perspective to screen, assess, monitor, and provide multiple levels of support to a suicidal youth to manage his or her suicidal thoughts and behaviors over time.

This illustrative case example of a SMHP (in this case, a school psychologist) responding to an adolescent student who reported suicidal thoughts and behaviors during school pulls together the elements we discuss in the book and demonstrates how to use the three suicide risk forms: screening, assessment, and monitoring. Completed forms are included in the body of the text; full-size forms are available for download in the online eResources. If you have not yet gone to the website to download these documents, please do so before reading this chapter.

Referral and Risk Screening

Mr. Sal Horizon, the school counselor and your colleague of 10 years, is knocking on your door. You have great respect for his expertise as a college counselor and his reputation among students is impeccable—they like him and trust him. He walks in and closes the door behind him. You're a bit surprised to see him looking distraught. He hands you the school's *Youth Suicide Risk Screening Form*. You glance at it and see that a 16-year-old student named James Burns reported that he "wished he were dead."

Before you can ask about the student's current location, Sal cracks a knowing smile and says, "Don't worry. Jimmy is safe—he's with the director of counseling." You are relieved. The crisis plan seems to be working (so far). And for all of his stress, Sal still has his usual affable sense of humor. "Okay," you say to him, "Give me what you've got on this student—his history, stressors, whatever".

Sal tells you that James (Jimmy) is a 16-year-old high school junior who has spent all three years at Rye High School. Sal tells you, "He's a really good kid—great student. Puts a lot of pressure on himself to get straight

Youth Suicide Risk Screening Form

Student name **James Burns**   Date of screen   **9/12/15**

	Past 24 hours	Past week	Past Month
1. Have you wished you were dead?	☒	☒	☒
2. Have you felt that you, your friends, or your family would be better off if you were dead?	☒	☐	☐
3. Have you had thoughts about killing yourself?	☒	☐	☐
4. Have you tried to kill yourself? ☒ No ☐ Yes	☐	☐	☐

    a. If yes, how?

    b. If yes, when and where?

    c. Did you stop yourself, or did someone stop you?

    d. How do you feel now that they stopped you?

5. Do you plan to kill yourself?   ☒ No   ☐ Yes
    a. If yes, how, when, and where?

If student checks "past 24 hours" or "past week" to any question, reports a suicide attempt at any time, or checks "yes" to question 5, a full suicide risk assessment **must** be conducted for safety. This may be done by school-based mental health staff or by referral based on school district policy.

Parents contacted?	☒ Yes	☐ No
Full assessment completed by school staff?	☒ Yes	☐ No
Outside referral for assessment made?	☐ Yes	☒ No

Referred to: _____   Phone / email: _____

Mr. Horizon – School Counselor   **September 12, 2015**
Screener name and credentials   Date

Adapted from the Ask Suicide-Screening Questions form (ASQ; Horowitz, 2012),
the Columbia Suicide Severity Rating Scale (C-SSRS; Posner, 2009) and the
Suicide Ideation Questionnaire-JR (SIQ-JR; Reynolds, 1997).

A's. He's mostly flown under the radar because he's such a good student. He's come to me really upset a couple of times over the past few years whenever he's gotten a grade lower than an A. You know the type. Math and science have always been his strongest subjects. He barely needs to study to get passing grades in these courses. Lately, though, things have really gone south for Jimmy. He's having difficulty concentrating. He complains about 'freezing' as soon as the test is put in front of him. For the first time ever, he has failed tests in English, Latin, and history."

Sal tells you that the family is intact, although the parents separated for a year when Jimmy was in the fifth grade. Jimmy has an older brother, who graduated from the same high school. His mother was born in Mexico and lived there until she was 11 years old. She grew up in a primarily Spanish-speaking neighborhood in the United States, but ever since she met Jimmy's father has been living and working in an exclusively English-speaking community. Jimmy's father was born here, of Irish and German ancestry, and grew up in a small town near where they currently live.

Sal knows that Jimmy played the drums in the past, but quickly realizes that he has not heard Jimmy talking about drumming with his friends as of late, nor did he perform in the recent school talent show. It is easy for Jimmy to stay under the radar as he has never been a behavior problem and has a nearly perfect discipline record with the exception of forgetting his school ID on occasion. This morning, Jimmy told Mr. Horizon that he just "can't get his act together" and that he is "stressed all the time." Your colleague is extremely worried about Jimmy, which alarms you as Sal is not one to overreact. You agree to meet with Jimmy to conduct a comprehensive suicide risk assessment based upon Mr. Horizon's screening.

Risk Assessment

Jimmy walks into your office appearing sad and forlorn. He looks at the ground as you politely ask him to sit in the chair facing you. You have your *Youth Suicide Risk Assessment Form* readily available as you are well aware that school district policy requires that you complete this form for each assessment conducted. You don't know Jimmy and he doesn't know you, and, in order for a risk assessment to be valid, the student needs to trust you. You ask Mr. Horizon to stay in the room for a few minutes. Jimmy trusts Mr. Horizon, and you want him to see that Mr. Horizon trusts you. This seems to work as Jimmy appears comfortable with your questions and answers them readily and with what seems to be honesty. After a few minutes, Sal says to Jimmy, "Jimmy, I gotta go. Tell your whole story, okay? I'll check on you later." Jimmy smiles, and says "Okay Mr. H."

Jimmy is a polite child who answers all of your questions with fairly limited prompting. He reports that he first started feeling sad in the fifth

Youth Suicide Risk Assessment Form

Student name **James Burns**   Date of assessment   **9/12/15**

Referral source (name / title): **Mr. Horizon / School Counselor**
Assessed by (name / title):   **Dr. Terri Erbacher, PhD / School Psychologist**
Reason for referral:

Jimmy sought out his school counselor with whom he had a good
relationship. As a high school junior, he had known his counselor since
freshman year. Jimmy told Mr. Horizon that he just does not feel like
living with this stress anymore.

Student description of problem (use student's words):

School is just too stressful. I'm overwhelmed all the time. I feel nervous
and miserable and it is never-ending.

I. IDEATION

Does the student report thoughts of suicide?	☒	Yes	❏	No
Timeframe:				
Right now	☒	Yes	❏	No
Past 24 hours	☒	Yes	❏	No
Past week	☒	Yes	❏	No
Past month	☒	Yes	❏	No
Past year / lifetime	☒	Yes	❏	No

When does the student first remember having thoughts of suicide?   **In 5ᵗʰ grade**
Describe ideation in student's words:

Jimmy first remembers feeling depressed and "bored with life" in 5ᵗʰ
grade. It became "really bad" in 8ᵗʰ grade when he realized he was "not
normal" and he wanted life to end. He just can't have fun doing
anything. Ever.

Frequency (every minute / hourly / daily /weekly): Right now? Every minute
Duration (a few seconds / minutes / hours / days): It has lasted a few days now
Intensity (not disruptive → completely disruptive): I cannot think about anything else
Location (where the ideation occurs): At school or doing homework

What stops or interrupts the ideation? When and where is it **not** present?

When I am with my mother or my girlfriend.

II. INTENT

How much does the student want to **die**? ❑ not at all ☒ somewhat ❑ a great deal
Describe intent in student's words:

"It's too overwhelming."

How much does the student want to **live**? ❑ not at all ☒ somewhat ❑ a great deal
When is the student's desire to live stronger? What is different when he or she wants to live?

"It's not."

III. PLAN

Does the student report a plan?	☒	Yes	❑	No
	❑	Specific	☒	Vague
	❑	Imminent	❑	Future imminent
Has the student written a suicide note?	❑	Yes	❑	No

How does the student envision dying?
❑ gun ❑ hanging ❑ cutting ☒ pills ❑ jumping ❑ suffocation ❑ other _____

Does the student have access to the means?	☒	Yes	❑	No
Does the student know how to use the means?	☒	Yes	❑	No
Where does the student envision dying?	No answer			
When does the student envision dying?	No answer			

Has the student made an attempt in the past?	❑	Yes	☒	No
How recently? _____				
Did someone interrupt it?	❑	Yes	❑	No
Did the student stop him or herself?	❑	Yes	❑	No
Did it result in hospitalization?	❑	Yes	❑	No

Describe the current **suicide plan** in the student's words:

I take medication for my depression. I would take all of them and overdose.

What would make it more likely that the student will follow through with the plan (**triggers**)?

More school work.

What could **reduce the likelihood** that the student will follow through with the plan?

I don't know.

IV. STRENGTHS AND RESOURCES
What are the student's **reasons for living**?

My mother.

What **family member** or adult does the student identify as a support?

mother.

What **friends / peers** does the student identify as supports (online or offline)

girlfriend.

What is the student good at / likes to do / enjoys doing? What does the student look forward to doing?

I used to enjoy drumming. I don't enjoy anything anymore.

V. RISK FACTORS (check all that apply)

❑ Prior suicide attempt	❑ Gun in the home	❑ Chronic illness
❑ Failing a grade / repeating a grade	☒ Dissatisfied with grades	❑ Conflict with staff
❑ Suspended from school	❑ Disciplinary crisis	❑ Conduct disorder
❑ Recent humiliation in front of peers	☒ Socially isolated	☒ Anxiety
❑ Recent suicide death of friend / family	❑ General dislike of school	☒ Stressful events
❑ Victim of intimate partner violence	❑ Sexual abuse	❑ Physical abuse
❑ Sleep disturbance / insomnia	❑ Victim of (cyber) bullying	☒ Substance abuse
☒ Depression / bipolar depression	❑ Perpetrator of (cyber)	❑ PTSD
☒ Perceived burden to others	bullying	❑ Legal involvement
❑ Other _____		

VI. PRESENTATION AT TIME OF ASSESSMENT (Check all that apply)
Emotional state

❑ Numb	☒ Depressed	☒ Anxious
❑ Irritable	❑ Angry	❑ Scared
❑ Other _____		

Cognitive state

☒ Hopeless about future	☒ Blaming self	❑ Blaming others
☒ Rigid thinking	❑ Poverty of speech	❑ Confused
❑ Auditory, visual, tactile hallucinations	❑ Poor insight	❑ Unrealistic
❑ Poor judgment	❑ Other _____	

Behavioral state

☒ Lethargic	❑ Agitated	❑ Impulsive
❑ Abnormal movements	❑ Threatening	❑ Risk-taking
❑ Other _____		

VII. ASSESSMENT OF SCHOOL ENVIRONMENT

School staff interviewed   Mr. Horizon

Documents reviewed   grades, progress reports

Recent changes in **schoolwork**?   ☒ Yes   ☐ No
Describe: Just recently, Jimmy has failed a few tests.
He is typically a very good student.

Recent changes in **emotions/mood**?   ☒ Yes   ☐ No
Describe: Jimmy has just appeared sad

Recent changes in **thoughts/cognitions**?   ☐ Yes   ☒ No
Describe:

Recent changes in **behaviors** (discipline)?   ☐ Yes   ☒ No
Describe: He is a very nice boy, no discipline problems

Changes in **appearance**?   ☐ Yes   ☒ No
Describe:

Changes in **peer interaction**?   ☒ Yes   ☐ No
Describe: Recently been withdrawing from friends

Any **environmental stressors**? (e.g. this calendar-year such as academic   ☐ Yes   ☐ No
testing or activities such as significant sports loss or upsetting assemblies,
classroom presentations, school disruptions or teacher changes, etc?)
Describe: The junior class has begun having college
prep presentations

Any **comments indicating suicidal ideation, self-destruction or death**?   ☒ Yes   ☐ No
Describe:
Jimmy says he does not want to live anymore.

VIII. ASSESSMENT OF PARENT(S)/GUARDIAN(S)

Parent/guardian interviewed   Mr. & Mrs. Burns

Has your child ever mentioned having thoughts of suicide or dying?   ☐ Yes   ☒ No
If so, when and how often?
Describe:

Jimmy has always had depression. We had no idea it was
this bad.

How likely do you think it is that he/she would act on these thoughts? Please describe:

"no idea."

Can you think of anything that has been very **stressful** for your child lately, such as the loss of a family member or change in family structure (e.g., parent moves in or out)? Please describe:

Nothing.

Have you noticed a change in what you would consider normal for your child in terms of his/her **behavior** - either significantly more active (e.g., engaging in risky behaviors or harming him/herself) or withdrawn (e.g., not participating in activities that he/she would normally)? Please describe:

No. Wait, he used to love drumming and has not been doing it with his friends.

Have you noticed a change in what you would consider normal for your child in terms of his/her **emotions** – either significantly more emotional (e.g., sad, angry, scared) or less emotional (e.g., quiet, withdrawn, unresponsive) than usual? Please describe:

No. He's always been a depressed kid.

Have you noticed a change in what you would consider normal for your child in terms of his/her **thoughts** – either significantly more preoccupied or significantly less able to concentrate and focus on any one thing?

Nope.

Does your child know anyone who has died by suicide or attempted suicide? If so, who and when?

No.

IX. RISK ASSESSMENT SUMMARY

1. **Low risk:** None or passing ideation that does not interfere with activities of daily living; reports no desire to die (i.e., intent), has no specific plan, exhibits few risk factors, and has identifiable protective factors.
2. **Moderate risk:** Reports frequent suicidal ideation with limited intensity and duration; has some specific plans to die by suicide but no reported intent. Demonstrates some risk factors but is able to identify reasons for living and other protective factors.
3. **High risk:** Reports frequent, intense, and enduring suicidal ideation. Reports specific plans, including choice of lethal methods and availability / accessibility of the method. Student presents with multiple risk factors and identifies few if any protective factors. If the student has written a suicide note, the student is immediately considered at high risk.

OVERALL RISK LEVEL (summary): Student meets criteria for **low / moderate / high** suicide risk based on the following information *(If a student falls between levels, err on the side of caution and assume higher risk category)*:

High Risk - Jimmy has had suicidal thoughts since 5ᵗʰ grade and they have been severe for 3 years. He is thinking about suicide constantly at this point. Jimmy has identified a suicide plan to overdose on his prescription pills, though he does not indicate specificity of time and place. He has identified a few protective factors, but currently reports extreme depression and anhedonia.

X. ACTIONS TAKEN / RECOMMENDATIONS

Actions taken should be a direct result of the risk level identified above in collaboration with your school district procedure. In all cases, parents should be notified to inform them you met with their child.

Parent/guardian contacted?	☒ Yes	☐ No
Released to parent/guardian?	☒ Yes	☐ No
Referrals provided to parent?	☒ Yes	☐ No
Safety plan developed?	☒ Yes	☐ No
Recommending removal of method/means?	☒ Yes	☐ No
If currently in treatment, contact made with therapist/psychiatrist?	☒ Yes	☐ No
Outpatient therapy recommended?	☒ Yes	☐ No
Recommending 24-hour supervision?	☒ Yes	☐ No
Hospitalization recommended?	☒ Yes	☐ No
Release of Information signed?	☒ Yes	☐ No
Copy of this assessment provided to referral?	☒ Yes	☐ No
Consultation received?	☒ Yes	☐ No

Other? Please describe:

Parents came to school for this evaluation so Jimmy was released to their care. Jimmy sees a psychiatrist for medication management - Parents signed release to communicate. Parents will lock and administer prescription medication.

Terri Erbacher, PhD - School Psychologist   9/12/15

Assessor's signature and credentials   Date

Reviewed by:

Mrs. Cathy Harris, School Principal

Name and credentials

Mrs. Harris   9/12/15

Signature   Date

Note: This form is intended for use by qualified mental health professionals who have been trained in how to conduct a youth suicide assessment. For a more in-depth explanation of how to use this form, please refer to chapter 6 of Erbacher, Singer & Poland (2015): Suicide in Schools: A Practitioner's Guide to Multi-Level Prevention, Assessment, Intervention and Postvention. New York: Routledge Press.

grade when he became "bored with life" and "nothing was fun anymore." His feelings of sadness intensified in the eighth grade when he began to feel he was "not the same as other kids" because of his depression. That was the first time he wanted life to end. He complained to his parents that he was having lots of stomachaches. When they took him to the doctor, she asked Jimmy if he had ever felt sad more days than not. He told his doctor he had problems sleeping, had stomachaches, and thought that people did not like him. His doctor talked with his parents about depression, and they agreed to start him on a trial of Zoloft. You ask him, "Did she ask you about thoughts of killing yourself?" "No," he replied, "She never asked that. I would have told her, but she didn't ask." He tells you that he has had suicidal thoughts since he realized he was "not normal" in eighth grade and he is afraid for his parents to know. The thought of potential abuse crosses your mind so you gently ask him about his relationship with his family. Jimmy tells you that he gets along really well with his mother and okay with his father. He says his dad is very strict, particularly about grades.

He describes his parents as good people who work hard to give him what he needs. But they are under financial stress as his father lost his job last year. Jimmy reports that his mother's Mexican heritage makes it a bit difficult to share his despair with her. His mother has been through a lot since her immigration, leaving behind her extended family, learning a new language, and living in poverty as her parents made something for themselves in America. Jimmy feels that his problems are trivial compared to all that she has gone through and does not want to burden her. His mother sees medication as a treatment for his physical illness (stomachaches) rather than for the underlying depression. Psychotherapy has never been considered. Jimmy tells you how stressed, overwhelmed, and miserable he feels and that it's never-ending. He is having trouble thinking of anything else, especially his school or homework. His suicidal thoughts and behaviors (STB) have increased. While they were occasional and fleeting in eighth grade, they became more common after that; for the last couple of days, he has begun thinking about suicide nearly every hour. You ask Jimmy what triggered him finding Mr. Horizon today, and he tells you that the college prep assembly held that morning got him thinking about his future. He feels like such a burden to his parents already; he cannot imagine asking them to pay for college. Your heart breaks for this young boy. His sense of despair comes through to you clearly as he shares his hopelessness after suffering in silence all year. You want to tell him it is all going to be okay, but you realize that doing so would derail your assessment and likely backfire: the minute you say "it will be okay," he will think of a dozen reasons why it is not going to be okay, reinforcing his depressed and hopeless view of life.

You know you have to ask him if he has devised a suicide plan. You take a deep breath and continue, "Jimmy, I am so sorry to hear you have been experiencing all this. I cannot imagine what you have been going through. I am so glad you are talking to me about it now. I really want to help you, so thank you for being honest. I am sure it is hard to talk about. When you think about suicide, have you thought about how you would do it? Do you have a plan?" Jimmy tells you that he has thought about taking pills. He takes medication for his depression and would plan to overdose. Jimmy has not envisioned where or when he would carry out this plan; he has not yet resolved to do it. You are simultaneously relieved that he has not yet formulated a more detailed plan and convinced that he needs more intensive help than he has been getting.

A comprehensive suicide risk assessment also gathers information on factors that protect from suicide risk. You have already heard some protective factors during the course of the assessment, such as a strong and supportive relationship with his mother and a passion for drumming (although one that appears to have waned). "Jimmy, I appreciate you sharing so many of the things that have been hard for you. I'm curious about some of the things that make you happy." "Nothing," he says. "I feel bad for my girlfriend. She's really sweet, but I think she's going to break up with me if I can't pull it together." You ask him, "When was the last time you did something that made you feel even slightly better?" "Last night, I guess . . . My best friend and I were Snapchatting. It was hilarious."

You explain to Jimmy that you'll need to call his parents. You are clear to him that he is not in trouble but that they need to know he is hurting. Mr. and Mrs. Burns come to school immediately and tell you that they are very concerned. While they always knew he was depressed, they had no idea he had thoughts of suicide. They are kind and comforting to Jimmy as mom hugs and kisses him. Dad is verbally comforting, telling Jimmy "things will be okay." They agree to take him to the hospital, but they want to handle it from here without the school's interference whatsoever. You explain the importance of working together, and they dismiss it as a "family problem that they will handle" and leave your office.

Hospitalization

After two days you have heard nothing from the family, even after several phone calls home to check in. On the third day, you get a phone call from the hospital's attending psychiatrist with an update on Jimmy's status. It is atypical to get a call directly from the psychiatrist, but the family signed a release of information allowing Dr. Hill to talk to you. He tells you that Jimmy's parents took him to the local crisis center, where he was assessed and determined to be appropriate for hospitalization. You again reach out to Jimmy's parents to no avail. You begin to wonder if they will change schools, perhaps putting him into a local nonpublic school. In the meantime, you coordinate with the academic liaison at the hospital to make sure Jimmy is provided work while there so that he does not fall any further behind academically than need be. Jimmy has all of his textbooks and also has access to the school's online database for class assignments. After another week passes, Dr. Hill informs you that Jimmy will be kept another 3 days, making this a full 14-day stay—lengthier than is typical and an indicator of the severity of Jimmy's problems. Dr. Hill tells you that he consulted with Jimmy's pediatrician, discontinued the Zoloft, and started Jimmy on Prozac and that while this new medication will take time to be effective, Jimmy is stable and ready to return to school the following Monday.

Re-Entry Into the School Environment

During Jimmy's hospitalization, you and your administrators reviewed the school's policies regarding re-entry. So that Jimmy's re-entry is as successful as possible you arrange a meeting with the school principal, the director of pupil services, you, Mr. Horizon, the school nurse, both parents, and Jimmy. You make a list of issues to be discussed regarding Jimmy's return to school:

- What will he tell his peers about where he was? What about closer friends?
- What would Jimmy and his family like to tell his teachers?
- How will he handle rumors about where he was during his absence?
- How will he catch up on missed schoolwork? What is the essential work that must be completed? What extended time will he have to complete makeup work without penalty?
- Do we need to modify his class schedule at all? Is he ready to return full time?
- Does he need tutoring or further support to complete academic work missed?
- How might teachers react to his return?
- What is the plan if Jimmy starts to feel depressed or have suicidal feelings again?
- How might Jimmy's medication impact him? What might the side effects be and how can he handle them?
- What is the plan if Jimmy starts to get upset in class?
- What communication will the school psychologist (also acting as the case manager) have with the family? With the outside treatment team? Will Jimmy's parents support this communication?
- What is the follow-up plan for mental health treatment both in and out of school?

When you call Jimmy's parents, you explain the purpose of the meeting, who will be present, the topics to be covered, and ask them if they have any concerns or questions prior to the meeting. At first they say they cannot come, then they ask a few procedural questions, and then they share that they are afraid to let Jimmy be in school. You assure them that Jimmy's safety is your top priority.

Jimmy's parents come to the meeting appearing very defensive. They first ask why the school needs to know anything. You work hard to maintain rapport with this distressed family by immediately addressing their concerns, the first of which is their privacy. Mr. and Mrs. Burns are extremely concerned about who knows what about their child, and Jimmy expresses fear of being singled out. You and your team assure them that the only ones who need to know the situation are the people in this room. Once this confidentiality is ensured, they relax. The family decides to simply tell teachers that he was sick and in the hospital, with no further detail. While it is preferable that teachers are aware of Jimmy's depression in order to watch closely for warning signs, the team agrees to this to maintain the trust of the parents. The pupil services director tells the parents that the school understands it will take time for Jimmy to adjust to his new medication, and he is given to the end of the semester to complete his missed work for full credit.

Jimmy tells you that Dr. Hill said he can call anytime and Jimmy says he feels comfortable doing so. You reinforce this as a positive option. The team agrees that you will see Jimmy once a week to support Dr. Hill's therapeutic treatments. Your first meeting will occur before Jimmy returns to class to get a sense of his current baseline functioning and talk about strategies for responding to student questions about his absence. As the case manager, you document the agreed upon action items from the meeting. If Jimmy gets upset in class, he will be allowed to leave class immediately and without explanation by flashing his red medical pass to the teacher. As per school policy, the teacher acknowledges seeing the pass by nodding and Jimmy can leave. As it is a medical pass, it fits with what teachers will know to be a medical hospitalization. The team agrees to meet again at the end of the semester to follow up with Jimmy's progress and make sure he is on the right track.

Creating a Safety Plan

The last order of business in the re-entry meeting is for the team to develop a safety plan for Jimmy.

Jimmy and you recall his most recent suicidal crisis when he was sitting in your office. He tells you that it was triggered primarily by feeling overwhelmed with school work and beginning to think about college. He realizes that others can observe when he is feeling this way as he withdraws from those he cares about and doesn't want to do anything fun, including play the drums. You use a method of Socratic questioning to ask Jimmy what has worked for him in the past when he has had hard

Safety Plan

Think of the most recent suicidal crisis. Write a one to two sentence description of what triggered the suicidal crisis.

Triggers

- School work
- Thinking about college

Suicidal thoughts and behaviors: What are the thoughts, emotions, or behaviors that let you (and those around you) know that you were in crisis?

Suicidal Thoughts Behaviors

- Withdrawing
- Not playing drums

Internal coping: What can you do on your own to distract yourself from suicidal thoughts? What do you like to do? What have you done in the past?

Internal Coping

- Drumming
- Play video games

External coping: Who can help distract you from your suicidal thoughts?

External Coping

- My mother
- My girlfriend

Plan: List your coping strategies from above, starting with the most enjoyable.

Safety Plan

- My mother or girlfriend
- Drumming
- Video Games

☒ I agree to remove lethal means from the house ___RB___ (initials)

Emergency numbers I will call in the event that my suicidal thoughts continue or get worse after using the coping strategies listed above:

People to call

- Safe and trusted adult: **Mom cell #867-5309**
- School personnel: **Mr. Horizon**
- National Suicide Prevention Lifeline: 1-800-273-TALK (8255)
- 911

If no one is available and I have tried all of the coping strategies listed above, and still I believe I might do something to end my life, I will go to the emergency room **Joy Crisis Center** or call 911.

By signing below I agree that I have been part of the creation of this safety plan and that I intend to use it when I am having thoughts of suicide. I realize that my signature below does not make this a legal contract, but rather a plan for my continued well-being and happiness.

James Burns	*James Burns*	10/4/15
Student	Signature	Date
Dr. Erbacher / Psychologist	*Dr. Erbacher*	10/4/15
School Personnel / Credential	Signature	Date
Mrs. Harris /School Principal	*Mrs. Harris*	**10/4/15**
Supervisor/Administrator / Credential	Signature	Date
Mr. Raymond Burns	*Mr. Raymond Burns*	10/4/15
Parent / Guardian	Signature	Date

times; Jimmy reports the internal coping strategies of playing drums and video games and, even more so, the support of his mother and girlfriend. Jimmy agrees to reach out to his mother or Mr. Horizon at school. Finally, Jimmy and his parents agreed to remove his access to medication at the present time. Jimmy's parents will monitor his Prozac for now, giving it to him each morning at breakfast. All parties signed the safety plan, and a copy is provided to Jimmy and his parents; you keep the original for your records.

Obtaining Baseline Information and Data

You meet with Jimmy individually in your office. When a youth is released from a hospital, determined to be safe in the community and able to return to school, there is no need to do a comprehensive suicide risk assessment. However, you are well aware that most students do not leave the hospital being free of all STB. You know that suicidality waxes and wanes, and you want a way to monitor this over time. Otherwise, how will you know when it increases? To gain a perspective of his baseline STB, you administer the *Suicide Risk Monitoring Tool* (which we will refer to as "the tool"). You'll administer the tool weekly, using it to assess progress and dictate treatment strategies. You chart the results of the tool to get a picture of where treatment should first be focused.

Upon initial glance at Jimmy's baseline data (see Figure 11.1), you immediately note that sadness/depression and feelings of burdensomeness are of most concern to you at this point in time. Hopelessness is also a warning sign of concern, followed by lack of connection. Jimmy does not report having a suicide plan, and while he reports high intent (strong desire to die) and says he thinks of suicide almost every day, these thoughts only last a few seconds. Compared to his initial suicide

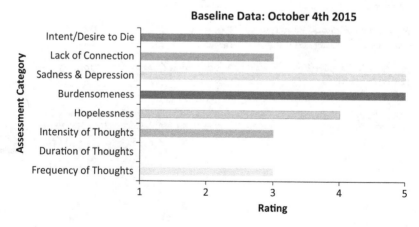

Figure 11.1 Baseline Data

Suicide Risk Monitoring Tool – Middle/High School Version

Student name __James Burns__   Date __10/4/15__

Completed by (name / title): __Dr. Terri Erbacher / School Psychologist__

I. IDEATION

Are you having thoughts of suicide?	☒ Yes	☐ No
Right now	☒ Yes	☐ No
Past 24 hours	☒ Yes	☐ No
Past week	☒ Yes	☐ No
Past month	☒ Yes	☐ No

Please circle / check the most accurate response:

How often do you have these thoughts? (Frequency): less than weekly / weekly / **daily** / hourly / every minute

How long do these thoughts last? (Duration): **a few seconds** / minutes / hours / days / a week or more

How disruptive are these thoughts to your life (Intensity): not at all= 1☐ 2☐ 3☒ 4☐ 5☐ =a great deal

II. INTENT

How much do you want to **die**? not at all= 1☐ 2☐ 3☐ 4☒ 5☐ =a great deal

How much do you want to **live**? not at all= 1☐ 2☐ 3☒ 4☐ 5☐ =a great deal

III. PLAN

Do you have a plan?	☐ Yes	☒ No
Have you written a suicide note?	☐ Yes	☒ No
Have you identified a method?	☐ Yes	☒ No
Do you have access to the method?	☐ Yes	☐ No	☒ N/A
Have you identified when & where you'd carry out this plan?	☐ Yes	☐ No	☒ N/A
Have you made a recent attempt?	☐ Yes	☒ No

If so, When / How / Where? _____

IV. WARNING SIGNS

How hopeless do you feel that things will get better? not at all= 1☐ 2☐ 3☐ 4☒ 5☐ =a great deal

How much do you feel like a burden to others? not at all= 1☐ 2☐ 3☐ 4☐ 5☒ =a great deal

How depressed, sad or down do you currently feel? not at all= 1☐ 2☐ 3☐ 4☐ 5☒ =a great deal

How disconnected do you feel from others? not at all= 1☐ 2☐ 3☒ 4☐ 5☐ =a great deal

Is there a particular trigger/stressor for you? If so, what? _____schoolwork_____

Has it improved? not at all= 1☒ 2☐ 3☐ 4☐ 5☐ =a great deal

V. PROTECTIVE FACTORS

REASONS FOR LIVING (things good at / like to do / enjoy / other)	SUPPORTIVE PEOPLE (family / adults / friends / peers)
drumming	mother
video games	

What could change about your life that would make you no longer want to die?

happiness

Purpose: This tool is meant to be a suicide risk management screening. It is not a comprehensive suicide risk assessment measure. At times, we must monitor ongoing suicidality of students who have already been assessed either by you, an outside mental health professional or in a hospital setting. Clinicians working with suicidal students often report being unsure when a student may need re-hospitalization or further intervention and when levels of suicidality are remaining relatively stable for that *individual* student. Monitoring suicidality and managing risk over time is the purpose of this form.

We have created two versions of this tool as older middle school and high school students are better able to identify responses when provided with more choices than elementary and early middle school students. With older middle school and high school students, complete this form with them the first time, explaining each area and ensuring they understand how to complete it. During subsequent sessions, they can complete the form independently, followed by a collaborative discussion of risk and treatment planning.

As you know your student best, we have created within this form a place to document the particular triggers or stressors for this individual. This will allow you to monitor and track their unique stressors over time.

V. LEVEL OF CURRENT RISK:

Recommendations for further treatment and management of suicide risk should be a direct result of the ratings of risk as identified below in collaboration with your school district procedure. In all cases, parents should be notified to inform them you met with their child.

Student meets criteria for low / moderate / high suicide risk based on the following information (If a student falls between levels, err on the side of caution and assume higher risk category):

1. Low risk: None or passing ideation that does not interfere with activities of daily living; reports no desire to die (i.e. intent), has no specific plan, exhibits few risk factors and has identifiable protective factors.
2. Moderate risk: Reports frequent suicidal ideation with limited intensity and duration; has some specific plans to die by suicide, but no reported intent. Demonstrates some risk factors, but is able to identify reasons for living and other protective factors.
3. <u>**High risk: Reports frequent, intense, and enduring suicidal ideation. Has written suicide note or reports specific plans, including choice of lethal methods and availability / accessibility of the method. Student presents with multiple risk factors and identifies few if any protective factors.**</u>

VI. ACTIONS TAKEN / RECOMMENDATIONS:

Parent/guardian contacted?	☒ Yes	☐ No
Released to parent/guardian?	☐ Yes	☒ No
Referrals provided to parent?	☐ Yes	☒ No
Safety plan developed?	☒ Yes	☐ No
Recommending removal of method/means?	☒ Yes	☐ No
If currently in treatment, contact made with therapist/psychiatrist?	☒ Yes	☐ No
Outpatient therapy recommended?	☒ Yes	☐ No
Recommending 24-hour supervision?	☒ Yes	☐ No
Hospitalization recommended?	☐ Yes	☒ No

Other? Please describe:

Jimmy was just released from the hospital, so while he remains at high suicide risk, he is under constant care of his parents, psychiatrist and new outpatient therapist. It is suggested to continue the current safety plan while his new medication regime activates within his system.

risk assessment, improvements are significant. However, his thoughts are still somewhat intense in their disruption to his life. When asked about protective factors, Jimmy reports that he is good at drumming and video games (you take note that he does not currently say he *enjoys* these things, just that he is good at them). He names his mother as his primary support at this time. When you ask Jimmy about his brother, he tells you that they are very close, but that his brother is "busy . . . off at college."

As the *Suicide Risk Monitoring Tool* provides guidance about selecting counseling techniques and intervention strategies, you and Jimmy develop a treatment plan collaboratively. You agree to first focus treatment goals on his feelings of sadness and depression, hoping that a positive impact here may help other areas as well. After all, Jimmy does have connections with friends, his mother, a girlfriend and his drumming circle, but he is too lethargic to use these connections at this time. You work in concert with Jimmy's outside therapist, and you agree to maintain frequent contact.

Monitoring Suicide Risk Over Time

The *Suicide Risk Monitoring Tool* is designed to be administered regularly (daily, weekly, monthly). The high school version is a self-report instrument assessing suicidal ideation and emotional well-being. The student rates each item on a 5-point Likert-type scale where 5 is the highest and 1 is the lowest. Week 1 provides a baseline and serves as a comparison for subsequent administrations. Each week, Jimmy fills out the tool, and you quickly score it and review it with him. Regular use of the tool along with clinical observation and interview increases the likelihood you will recognize spikes in suicide risk, indicators of the need for a higher level of care. You continue to work with Jimmy throughout the year. As this was such a complicated case, your supervisor, the director of pupil services, asks for a detailed review of the case as you approach the summer months. Because you have used the tool at each meeting, you are able to graph the change in Jimmy's status over seven months. Knowing how much your administrators like seeing progress monitoring data in graph form, you present the following report on Jimmy's suicidal thoughts and behaviors:

Warning Signs

You begin by discussing Jimmy's suicidal warning signs (see Figure 11.2); these were the clearest indicators of how he was feeling, and you used them to guide treatment.

After baseline on October 4, Jimmy's STB decreased slightly. They increased slightly the following week as Jimmy reported that everything was still "boring," feeling a bit defeated as things were not improving fast

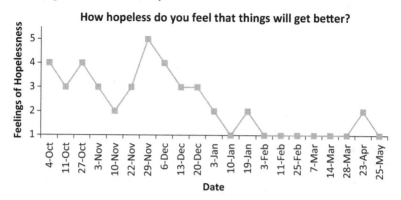

Figure 11.2 Hopelessness

enough. You normalized this for him explaining it's common to feel like change is not happening fast enough during intense treatment. Jimmy's feelings of hopelessness increased on November 29, appeared to stabilize through February and March, and again increased slightly in April. Your supervisor wonders aloud about a pattern with these two dates as he anticipates the next graphs.

Connection is something that is internally important to Jimmy, so this was one of the first areas to improve (see Figure 11.3). While his lack of connection increased significantly on November 29, he quickly re-stabilized. Now your supervisor turns to you with a look of wonder about what went on in November. You tell him that Jimmy and his girlfriend broke up toward the end of October once Jimmy returned to school. He felt that it was all just too much to deal with and that he needed to focus on his schoolwork and "getting better." During the week of November 29, Jimmy found out that his ex-girlfriend had been pregnant and decided to have an abortion without telling him about it. He felt alone, defeated, and helpless. He also felt guilty that he was not there for her and ashamed that he had "done this to her." He still loved her and felt awful that she had to go through that experience without his support. The feelings of helplessness and distress increased his STB. You shared the information about his increased suicide risk with his mother; Dr. Hill and the re-entry team agreed to continue treatment as is. Jimmy's withdrawal became the focus of your treatment as you realized that Jimmy has a tendency to withdraw from those he cares about most when he is upset or ashamed. Jimmy's lack of connection decreased the following week and became stable the week after that. Jimmy realized the importance of his connections and as can be seen, he maintained them from that point forward.

Your supervisor notices that feelings of being a burden seemed to stay relatively high for quite some time (see Figure 11.4). You discuss Jimmy's background and the financial duress of his parents and how Jimmy was

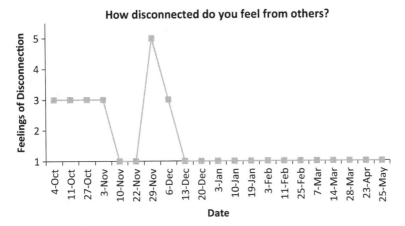

Figure 11.3 Disconnection

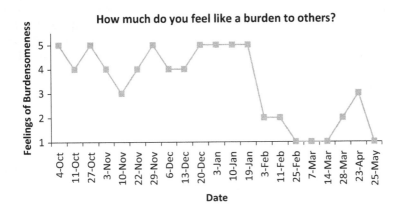

Figure 11.4 Burdensomeness

beginning to think about his future with the idea of college looming. He really wants to go to college, but realizes his parents cannot afford it. He also realizes that his depression is a lifelong mental health problem that he will continue to need to deal with. When he is sad and lethargic, he feels like a burden to his parents and that he is not contributing to their household. Sometimes it is the unexpected extra-therapeutic events that make the biggest difference in a person's well-being. For Jimmy, it was a realization that his life was a gift, rather than a burden. He had this realization after his brother nearly died the week of February 25 after attempting to take his own life. Jimmy and his brother have a close relationship and since his brother's attempt, Jimmy reported that he has been up late talking to his brother and "helping him out." Jimmy clearly felt good about being able to help his brother talk through some tough stuff. Jimmy's rating of burdensomeness dropped to "not at all" and remained stable after this time (with the exception of the anticipation of college expenses creeping up). After his brother's suicide attempt, Jimmy reported to you that he felt he was "out of his super-dark place" Jimmy's coping strategies have improved dramatically.

As you quickly observe in Figure 11.5, depression follows a similar pattern in that it improves but often never quite goes away. You and your supervisor discuss the possibility of securing further services for Jimmy in the community over the summer because he will not have school support during this time. He continues to see his outside therapist but would benefit from a summer program so that he is not home alone all day, which can lead to ruminating on the things that stress him. A significant dip in his depressive feelings is noticed on February 3, a time when there was also a significant decrease in feelings of being a burden and hopelessness, and his STB became less disruptive to his life. At that time, you were working with Jimmy on writing positive affirmations, a strategy he really took to as he began writing them four times a day since they were so helpful. Jimmy also began using a breathing-to-relax application (Breathe2Relax) on his iPad and visiting an online universal laughing room (http://doasone. com/BreathingRooms.aspx?RoomID=3) that allows him to share this joyful emotional response with others around the world. It is hard not to laugh back.

From reviewing Figure 11.6, it is evident that Jimmy's frequency of suicidal thoughts never went beyond a 3 (thinking about suicide daily). Your supervisor notices that Jimmy's suicidal thoughts decreased in January and were relatively stable until April 23. You point out that due to his stabilization throughout January, February, and March, you decreased the frequency of administering the *Suicide Risk Monitoring Tool* to bi-weekly and then monthly.

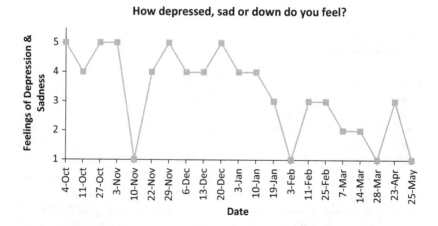

Figure 11.5 Depression/Sadness

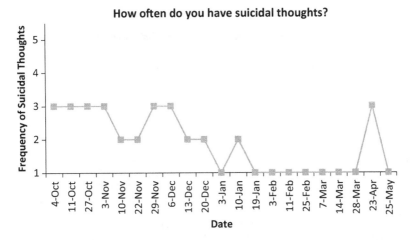

Figure 11.6 Frequency of Suicidal Thoughts

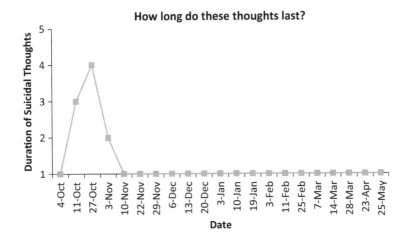

Figure 11.7 Duration of Suicidal Thoughts

While Jimmy has had multiple STBs, his thoughts typically did not last long in duration (see Figure 11.7). A red flag goes up for your supervisor about October 27 as he is seeing an increase in the intensity and duration of Jimmy's suicidal thoughts (and increased intent as will be seen) and there had been an increase in multiple warning signs (depression, burdensomeness, and hopelessness) as well. These comparisons give you a better understanding of Jimmy's current STB, and your supervisor asks about this date.

You remind your supervisor of the meeting that day when Jimmy was sent to you by the school's disciplinarian after being caught with alcohol at a school pep rally. Jimmy denied drinking, which was confirmed as likely by the nurse taking his vitals. However, he had a flask with vodka

Suicide Risk Monitoring Tool – Middle/High School Version

Student name __James Burns__   Date __10/27/15__

Completed by (name / title): __Dr. Terri Erbacher / School Psychologist__

I. IDEATION

Are you having thoughts of suicide?	☐ Yes	☒ No	
Right now	☐ Yes	☒ No	
Past 24 hours	☐ Yes	☒ No	
Past week	☒ Yes	☐ No	
Past month	☒ Yes	☐ No	

Please circle / check the most accurate response:

How often do you have these thoughts? (Frequency): less than weekly / weekly / **daily** / hourly / every minute

How long do these thoughts last? (Duration): __a few seconds__ / minutes / hours / days / a week or more

How disruptive are these thoughts to your life (Intensity): not at all= 1☐ 2☐ 3☐ 4☐ 5☒ =a great deal

II. INTENT

How much do you want to **die**?   not at all= 1☐ 2☐ 3☒ 4☐ 5☐ =a great deal

How much do you want to **live**?   not at all= 1☐ 2☐ 3☒ 4☐ 5☐ =a great deal

III. PLAN

Do you have a plan?	☒ Yes	☐ No	
Have you written a suicide note?	☐ Yes	☒ No	
Have you identified a method?	☐ Yes	☒ No	
Do you have access to the method?	☐ Yes	☐ No	☒ N/A
Have you identified when & where you'd carry out this plan?	☐ Yes	☒ No	☐ N/A
Have you made a recent attempt?	☐ Yes	☒ No	

If so, When / How / Where? _____

IV. WARNING SIGNS

How hopeless do you feel that things will get better?   not at all= 1☐ 2☐ 3☐ 4☐ 5☒ =a great deal

How much do you feel like a burden to others?   not at all= 1☐ 2☐ 3☐ 4☐ 5☒ =a great deal

How depressed, sad or down do you currently feel?   not at all= 1☐ 2☐ 3☐ 4☐ 5☒ =a great deal

How disconnected do you feel from others?   not at all= 1☐ 2☐ 3☐ 4☐ 5☒ =a great deal

Is there a particular trigger/stressor for you? If so, what? _____ schoolwork _____

Has it improved?   not at all= 1☐ 2☐ 3☒ 4☐ 5☐ =a great deal

V. PROTECTIVE FACTORS

REASONS FOR LIVING *(things good at / like to do / enjoy / other)*	SUPPORTIVE PEOPLE *(family / adults / friends / peers)*
drumming	my mother
video games	my father

What could change about your life that would make you no longer want to die?

To be able to get stuff like homework done so I can relax and enjoy my life and have more fun. Ongoing happiness. No more depression and less anxiety. Having some control over what happens.

Purpose: This tool is meant to be a suicide risk management screening. It is not a comprehensive suicide risk assessment measure. At times, we must monitor ongoing suicidality of students who have already been assessed either by you, an outside mental health professional or in a hospital setting. Clinicians working with suicidal students often report being unsure when a student may need re-hospitalization or further intervention and when levels of suicidality are remaining relatively stable for that *individual* student. Monitoring suicidality and managing risk over time is the purpose of this form.

We have created two versions of this tool as older middle school and high school students are better able to identify responses when provided with more choices than elementary and early middle school students. With older middle school and high school students, complete this form with them the first time, explaining each area and ensuring they understand how to complete it. During subsequent sessions, they can complete the form independently, followed by a collaborative discussion of risk and treatment planning.

As you know your student best, we have created within this form a place to document the particular triggers or stressors for this individual. This will allow you to monitor and track their unique stressors over time.

V. LEVEL OF CURRENT RISK:

Recommendations for further treatment and management of suicide risk should be a direct result of the ratings of risk as identified below in collaboration with your school district procedure. In all cases, parents should be notified to inform them you met with their child.

Student meets criteria for low / moderate / high suicide risk based on the following information (If a student falls between levels, err on the side of caution and assume higher risk category):

1. Low risk: None or passing ideation that does not interfere with activities of daily living; reports no desire to die (i.e. intent), has no specific plan, exhibits few risk factors and has identifiable protective factors.
2. Moderate risk: Reports frequent suicidal ideation with limited intensity and duration; has some specific plans to die by suicide, but no reported intent. Demonstrates some risk factors, but is able to identify reasons for living and other protective factors.
3. <u>High risk: Reports frequent, intense, and enduring suicidal ideation. Has written suicide note or reports specific plans, including choice of lethal methods and availability / accessibility of the method. Student presents with multiple risk factors and identifies few if any protective factors.</u>

VI. ACTIONS TAKEN / RECOMMENDATIONS:

Parent/guardian contacted?	☒ Yes	☐ No
Released to parent/guardian?	☒ Yes	☐ No
Referrals provided to parent?	☐ Yes	☐ No
Safety plan developed?	☒ Yes	☐ No
Recommending removal of method/means?	☒ Yes	☐ No
If currently in treatment, contact made with therapist/psychiatrist?	☒ Yes	☐ No
Outpatient therapy recommended?	☐ Yes	☐ No
Recommending 24-hour supervision?	☐ Yes	☐ No
Hospitalization recommended?	☐ Yes	☐ No

Other? Please describe:

James continues to have suicidal thoughts that are still strong in frequency and intensity due to a recent traumatic event. He feels like a burden, is depressed and hopeless. Improved relationship with father. He can better identify triggers. Parents and outside therapist contacted and safety plan otherwise remains intact. Added removal of alcohol.

on his person. You and the team met with Jimmy to hear his side of the story. He apologized and said he was ashamed. Upon completion of the *Suicide Risk Monitoring Tool,* it was evident that his STB had increased significantly. You decided it was important at that time to inform his parents and his outside therapist because you were very concerned that he was going backwards. He did not have a suicide plan at that point so, as a team, you decided immediate hospitalization was not warranted.

His outside therapist agreed to meet with Jimmy that same night, and his parents came to pick him up at school rather than him taking the bus. They were grateful for the communication and collaboration and reported that they had not noticed any behaviors worsening at home. You spoke with Dr. Hill the next day, who expressed concern because suicide risk is significantly increased with alcohol. Jimmy's parents agreed to monitor this closely, and Dr. Hill proposed continuing the current treatment plan for another two weeks until the Prozac started taking effect. In the meantime, you and Jimmy discuss the dangers of taking medication *and* drinking alcohol. He agreed to add the removal of all alcohol to his safety plan, and you both signed it again.

Your supervisor notices the first significant dip in the intensity of Jimmy's suicidal thoughts appears on November 10 (see Figure 11.8). In fact, all warning signs decreased in severity on that date. This improved functioning was significant. Jimmy had always been interested in video games, and his college counselor, Mr. Horizon, had found an interesting college program for him where he would learn the skill of programming these games. Jimmy could not have been more excited that such a program even existed! At the same time, the wrestling season began, and Jimmy was happy to be running and working out again (increased endorphins) and socializing with his wrestling buddies. You decided it was important to share the good news of Jimmy's overall decrease in warning signs with his parents and Dr. Hill. Each small victory is a success.

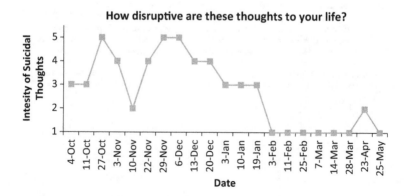

Figure 11.8 Intensity of Suicidal Thoughts

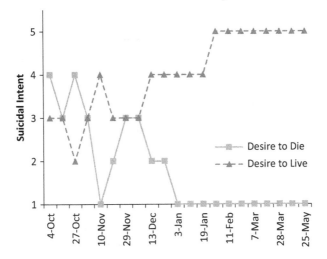

Figure 11.9 Suicidal Intent

You discuss Figure 11.9 with your supervisor and note that Jimmy's desire to die directly opposes his desire to live (some dates omitted on the graph due to space considerations). This is not always the case; students can have *both* a strong desire to live and a strong desire to die. January 3 was momentous for you because it was the day his desire to die decreased to none. When you saw him after the winter break, Jimmy expressed relief that his teachers had not assigned any projects, and he spent the time relaxing with family and friends. It is important to note that on April 23, when he was feeling stressed about the end of school and thoughts of college visits over the summer, his desire to die did not increase and his desire to live did not decrease. This shows that when faced with normal life stressors, he wanted to live through them. This was such a positive leap for Jimmy.

Conclusion

You and Jimmy decided that it would be reasonable to decrease meetings from bi-weekly to monthly after his scores stabilized for several weeks. By the end of the year, he no longer reported any suicidal ideation and he had increased his protective factors dramatically. Jimmy was back together with his girlfriend ("the love of his life"), and she supported him when he was feeling down. On the last day of treatment, May 25, Jimmy was no longer feeling as if he were a burden and he had no feelings of depression. While schoolwork continues to overwhelm him at times, it no longer serves as a significant trigger for his STB. You remind Jimmy that his depressive feelings can come and go. Before Jimmy leaves for summer break, you confirm that he will continue to see Dr. Hill over

Suicide Risk Monitoring Tool – Middle/High School Version

Student name **James Burns**　　　　　　　　　　　　　　　Date **5/25/16**

Completed by (name / title): **Dr. Terri Erbacher / School Psychologist**

I. IDEATION

Are you having thoughts of suicide?	❑ Yes	☒ No		
Right now	❑ Yes	☒ No		
Past 24 hours	❑ Yes	☒ No		
Past week	❑ Yes	☒ No		
Past month	❑ Yes	☒ No		

I'm not

Please circle / check the most accurate response:

How often do you have these thoughts? (Frequency): less than weekly / weekly / daily / hourly / every minute

How long do these thoughts last? (Duration):　　　　a few seconds / minutes / hours / days / a week or more

How disruptive are these thoughts to your life (Intensity): not at all= 1☒ 2❑ 3❑ 4❑ 5❑ =a great deal

II. INTENT

How much do you want to **die**?　　　not at all= 1☒ 2❑ 3❑ 4❑ 5❑ =a great deal

How much do you want to **live**?　　　not at all= 1❑ 2❑ 3❑ 4❑ 5☒ =a great deal

III. PLAN

Do you have a plan?	❑ Yes ☒ No	
Have you written a suicide note?	❑ Yes ☒ No	
If you have a plan, have you identified a method?	❑ Yes ☒ No	
Do you have access to the method?	❑ Yes ❑ No	☒ N/A
Have you identified when & where you'd carry out this plan?	❑ Yes ❑ No	☒ N/A
Have you made a recent attempt?	❑ Yes ☒ No	

If so, When / How / Where? _____

IV. WARNING SIGNS

How hopeless do you feel that things will get better?　　not at all= 1☒ 2❑ 3❑ 4❑ 5❑ =a great deal

How much do you feel like a burden to others?　　　　not at all= 1☒ 2❑ 3❑ 4❑ 5❑ =a great deal

How depressed, sad or down do you currently feel?　　not at all= 1☒ 2❑ 3❑ 4❑ 5❑ =a great deal

How disconnected do you feel from others?　　　　　not at all= 1☒ 2❑ 3❑ 4❑ 5❑ =a great deal

Is there a particular trigger/stressor for you? If so, what? _____**schoolwork**_____

Has it improved?　not at all= 1❑ 2❑ 3❑ 4❑ 5☒ =a great deal

V. PROTECTIVE FACTORS

REASONS FOR LIVING *(things good at / like to do / enjoy / other)*	SUPPORTIVE PEOPLE *(family / adults / friends / peers)*
Drumming, wrestling	my family (mother/father)
video games	my girlfriend
hope for a better future	friends
more to enjoy in life - happiness	
career - hope to make video games	

What could change about your life that would make you no longer want to die?

I don't feel that way.

Purpose: This tool is meant to be a suicide risk management screening. It is not a comprehensive suicide risk assessment measure. At times, we must monitor ongoing suicidality of students who have already been assessed either by you, an outside mental health professional or in a hospital setting. Clinicians working with suicidal students often report being unsure when a student may need re-hospitalization or further intervention and when levels of suicidality are remaining relatively stable for that *individual* student. Monitoring suicidality and managing risk over time is the purpose of this form.

We have created two versions of this form as older middle school and high school students are better able to identify responses when provided with more choices than elementary and early middle school students. With older middle school and high school students, complete this form with them the first time, explaining each area and ensuring they understand how to complete it. During subsequent sessions, they can complete the form independently, followed by a collaborative discussion of risk and treatment planning.

As you know your student best, we have created within this form a place to document the particular triggers or stressors for this individual. This will allow you to monitor and track their unique stressors over time.

V. LEVEL OF CURRENT RISK:
Recommendations for further treatment and management of suicide risk should be a direct result of the ratings of risk as identified below in collaboration with your school district procedure. In all cases, parents should be notified to inform them you met with their child.

Student meets criteria for low / moderate / high suicide risk based on the following information (If a student falls between levels, err on the side of caution and assume higher risk category):
   1. **Low risk: None or passing ideation that does not interfere with activities of daily living; reports no desire to die (i.e. intent), has no specific plan, exhibits few risk factors and has identifiable protective factors.**
   2. Moderate risk: Reports frequent suicidal ideation with limited intensity and duration; has some specific plans to die by suicide, but no reported intent. Demonstrates some risk factors, but is able to identify reasons for living and other protective factors.
   3. High risk: Reports frequent, intense, and enduring suicidal ideation. Has written suicide note or reports specific plans, including choice of lethal methods and availability / accessibility of the method. Student presents with multiple risk factors and identifies few if any protective factors.

VI. ACTIONS TAKEN / RECOMMENDATIONS:

Parent/guardian contacted?	☒ Yes	☐ No
Released to parent/guardian?	☐ Yes	☐ No
Referrals provided to parent?	☐ Yes	☐ No
Safety plan developed?	☐ Yes	☐ No
Recommending removal of method/means?	☐ Yes	☐ No
If currently in treatment, contact made with therapist/psychiatrist?	☐ Yes	☐ No
Outpatient therapy recommended?	☐ Yes	☐ No
Recommending 24-hour supervision?	☐ Yes	☐ No
Hospitalization recommended?	☐ Yes	☐ No

Other? Please describe:

Parents contacted to share improvements. Improved relationship with father and Jimmy now has identified career aspirations to develop video games. While he continues to worry about his family finances, he no longer feels like a burden for wanting to go to college.

the summer and that he still has a copy of his safety plan to ensure he knows what to do and who to call should his STB increase. Jimmy also has shared with you that his relationship with his father is improving, and he now includes him in his circle of supportive people. Jimmy is spending more time with friends again and is playing drums (and yes, he once again *enjoys* it!). He also reports many other reasons for living including a possible career developing video games, having hope of a brighter future, and actually experiencing happiness.

12 Suicide in Schools

Resources

Find Dr. Erbacher's quarterly newsletter at http://www.delcosuicidepre
vention.org.

Websites

National Association of School Psychologists: http://www.nasponline.org

National Association of Secondary School Principals, *Taking the Lead on Suicide Prevention and Intervention in the Schools*: http://www.nasponline.org/
resources/principals/index.aspx. This will be a helpful resource to share with
your school administrators.

Save a Friend: Tips for Teens to Prevent Suicide: http://www.nasponline.org/
resources/crisis_safety/savefriend_general.aspx

Times of Tragedy: Preventing Suicide in Troubled Children and Youth, Part I:
http://www.nasponline.org/resources/crisis_safety/suicidept1_general.aspx

Awareness/Prevention for Professionals

Active Minds empowering youth on college campuses: http://www.activeminds.org

Aevidum to empower students: http://aevidum.com

American Association of Suicidology: http://www.suicidology.org

American Foundation for Suicide Prevention: http://www.afsp.org

American Psychological Association Children & Trauma: http://www.apa.org/
pi/families/resources/children-trauma-update.aspx

Center for Disease Control: http://www.cdc.gov

Delaware County Suicide Task Force: http://www.delcosuicideprevention.org

Jason Foundation Suicide Prevention Program: http://www.jasonfoundation.com

Minding your Mind: http://www.mindingyourmind.org

National Alliance on Mental Illness: http://www.nami.org

National Council on Suicide Prevention: http://www.ncsp.org

National Institute of Mental Health: http://www.nimh.nih.gov/suicidepreven
tion/index.cfm

National Mental Health Association: http://www.nmha.org

National Organization of People of Color Against Suicide: http://www.nopcas.com

National Suicide Prevention Resource Center: http://www.sprc.org

QPR Institute: http://www.qprinstitute.com

Signs of Suicide Prevention Program: http://www.mentalhealthscreening.org/
highschool/

Speaking of Suicide: http://www.speakingofsuicide.com

Substance Abuse and Mental Health Services Administration: http://www.sam hsa.gov

Suicide Awareness/Voices of Education: http://www.save.org

Pennsylvania Youth Suicide Prevention Initiative: http://www.paspi.org/Train ing.php

U.S. Department of Health and Human Services, National Strategy on Suicide Prevention: http://www.mentalhealth.samhsa.gov/suicideprevention/

Yellow Ribbon Youth Suicide Prevention Program: http://www.yellowribbon.org

Connect With Local Contacts

Suicide Prevention Resource Center (SPRC): Provides an alphabetical listing of states and territories along with contact information for the person(s) who are taking the lead in the state plan development or implementation process: http://www.sprc.org/states/all/contacts

For Survivors of Suicide

American Association of Suicidology—Clinicians as Survivors of Suicides: mypage. iusb.edu/~jmcintos/therapists_mainpg.htm

Center for Loss and Bereavement: http://www.bereavementcenter.org

Compassionate Friends for Parents Who Lost Children: http://www.compassion atefriends.org

Dougy Center for Grieving Children and Families: http://www.dougy.org

Friends and Families of Suicides: http://www.friendsandfamiliesofsuicide.com

Grief Loss Recovery: http://www.recover-from-grief.com

National Suicide Prevention Lifeline: http://www.suicidepreventionlifeline.org

Online Healing for Grief: http://www.journeyofhearts.org

Parents of Suicides: http://www.parentsofsuicide.com

Suicide Memorial Wall: http://www.suicidememorialwall.com

Survivors of Suicide (SOS): http://www.survivorsofsuicide.com

Contemplating Suicide?

Go here: http://www.metanoia.org/suicide

Websites for Teens

Facts for Teens: Teen Suicide: http://www.safeyouth.org/scripts/teens/docs/ suicide.pdf

Go Ask Alice!: http://www.goaskalice.columbia.edu

Hospice: http://www.hospicenet.org/html/teenager.html

Jason Foundation: http://www.jasonfoundation.com/student.html

Jed Foundation: https://www.jedfoundation.org/students

The ME Project: http://meproject.org

National Institute of Mental Health: http://www.nimh.nih.gov/publicat/ friend.cfm

Reach Out: http://www.reachout.com

Samariteens: http://www.samaritansofboston.org/samariteens.html

Suicide Prevention Lifeline: http://www.suicidepreventionlifeline.org

TeensHealth Answers & Advice: http://kidshealth.org/teen
Trevor Project: http://www.thetrevorproject.org

For Parents

Parent Awareness Series: http://www.sptsnj.org/pdfs/parent-awareness-hand-out.pdf

Professional Videos

School-based suicide prevention: A matter of life and death by Jan Ulrich. Visit: http://www.sprc.org/library_resources/items/school-based-suicide-preven tion-matter-life-and-death
Training videos for schools, colleges and clinicians by Dr. Scott Poland. Visit: http://www.nova.edu/suicideprevention/training-videos.html

Twitter—Who to Follow

Active Minds, Inc. @Active_Minds
American Association of Suicidology @AASuicidology
American Foundation for Suicide Prevention @afspnational
Bazelon Center @BazelonCenter
Dart Center for Journalism & Trauma @DartCenter
End The Stigma @EndTheStigma
IMAlive Crisis Chat @_IMAlive
International Association for Suicide Prevention (IASP) @IASPinfo
It Gets Better @ItGetsBetter
National Alliance on Mental Illness (NAMI) @NAMICommunicate
National Institute of Mental Health (NIMH) @NIMHgov
Social Work Podcast @socworkpodcast
Suicide Prevention Resource Center @SPRCtweets
Suicide Prevention Social Media Chat @SPSMChat
SuicidePreventionAUS @SuicidePrevAU
The Substance Abuse and Mental Health Services Administration @samhsagov
The Trevor Project @TrevorProject
To Write Love On Her Arms (TWLOHA) @TWLOHA
Young Minds Advocacy Project @YoungMindsAdvoc

Bibliotherapy

More books, resources, and readings can be found on the following sites:
http://www.afsp.org
http://www.suicide.org/suicide-books.html
http://www.forsuicidesurvivors.com/Good-Books-for-Survivors-of-Suicide.html

Books for Professionals

Berman, A. L., Jobes, D. A., & Silverman, M. M. (2006). *Adolescent Suicide: Assessment and Intervention* (2nd ed.)
Brent, D. A., Poling, K. D., & Goldstein, T. R. (2011). *Treating Depressed and Suicidal Adolescents: A Clinician's Guide*

Cohen, J. A., Mannarino, A. P., & Deblinger, E. (2006). *Treating Trauma and Traumatic Grief in Children and Adolescents*

Dunne, E., McIntosh, J., & Dunne-Maxim, K. (1987). *Suicide and Its Aftermath, Understanding and Counseling the Survivors*

Figley, C. R. (1999). *Traumatology of Grieving: Conceptual, Theoretical and Treatment Foundations*

Goldsmith, S. (2002). *Reducing Suicide: A National Imperative*

Goldston, D. B. (2003). *Measuring Suicidal Behavior and Risk in Children and Adolescents*

Jamison, K. R. (1999). *Night Falls Fast: Understanding Suicide*

Johnson, K. (1998). *Trauma in the Lives of Children: Crisis and Stress Management Techniques for Counselors, Teachers and Other Professionals*

Joiner, T. (2005). *Why People Die by Suicide*

Juhnke, G. A., Granello, D. H., & Granello, P. F. (2011). *Suicide, Self-injury and Violence in the Schools: Assessment, Prevention and Intervention Strategies*

Kerr, M. M. (2003). *Postvention Standards Manual: A Guide for a School's Response in the Aftermath of a Sudden Death*

Leach, M. M. (2006). *Cultural Diversity and Suicide: Ethnic, Religious, Gender and Sexual Orientation Perspectives*

Lehmann, L., Jimerson, S., & Gaasch, A. (2001). *Teens Together Grief Support Group Curriculum: Adolescence Edition*

Leong, F. T. L., & Leach, M. M. (2008). *Suicide Among Racial and Ethnic Minority Groups*

Lester, D. (1992). *Why People Kill Themselves*

Lowenstein, L. (2006). *Creative Interventions for Bereaved Children*

Maltsberger, J. T., & Goldblatt, M. J. (Eds.). (1996). *Essential Papers on Suicide*

Maris, R., Berman, A., & Silverman, M. (2000). *Comprehensive Textbook of Suicidology*

Miller, D. (2011). *Child and Adolescent Suicidal Behavior: School-Based Prevention, Assessment and Intervention*

Poland, S. (1989). *Suicide Intervention in the Schools*

Rudd, M. D., Joiner, T., & Rajab, M. H. (2001). *Treating Suicidal Behavior: An Effective, Time-Limited Approach*

Shea, S. C. (1999). *The Practical Art of Suicide Assessment*

Shneidman, E. (1996). *The Suicidal Mind*

Stroebe, M. S., Hansson, R. O., Schut, H., & Stroebe, W. (Eds.). (2008). *Handbook of Bereavement Research and Practice*

Trozzi, M., & Massini, K. (1999). *Talking With Children about Loss*

Webb, N. B. (2011). *Helping Bereaved Children: A Handbook for Practitioners*

Wenzel, A., Brown, G. K., & Beck, A. T. (2009). *Cognitive Therapy for Suicidal Patients: Scientific and Clinical Applications*

Worden, J. W. (1996). *Children and Grief: When a Parent Dies*

Worden, J. W. (2008). *Grief Counseling and Grief Therapy: A Handbook for the Mental Health Practitioner* (4th ed.)

Wright, H. (1993). *Crisis Counseling: What to Do and Say During the First 72 Hours*

Books for Survivors of Suicide

Bolton, I. (1983). *My Son, My Son: A Guide to Healing After a Suicide in the Family*

Chalifour, F. (2005). *After*

Chance, S. (1997). *Stronger Than Death: When Suicide Touches Your Life*

Cobain, B., & Larch, J. (2006). *Dying to Be Free: A Healing Guide for Families after a Suicide*

Harrison, J. (2006). *Incomplete Knowledge*

Hopely, M. (2013). *The People You Meet in Real Life*

Kosminsky, P. (2007). *Getting Back to Life When Grief Won't Heal*

Loehr, C.A. (2006). *My Uncle Keith Died*

Lukas, C. (2008). *Blue Genes: A Memoir of Loss and Survival*

Lukas, C., & Seiden, H. (2007). *Silent Grief: Living in the Wake of Suicide*

Treadway, D.C. (1996). *Dead Reckoning: A Therapist Confronts His Own Grief*

Wickersham, J. (2008). *The Suicide Index: Putting My Father's Death in Order*

For Men

Cox, P. (2002). *When Suicide Comes Home: A Father's Diary and Comments*

Golden, T.R. (1996). *Swallowed by a Snake: The Gift of the Masculine Side of Healing*

Poetry/Inspirational

Greenleaf, C. (2006). *Healing the Hurt Spirit: Daily Affirmations for People Who Have Lost a Loved One to Suicide*

Smith, H.I. (2006). *A Long-Shadowed Grief: Suicide and Its Aftermath*

Staudacher, C. (1994). *A Time to Grieve: Meditations for Healing After the Death of a Loved One*

Social Work Podcast Episodes

Singer, J.B. (Producer). (2007, January 29). Crisis intervention and suicide assessment: Part 2—intervention and crisis assessment [Episode 4]. Social Work Podcast [Audio podcast]. Retrieved from http://socialworkpodcast. com/2007/02/crisis-intervention-and-suicide.html

Singer, J.B. (Producer). (2007, October 15). Dialectical Behavior Therapy: Interview with Sabrina Heller, LSW. [Episode 26]. Social Work Podcast [Audio podcast]. Retrieved from http://socialworkpodcast.com/2007/10/ dialectical-behavior-therapy-interview.html

Singer, J.B. (Producer). (2010, February 21). Suicide and Black American males: An interview with Sean Joe, PhD, LMSW [Episode 56]. Social Work Podcast [Audio podcast]. Retrieved from http://socialworkpodcast.com/2010/02/ suicide-and-black-american-males.htmlSinger, J.B. (Producer). (2011, December 5). Lonely at the top: Interview with Thomas Joiner, PhD [Episode 70]. Social Work Podcast [Audio podcast]. Retrieved from http://www.social workpodcast.com/2011/12/lonely-at-top-interview-with-thomas.html

Singer, J.B. (Producer). (2012, August 10). Non-suicidal self-injury (NSSI): Interview with Jennifer Muehlenkamp, PhD [Episode 73]. Social Work Podcast [Audio podcast]. Retrieved from http://www.socialworkpodcast. com/2012/08/non-suicidal-self-injury-nssi-interview.html

Singer, J.B. (Producer). (2012, September 11). The Chronological Assessment of Suicide Events (CASE) Approach: Interview and role play with Shawn Christopher Shea, MD [Episode 74]. Social Work Podcast [Audio podcast]. Retrieved from http://www.socialworkpodcast.com/2012/09/the-chronological-assessment-of-suicide.html

Index